PHILOSOPHY OF HISTORY
AND THE PROBLEM OF VALUES

A native of Austria, Alfred Stern received his Ph. D. at the University of Vienna. He has given courses at the Sorbonne in Paris, the Institut des Hautes Etudes de Belgique in Brussels, the Universidad Nacional de México, the Ecole Libre des Hautes Etudes in New York, the University of Southern California in Los Angeles, and he is now Professor of Philosophy and Languages at the California Institute of Technology in Pasadena.

Professor Stern is the author of many books and articles published in English, French, German, Spanish, Japanese, etc. Among his works are *Die philosophischen Grundlagen von Wahrheit, Wirklichkeit, Wert* (Munich, 1932); *Filosofía de la Política* (Mexico, 1943); *Philosophie du Rire et des Pleurs* (Paris, 1949; Buenos Aires, 1950); *Filosofía de los Valores* (Mexico, 1944; Buenos Aires, 1960); *Sartre—His Philosophy and Psychoanalysis* (New York, 1953; Buenos Aires 1951 and 1962; Tokyo, 1956), etc. 1964

PHILOSOPHY OF HISTORY

AND THE PROBLEM

OF VALUES

by

ALFRED STERN, PH.D.,

Professor of Philosophy and Languages
California Institute of Technology,
Pasadena, California

1962

MOUTON & CO - 'S-GRAVENHAGE

Printed in The Netherlands by P. H. Klop, Printers, The Hague.

To Marigloria,
my beloved wife

TABLE OF CONTENTS

INTRODUCTION 7

I. THE NEW HISTORICAL SENSE 9

II. HISTORICAL REALITY 17

III. THE PHILOSOPHY OF HISTORY — ITS ORIGIN AND AIMS . . 39

IV. HISTORICAL KNOWLEDGE 71

V. HISTORICAL KNOWLEDGE AND VALUES 100

VI. HISTORICISM, NATURAL RIGHT AND VALUES 138

VII. THE LIMITS OF HISTORICISM 182

VIII. HISTORICAL PROJECTS AND VALUES 202

INDEX OF NAMES 245

INTRODUCTION

This book tries to bring philosophy of history down to earth by showing that, in our epoch of gigantic ideological struggles and historical changes engaging the future of mankind, philosophy of history is everybody's concern. Our individual destinies depend to a large extent on the fate of the collectivity within which we live. Thus, philosophy of history becomes an essential part of our philosophy of life.

The author is convinced that philosophy of history is intimately linked with the field of values. Even a superficial approach to the problems of present history reveals that a choice between the different ideologies struggling in our day for supremacy is a choice between different *sets of values*. The examination of the relationships between philosophy and history and philosophy of values has not yet been undertaken on a broad front. It will be attempted in this book.

A few words should be said about the method our inquiry will follow. It is the author's conviction that any philosophical research lacking historical foundation is dilettantish. A scientist may well proceed without taking into account the history of his science, for past scientific theories are almost all obsolete because of their inability to cope with newly discovered empirical data. Philosophy, however, has to deal with the human condition in the world, the condition of a living, conscious, suffering individual who knows that he has to die. This basic human condition has not changed in history. Different philosophies only constitute different possibilities of conceptualizing and explaining this human condition, and, although the styles of these conceptualizations have changed in the course of history, past philosophical theories are not necessarily obsolete, for they still may be applicable to the unchanged basic human condition.

Thus, before a philosopher proposes a new doctrine of his own, he must discuss the most significant doctrines advanced before him; he must take into account their valid elements, reveal their shortcomings and refute their errors. Only then is he entitled to propose better solutions of his own. Thus, my doctrine will be developed gradually by a method half historical half dialectical. In the last two chapters, my doctrine will come to its final conclusions and will be synthesized into systematic unity. When explaining and discussing the doctrines of other thinkers, I shall keep in mind Seneca's maxim: *"soleo enim et in aliena castra transire, non tamquam transfuga, sed tamquam explorator"*[1] — I am in the habit of crossing over even into alien camps not as a deserter but as an explorer.

---

[1] *L. Annaei Senecae ad Lucilium Epistulae,* II, 5.

I. THE NEW HISTORICAL SENSE

One of the characteristic features of our time is the growth of its historical sense. The reason for this development is clear: we have lived more history than any other epoch in the evolution of mankind. In the past, during that short period of historical stability which — *cum grano salis* — characterized the forty-three years between the Franco-Prussian War of 1870/71 and World War I, a person could live without being interested in history. In our day such an attitude is no longer possible. We may try in vain to take no interest in history, but history takes an interest in us, in each of us. The last half century showed us that to understand history is of equal importance to those who make it and to those who endure it. Both need to know, in order to foresee and to act.

Does this bring us back to historical pragmatism, which, for a long time, has been abandoned? Intimately linked with the axiom of the immutability of human nature, historical pragmatism considered history as a collection of examples of practical use to mankind. For Polybius, the lesson given by history was, above all, a moral lesson for the benefit of the future ruler. By learning, thanks to the study of history, about the grandeurs and miseries of his own predecessors and of foreign princes, a ruler becomes able, according to Polybius, to endure with firmness the changes of fortune which — as Machiavelli was to tell us later — is a capricious lady. *Vultus fortunae varietur imagine lunae: crescit, decrescit, constans persistere nescit* — the face of fortune changes with the likeness of the moon: it waxes and wanes and cannot remain constant.

With Machiavelli, historical pragmatism became an object lesson. Since human nature is invariable, he said, all the ages are alike. Whoever knows one knows them all. When confronted with a concrete situation, the statesman will always find an analogous case in history. Machiavelli concluded that nothing would be more dangerous for a prince than to disregard the teachings of history. In his *Discours sur l'Histoire Universelle à Monseigneur le Dauphin*, Bossuet summed up the fundamental ideas of historical pragmatism by writing:

> Even if history were useless to other people, it would still be necessary for princes to study it ... If experience is necessary to acquire that wisdom which makes the good ruler, there is nothing more useful for their instruction than to combine their every-day experiences with the examples of past centuries.[1]

At the beginning of the nineteenth century, Hegel rebelled against historical pragmatism with the following arguments:

> One advises rulers, statesmen, nations to heed the lessons of history. ... But every period has such peculiar circumstances, each is to so large an extent an individual situation that one must and can decide only from within it and by growing out of it. In the tumult of world affairs, no general principle and no remembrance of similar conditions help us, for a pale memory has no power against the vitality and liberty of the present.[2]

Benedetto Croce struck an even heavier blow against historical pragmatism by showing that the present does not seek from history lessons to teach it what it should do but only the justification of what it has done. And Nietzsche went so far as to affirm that, far from imitating the examples of the past, the great action can develop only in a non-historic, anti-historic atmosphere. He who acts has to forget the past; otherwise he would be paralyzed by hesitation. In order to be able to act, the man of action must be unjust towards the past and see only his right to create a new future.[3]

There is yet another aspect of historical pragmatism much more concrete than that of Machiavelli, Bossuet and all their disciples: this is the pragmatism of the "monumental" conception of history. The term was coined by Nietzsche. The "monumental" conception of history gets its inspiration from the great examples of the past in order to be able to believe in the possibility of similar realizations in the future. Whoever adopts the monumental conception of history concludes that the grandiose action, having occurred once, has demonstrated its possibility and could therefore occur again in the future.

The way in which the youth of the nineteenth century saw Napoleon is certainly one of the most typical examples of a monumental conception of history. The fact that a Napoleon had been possible gave young

---

[1] *Oeuvres complètes de Bossuet* (Paris, 1836), tome X, p. 151.
[2] G. W. F. Hegel, *Sämtliche Werke* (edit. Glockner), Band 11, "Vorlesungen über die Philosophie der Geschichte", p. 31 (Stuttgart, 1928).
[3] F. Nietzsche, *Gesammelte Werke* (München, 1922), Band VI, "Vom Nutzen und Nachteil der Historie für das Leben", p. 238.

people between 1820 and 1895 the confidence that he would be possible again; it gave them faith in human grandeur and sometimes even the secret hope that they themselves might have been predestined to become the Bonapartes of their times. On Balzac's desk there was a portrait of that emperor who had converted his will into the law of a whole continent. Under this portrait young Balzac wrote the well known words: "What he has begun with the sword, I shall achieve with the pen."

For the Balzacian hero, Rastignac, who, from the height of the *Père Lachaise* cemetery, defied Paris by shouting "Now, let's fight it out!" (*"À nous deux, maintenant!"*) Napoleon was a "professor of energy." Dostoevski's Raskolnikoff was also haunted by the monumental example of Napoleon when he tried to find out whether he, the intellectual, was still capable of acting.

In his book, *Russian Realism in World Literature*,[4] George Lukács draws our attention to the fact that in many nineteenth century novels Bonaparte appears as the great example of the possibilities offered to extraordinary talents by a democratic society of reaching the highest levels of power. In this monumental conception of history, Napoleon became the standard against which to measure the democratic character of a society.

Although some forms of this monumental conception of history have survived, historical pragmatism in the narrow sense of a Machiavelli or a Bossuet has completely disappeared. Several factors contributed to this disappearance: Darwin's theory of evolution and modern Historicism with its insistence on the individuality and singularity of each nation and each historical situation shook the concept of a human nature, immutable through the ages, whose reactions would be the same under analogous conditions. And Bergson taught us that a living being which develops freely creates at every moment something new. From this springs the impossibility of foreseeing human actions under different historical constellations.

After the abandonment of the doctrine of the immutability of human nature thinkers of existentialist orientation like Heidegger, Ortega y Gasset and Sartre finally eliminated the very concept of human nature. They replaced the supra-temporal man "in general" of the Stoïcs by the man of a cetrain epoch and a certain place — that is to say by man *hic and nunc*. Instead of a human nature, they speak of "human reality" or "human condition."

---

[4] G. Lukács, *Der russische Realismus in der Weltliteratur* (Berlin, 1952), p. 135.

When, at the beginning of our reflexions, we said that, in our day, the comprehension of history is equally important to those who make it and to those who endure it, when we said that both need to know in order to foresee and to act, this did not imply a revival of historical pragmatism. We do not believe that historical analogies are a sure guide in life and we do not think that the monumental conception of history is of interest to the bulk of our contemporaries. This conception of history as an *adventure* may haunt the minds of certain exalted youths who are impressed by the bloody monuments of a Hitler or a Mussolini. That is all.

Far from being an *adventure,* history was recognized by most of our contemporaries as a *destiny,* a tragic collective destiny from which the individual can hardly escape. If they recognize the importance of understanding history, it is less *past* than *present* history, less the *historia rerum gestarum* than history as *res agendae,* as the whole of the collective forces which act and, while acting, engulf us. After having gone through two world wars and being confronted with the threat of a third one, my generation finally learned to understand history as a perpetual collective development of which each individual is, willy nilly, a part. At the cost of great sacrifices, we now understand that history is a rapid, turbulent river, flowing from the past through the present, toward the future an dragging us along in spite of ourselves.

To understand this history in the sense of knowing in order to foresee and to act simply means to have studied its forces and currents in the immediate past in order to be able to anticipate, with some probability, to which side we shall be thrown by the next wave.

This anticipation is possible. It is not necessary to be what Hegel called "a Manager of the World Spirit" *(ein Geschäftsführer des Weltgeistes)*[5] to foresee, under certain circumstances, the next phase of historical evolution. Any intelligent observer of the German scene from 1918 to 1932 could anticipate the tragic events which occurred between 1933 and 1945. Having studied the forces and direction of the historical currents of their epoch, some of these observers were even able to elude the gigantic wave *in statu nascendi* — for example by anticipated expatriation. The German writer, Erich Maria Remarque, left Germany several years before Hitler seized power. In 1932, the German Jewish historian and writer, Emil Ludwig, acquired Swiss citizenship, so that — as he expressed it — he would no longer be called a "German" during a second World War. This war broke out seven years later. Thus, the proverb

---

[5] G. F. W. Hegel, *Sämtliche Werke*, Band XI, p. 61.

historia vitae magistra ("history is life's teacher") has not lost its validity. It not only makes us more erudite but also more cautious.

Some years ago newspapers discussed the cases of some prominent Frenchmen who had emigrated to Canada or to South America in order to escape World War III. Was this anticipation right or wrong? History will judge. Anyway, these people have acquired a new sense unknown to their fathers: a historical sense which guides them in life. Just as the sea-gull has a sense for meteorological storms, man, in the middle of the twentieth century, has developed a sense for historical storms: he feels the coming of wars and revolutions.

Let us describe more precisely that new historical sense: in what respect is it different from that about which people began to talk almost a century and a half ago?

In 1814, the famous German jurist Friedrich Carl von Savigny, the founder of the historical school of law, defined the historical sense as the faculty "of firmly grasping the specific character *(das Eigentümliche)* of each epoch and of each juridical form".[6] This historical sense was purely theoretical. *Our* historical sense which is both theoretical and practical is, above all, the consciousness of man's temporality, his historicity — not as an individual, but as a member of a collectivity. Our new historical sense is the consciousness that the collectivity to which we belong has a past, that it has a future and that its present is a connecting link between these two dimensions; it is the consciousness that the present we are living in is laden with the heritage of the collective past and that it carries in its womb the germ of the future. Our historical sense is the consciousness that we are a part of this evolution of the collective past towards a collective future and that — to a large extent — it determines the course of our individual lives.

It is possible that the acquisition of this historical sense is a questionable gain for human happiness. Nietzsche envied the animals, unhistorical beings, which know neither past nor future and live only in the present. Having no memory of a grievous past and no conception of a fearful future, they must be happy. In order for happiness to be happiness, one thing is indispensible: "... the ability to forget, or expressed in a more erudite form, the faculty of feeling ... in a non-historic way."[7]

Hegel tried to invalidate this thesis in advance by declaring that world history is not the domain of happiness and that the periods of

---

[6] F. C. von Savigny, *Vom Berufe unserer Zeit für Gesetzgebung und Rechtswissenschaft* (Heidelberg, 1814), p. 48.
[7] Nietzsche's *Gesammelte Werke* (München, 1922), Band VI, p. 234.

felicity are the "empty pages of history".[8] Since the pages of the history of our century are full to the point of overflowing, we may understand why we are not happy. It is the price we have to pay for acquiring the historical sense.

It is obvious that the historical sense of our epoch has no longer anything in common with that erudite antiquarianism which threatens to change the past into a kind of gravedigger of the present: it has nothing in common with that sterile rumination which has been criticized so often, for instance, by Nietzsche, by Goethe and by Descartes. Let us not forget the remark of the father of modern philosophy that "if one is too curious about things which have been practised in past centuries, one usually remains very ignorant of those which are practised in this one".[9]

What we call the "new" historical sense is very close to that phenomenon which Sartre calls the discovery of man's historicity. According to the famous Existentialist, this discovery was made by the majority of Frenchmen from the year 1930 on. Up to that moment, says Sartre, they had secretly thought that to be historical was good for the dead. But the international crisis, especially the invasion of China by the Japanese, the rising of Nazism in Germany and, the Spanish civil war, opened their eyes. In his essay *"Qu'est-ce que la littérature?"* ("What is Literature?"), Sartre described in the following way that awakening of the consciousness of man's historicity in the French mentality:

> Suddenly it became necessary to envisage those first years of World Peace as the last years of the period between-two-wars; ... We noticed that our individual lives which had seemed to depend only upon our efforts, our virtues and defects, ... were governed ... by obscure collective forces .. At a single blow we felt ourselves bluntly *'situated'*. ... There was a collective adventure which appeared in the future and which was going to be *our* adventure. Historicity reflowed upon us. In everything we touched, in the air we breathed .. we discovered something like a taste of history ... The pressure of history revealed to us suddenly the interdependence of nations...an incident in Shanghai was a scissors' cut into our destiny — but at the same time it placed us back, in spite of ourselves, into our national collectivity.[10]

This masterful description by Sartre of the discovery of man's histori-

---

[8] G. W. F. Hegel, *Sämtliche Werke* (ed. Glockner) (Stuttgart, 1928), Band XI, p. 56.
[9] R. Descartes, *Discours de la méthode* (Paris, 1898), I, p. 13.
[10] J.-P. Sartre, *Situations*, II, "Qu'est-ce que la littérature?" (Paris, 1948), pp. 241—244.

city by the French expresses concretely what we have tried to define abstractly under the name of the new historical sense.

In the American mentality the historical sense awakened a little later, but, nevertheless, with great vigor, after the end of World War II. Since Russia had emerged from this war as a first-rate world power based on an ideology opposed to that of the United States, the Americans finally understood that their style of living — the famous "American way of life" — was not a natural product like the earth, but an historical product resulting from certain circumstances of their collective past. In a changing historical world the survival of these circumstances and of their product is no longer considered absolutely certain.

In the Soviet Union, the historical spirit has been solidly established since the October revolution of 1917, for Dialectical Materialism, the official state philosophy, is a fundamentally historical conception of society and even of nature. "According to this conception", said Engels toward the end of the nineteenth century, "socialism was no longer an accidental discovery of this or that ingenious brain, but the necessary outcome of the struggle between historically developed classes."[11]

More recently, Stalin wrote:

> The dialectical method regards as primarily important not that which, at the given moment, seems to be durable and yet is already beginning to die away, but that which is arising and developing, even though at the given moment it may not appear to be durable.[12]

This dialectical method which regards things from an evolutionary angle, this way of investigating what they were and what they are likely to become, is a fundamentally historical method.

Although in different ways, the historical sense predominates today in France, in the United States and in Russia. In other countries similar tendencies are noticeable.

However, in different countries and in different classes this historical sense has different emotional tonalities, just as it had a different character in other historical epochs. The historical sense of the representatives of the Enlightenment was full of gratitude for the heritage received from history and full of confidence in its future. Voltaire never tired of expressing the happiness he felt as the child of an enlightened century which — with its art of living, its social pleasures, its liberties — including the "liberties of the table" — had vanquished the barbarity of

[11] F. Engels, *Socialism Utopian and Scientific* (New York, 1934), p. 52.
[12] Stalin, *On Dialectical and Historical Materialism* (New York, 1940), p. 8.

ancient times. From the triumph of the culture of the sciences, inaugurated in the sixteenth century, Condorcet drew his conviction of an indefinite progress of mankind.

Summing up these feelings of gratitude and of optimism on the part of the philosophers of the Enlightenment with regard to history, Friedrich Schiller wrote in 1789:

> Unknowingly and without aiming at it, all previous centuries endeavoured to bring about our humanitarian century. We possess all the treasures which diligence and genius, reason and experience have harvested during the long life of mankind.[13]

Although our epoch is the heir of even richer treasures, it does not have that feeling of gratitude with regard to history. Worse than that! With nuclear science, the last result of the industrial revolution, our age seems to have inherited a Pandora's box, concealing forces which it cannot control. The emotional tonality of the new historical sense such as it predominates in the middle of the twentieth century — at least in the Western democracies — is determined by the fear of our contemporaries that they will no longer be able to dominate the historical forces released by their own dynamism and by man's feeling of being crushed by the forces of history, although they are human forces.

---

[13] F. Schiller, *Sämtliche Werke* (Stuttgart, 1813), Band VII, "Was heisst und zu welchem Ende studiert man Universalgeschichte?", pp. 30—31.

II. HISTORICAL REALITY

Up to now we have used the term "history" in the usual sense, as it is understood by everybody. Now a more precise definition becomes necessary. What characterizes the great majority of current definitions of history is the fact that they imprison their object in the past. Herodotus, father of history, began his first book by writing:

> What Herodotus, the Halicarnassian, has learnt by inquiry is here set forth: in order that the memory of the *past* may not be blotted out from among men by time ...[1]

This same tendency to limit history to the knowledge of the past is obvious among the majority of contemporary thinkers. André Lalande, for example, defines history as the "knowledge of the different stages successively achieved in the *past* by any sort of object of knowledge: a nation, an institution, a living species, a science, a language, etc."[2] For Raymond Aron "history in a narrow sense is the *science of the human past*"[3] and for Henri-I. Marrou it is the "knowledge" of this past *(la connaissance du passé humain).*[4] Faustino Ballvé defines history as *estudio de la vida de la humanidad por documentos*[5] — the study of the life of humanity by documents —, for Huizinga it is "the intellectual form in which a civilization renders account to itself of its *past*",[6] and according to Collingwood history deals with *"res gestae"*, i.e., with "actions of human beings that have been done in the *past*".[7]

Each of these definitions has its merits. What interests us at this moment is, however, the fact that they all limit history to the past.

[1] Herodotus, Book I.
[2] A. Lalande, *Vocabulaire technique et critique de la philosophie* (Paris, 1928), I, p. 303.
[3] R. Aron, *Introduction à la philosophie de l'histoire* (Paris, 1938), p. 17.
[4] H.-I. Marrou, *De la connaissance historique* (Paris, 1956), p. 32.
[5] F. Ballvé, *Diez Lecciones de Economía* (Mexico, 1956), p. 1.
[6] J. Huizinga, "A Definition of the Concept of History", *Philosophy of History* (Oxford, 1936), p. 9.
[7] R. G. Collingwood, *The Idea of History* (Oxford, 1946), p. 9.

This insistence on the past among ancient and modern thinkers becomes conceivable as soon as one realizes the original significance of the word history. In Greek ἱστορία means inquiry, research, investigation. Now, an inquiry is only possible into that which has become *real* which is exactly what the *past* is. A future history is not possible; it would only be a product of the imagination: a fable, a novel. However, according to its conception — and it is Voltaire who says so — *l'histoire est le récit des faits donnés pour vrais, au contraire de la fable qui est le récit des faits donnés pour faux ou fictifs*",[8] that is history is an account of facts presented as true, contrary to the fable which is an account of facts presented as false or fictitious. Since we cannot always clearly distinguish between true and false, between fact and fable, we may perhaps have recourse to the more modest definition of history by Galbraith as "the *past*, so far as we know it".[9] This latter definition accords with Karl Jaspers' statement that "history is ... the *enlightened past*" *(helle Vergangenheit)*.[10]

Although a history of the future is impossible, a history of the past does not seem to be the only conceivable one, because one could also imagine a *history of the present*. The latter was, indeed, affirmed by some of the world's greatest historians. For what else were men like Herodotus, Thucydides or Julius Caesar doing but writing the histories of their present? Hegel considered that kind of history as legitimate and even superior to one based on tradition. He called it *"ursprüngliche Geschichte"* — original history. Among its products he admired especially the French *mémoires*, for example those of Cardinal de Retz, which he classed as a "masterpiece". Among the Germans, he added, such masters are very rare.[11]

Hegel affirmed the history of the present in yet another, rather metaphysical sense. Since, according to this thinker, all events of universal history are only manifestations of the *Mind (Geist)* or the *Idea,* and since the Idea is "eternally present", it folows that all events, even those of the past, are present. Universal Mind is immortal, says Hegel; consequently, there is no past and no future but only an "essential now".

Thus, it is understandable that, in our day, Hegel's greatest disciple, the Italian philosopher, Benedetto Croce, contends that *"ogni vera storia*

---

[8] *Oeuvres complètes de Voltaire* (Paris, 1879), tome XIX, III, p. 346.
[9] V. H. Galbraith, "Why We Study History", *Hist. Assoc. Publication*, 1944, 131.
[10] K. Jaspers, *Vom Ursprung und Ziel der Geschichte* (Zürich, 1949), p. 50.
[11] G. W. F. Hegel, *Sämtliche Werke* (ed. Glockner), 1928, Band XI, p. 28.

è storia contemporanea"[12] — every true history is contemporary history. For Croce, the criterion of the present character of a history is that of corresponding to a present interest. Croce considers as "present" any history — even that of a remote past — which, at this moment, is thought by us. It must "vibrate in the historian's soul" — then it is "present", even if it took place centuries ago. The famous American historian, Carl Becker, shares Croce's opinion.

The idea of "present history" has always fascinated the minds of original thinkers. Among them the Spanish philosopher José Ortega y Gasset certainly holds a prominent position. If everyone among us asks himself why his life is such as it is, he will find the ultimate cause in the society where he lives and in that which this society has been in the past: in its beliefs, feelings, preferences. It is impossible to understand the European or American Rationalist of today, if one does not know what his ancestor has been — namely the medieval Christian. And the latter is conceivable only when the antique Stoïc is taken into consideration. Ortega concludes by saying that

> history is the systematic science of that radical reality which is my life. Consequently, it is the science of the most rigorous *present*. If it were not science of the present, where would we find that past which one can ascribe to it as its subject matter?[13]

Here, we are confronted with another conception of history as a discipline of the present, a very suggestive and original one. For Ortega, the past is not an abstract, inert thing; it is a living force which sustains our present. *"El pasado no está allí, en su fecha, sino aquí, en mí. El pasado soy yo — se entiende, mi vida"*[14] — the past is not there, at its date, but here, in myself. I am the past, that is to say, it is my life.

This is certainly entirely true. But let us now return to present history in the sense which Hegel called *"ursprüngliche Geschichte"* — the history which takes place before our eyes and of which we are witnesses. This kind of history was affirmed, without restriction, by another prominent modern thinker: the Frenchman Léon Brunschvicg. Refuting, during a meeting of the *Société Française de Philosophie*, the objections of his colleague Beaulavon, Brunschvicg declared:

> In abstracto, contemporary history ... seems to be the only possible one. The doctrines of *which* philosophers and of

[12] B. Croce, *Teoria e storia della storiografia* (Bari, 1927), p. 4.
[13] J. Ortega y Gasset, *Obras completas* (Madrid, 1950—52), t. VI, "Historia como sistema", p. 45.
[14] *Ibid.*, t. VI, p. 45.

> *which* scientists are we ... authorized to interpret if not of
> those we have the good fortune of knowing personally and
> whose thoughts we can grasp in pure *statu nascendi,* as we
> have done here for more than twenty years?[15]

If this is true for the history of ideas, it is, perhaps, not always true
for political and military history. The eminent French historian, Marrou,
says that "he tries to know much more than has been known by any
contemporary of the epoch studied and more than any contemporary is
capable of knowing. ... The historian must succeed in subjecting the
past to that rational gaze which understands, grasps and (in a way)
explains ..."[16]

However this may be, in a strict sense even present history is no
longer present at the moment at which it is written. Also, the men of
action who made history — a Julius Caesar, a Foch, a Clemenceau, a
Churchill or an Eisenhower — wrote it *post festum.* While history is
happening, says Etienne Gilson, one does not yet narrate it. "As soon as
Clio begins to speak, and were it only one second later, that which she
is speaking about has ceased to exist."[17] Then begins the reconstruction
with all its hazards, such as forgetfulness, the conclusions from the
effects to the causes, which are only probable, the rationalization of the
motives, the reinterpretation of the past in the light of the present and
its preoccupations.

In his *Philosophy of Law,* Hegel pronouced the celebrated sentence
that "the owl of Minerva takes its flight only when the shades of night
are gathering."[18] Only *post festum,* after the event, can philosophy begin its erudite work of interpretation. Thus, philosophy arrives always
"too late" to influence the course of events.

With these words the ultra-conservative Hegel wanted to discourage
the young, enthusiastic followers of philosopical doctrines aiming at a
reform of the political realities of the absolute Prussian monarchy. It
was to fulfil this task that Hegel had been called to the University of
Berlin in 1818 by the Prussian Minister of Education, von Altenstein.

However, Hegel's point of view did not take into account the true
influence exerted by philosophy on the great historical events. A witness
of the French revolution which he admired as the supreme triumph of
reason and the idea of right in political reality, Hegel had been, after all,

---

[15] L. Brunschvicg, *Ecrits philosophiques,* tome II, "Histoire et philosophie" (Paris,
1954), p. 116.
[16] H.-I. Marrou, *De la connaissance historique* (Paris, 1956), pp. 47—48.
[17] E. Gilson, *L'école des muses* (Paris, 1951), p. 12.
[18] G. W. F. Hegel, *Grundlinien der Philosophie des Rechts* (Stuttgart, 1928), p. 37.

in a position to see the formidable influence of philosophical ideas —
those of Rousseau and his confrères of the *Encyclopédie* — on the march
of history.

Evidently, Hegel could not foresee that his own system was going to
constitute another, no less impressive, example of the decisive influence
of philosophical ideas on political history. It is well known that Fascism
drew its inspiration from the right wing Old-Hegelians, while Communism is the intellectual child of the leftist Young-Hegelians. It was
said that the two opposing Hegelian factions met finally in the mortal
embrace of the battle of Stalingrad.

But if Hegel's reference to Minerva's owl is not valid for philosophy,
it seems to describe perfectly the function of historiography. The latter,
indeed, begins its work of interpretation only when the fact is accomplished. It is truly always in arrears with respect to the event. *Narrated*
history can only be a history of the past.

Sartre's philosophy accentuated this retrospective character of history.
For Sartre, there could not be any history of the present, since "the
present is not".[19] The present, he says, is a perpetual flight from being.
To him history is the science which studies the essences of men. But
man's essence is his past, according to Hegel's famous dictum, reaffirmed by Sartre: *Wesen ist, was gewesen ist.* Man first exists, appears in a
world and is afterwards defined as this or that being. During his whole
lifetime he develops his essence which is only completely crystallized at
the moment of his death. Thus, history can only judge the dead. The
living, thanks to their liberty and their future which is always open,
perpetually suspend a final verdict. The historian who wrote the history
of Pétain in 1919 had to rewrite it in 1951. And even then he had to
realize that the "meaning" of that history will remain in suspense and
will be reinterpreted in the light of the projects of future historians and
those of their societies. Therefore, Sartre says *"le sens du passé social est
perpétuellement en sursis"*[20] — the meaning of the social past is always
on reprieve. For the Sartrian Existentialist, history is possible only as
a history of the dead, it is an autopsy, a mortuary surgery where the
dead are "a prey of the living" *(en proie aux vivants).*

Before Sartre, other thinkers insisted on this retroactive effect of the
present and the future on the past. Bergson spoke of a *"mirage du pré-
sent dans le passé"* — a mirage of the present in the past — and showed
how Romanticism acted, retroactively, on classicism. "Retroactively it

[19] J.-P. Sartre, *L'être et le néant* (Paris, 1943), p. 168.
[20] *Ibid.*, p. 582.

created its own prefiguration in the past and an explanation of itself by its antecedents."[21]

In an analogous way, Léon Brunschvicg showed how Einstein's theory of general relativity justified, retrospectively, Leibniz' and Huygens' critiques of Newton.

Ernst Troeltsch, likewise, insisted on the plastic character of the past formed and reformed by the future.

> As in the physical sciences every calculation of a motion depends on the position of the observer, thus in history every standard is irremediably determined by the spot where one is located and at which it originates. It originates always as a living connection with the formation of the future.[22]

Here, we are confronted with a theory of historical relativity analogous to the one which Einstein established in the physical world. We shall discuss this later. For the moment let us take note of the fact that for Troeltsch, as for Bergson, Brunschvicg, Sartre and other thinkers — William Stern and Carl Becker are among them — the meaning of the past is always in suspense and a prey of the present. Our present situation and our projects regarding the future influence our interpretation of the historical past. History will be the narrative of necessary violence, if that which the present tries to justify is the violence it uses. History will be the condemnation of violence, if that which the present tries to justify is its opposition to violence. Being an instrument of action, says Benedetto Croce, history is always the justification of the present.[23]

We have seen that, from the most diverse angles, history seems to be limited to the presentation, the interpretation and the reinterpretation of the *past*. Although our attitudes towards this past vary according to our present interests and future expectations, the object of history seems to be confined to the past.

However, in my opinion, this is true only as far as history as knowledge is concerned and not with respect to history as reality. There are, indeed, two histories: the one which is narrated and the one which is happening. That which is narrated can, evidently, only refer to that which happened in the past, be it only one moment before. This is history as knowledge, history told orally or in written documents. But this history as knowledge has an object: history as reality. As far as the latter is concerned, it evidently has a past, a present and a future; it flows from the past to the present and projects itself toward the future.

[21] H. Bergson, *La pensée et le mouvant* (Paris, 1934), p. 23.
[22] E. Troeltsch, *Der Historismus und seine Probleme* (Tübingen, 1922), p. 169.
[23] B. Croce, *Il Carattere della Filosofia moderna* (Bari, 1941).

The duality is often veiled by the fact that common language has only a single word to designate history as knowledge and history as reality. Hegel noticed this strange linguistic fact and declared:

> History unites in our language the objective as well as the subjective side; it means the *historiam rerum gestarum* as well as the *res gestas* themselves; it is that which happened no less than the historical narration.[24]

In using the words "in our language" *(in unserer Sprache)* Hegel meant "in the German language". However, the situation is similar in other languages. In the concept of history none of the great modern languages — neither English, nor French, nor Spanish, nor Italian, nor (as I am told) Russian — ordinarily separates the aspect of reality from the aspect of knowledge. To be sure, in several of these languages scholars tried to introduce an erudite terminology which distinguishes these two aspects of history, but these attempts were not very successful.

In German the term *Geschichte*, coming from *Geschehen* (happening), is often reserved for history as reality, while several terms have been created for the designation of history as knowledge. Hegel called it *Geschichtserzählung* (historical narration), Nietzsche and Heidegger designated it as *Historie*, Simmel as *Historik*, Scheler used both of these terms. Furthermore, the term *Geschichtsschreibung* is used to designate written history. The multiplicity of these terms in German shows that awareness of the ambivalence in the concept of history is rather widespread among the philosophers and historians with German as their language.

In French, the distinction between *Histoire* with a capital for the designation of the events and *histoire* with a small letter to qualify the work of the historians does not seem ideal to me. Being only a distinction in writing, it cannot be orally expressed. The terms *"historialité"* and *"historial"*[25] proposed by Régis Jolivet seem to me somehow spurious.

The Italian distinction between *storia* and *storiografia* — the former to designate history as reality, the latter for history as knowledge — is an excellent terminology and susceptible to transposition into other languages. One finds, indeed, in English the analogous term *historiography*, in French the term *historiographie* and in Spanish the word *historiografía*. These terms are mostly used in translations of Italian writings. In the following, I shall use the term *historiography* whenever

---

[24] G. W. F. Hegel, *Sämtliche Werke* (ed. Glockner) (Stuttgart, 1928), Band XI, p. 97.
[25] R. Jolivet, "Définition et sens de l'histoire", *L'Homme et l'histoire* (Paris, 1952), p. 11.

it is necessary to contrast the history which is narrated with that which happens.

Let us, however, not forget an important warning of Hegel's which draws our attention to the fact that the synthesis of the two meanings of history in one word is not a "superficial hazard", but corresponds to a higher necessity. The terminological distinctions which we just mentioned are, indeed, somehow artificial, introduced by philosophers. "But the genius of each of these languages — says Professor Marrou — always refused to integrate such distinctions in living usage; they did so with good reason (*à bon droit*), for the first aspect (history as reality) does not exist in a pure condition or, at least, it is incomprehensible, unless in the form of the second"[26] — that is to say, in the form of history as knowledge.

Here, we are, indeed, confronted with a difficult aspect of the problem; for, evidently, the history which happened exists for us only in that which is narrated. And since, besides narrated or written history, we do not have any with which we could compare it — for history as reality no longer exists — certain ultracritical philosophers go so far as to call in question the existence of a historical reality. The fact seems to confirm Cicero's ironical dictum: *Nihil tam absurde dici potest quod non dicatur ab aliquo philosophorum* — nothing so absurd can be said which would not have been said by some of the philosophers.[27]

The eminent historian Marrou does not go as far. Nevertheless, he distrusts the concept of historical reality, since it does not exist "in pure condition" (*à l'état pur*), but only in the form of historical knowledge. He is convinced that historical knowledge has an object, that it refers to a reality — the past — but he considers this reality as a "noumenon" in the Kantian sense, impossible to be known such as it is "in itself," for as soon as historical reality is known, it is historical knowledge and no longer historical reality.

The final conclusion of Marrou — which he shares with Karl Jaspers — is that God alone can know historical reality authentically and totally. Being, according to his own confession, "more theologian than philosopher", Professor Marrou asks himself whether philosophy of history is not exposed to the danger of committing the sin of "immoderation" and "hybris".[28]

---

[26] H.-I. Marrou, "Philosophie critique de l'histoire et sens de l'histoire", *L'homme et l'histoire* (Paris, 1952), p. 7. In his book *De la connaissance historique* (Paris, 1956), pp. 38—41, Prof. Marrou adopts a similar position.

[27] Cicero, *De Divinatione*, II, 58.

[28] H.-I. Marrou, "Philosophie critique de l'histoire", p. 9.

In his *Introduction à la philosophie de l'histoire,* Professor Raymond Aron pushes the critical scruples as far as to refuse to admit any linguistic distinction between history as knowledge and history as reality.

> Since knowledge of the past is an aspect of historical reality, we shall not separate the reflexion on the science and the description of the happening. Neither theory nor language should dissociate subject and object.[29]

There is no question of our here being confronted with an authentic epistemological problem of history. It is a consequence of Kant's criticism which Hegel was the first to recognize, but without seeking a solution. For, in his *Philosophie der Geschichte,* Hegel drew our attention to the fact that the historian "is not passive with his thought, but brings his categories along with him and sees the real through them".[30]

The Neo-Kantians were the first philosophers who tried to solve this epistemological problem of history. We shall discuss it later.

It was again Hegel who identified history as reality and history as knowledge by declaring that the former occurs with the latter.

> The periods ... which elapsed for the nations before historiography may have been filled with revolutions, migrations and the wildest transformations: nevertheless, they were without objective history, because they had no subjective history, no historical narration.[31]

This is a very strange idea which is not generally accepted. Heidegger, for example, declares that historicity does not need historiography. Periods without historiography are not always non-historical, he adds.[32] Other thinkers, however, adopt a point of view very close to Hegel's. For Croce, history means only comprehension by means of an *account;* it is basically historiography. The account is linked to the document and *"una storia senza relazione col documento sarebbe ... inesistente in quanto storia"*[33] — a history without reference to the document would be inexistent as history. Similarly, Karl Jaspers declares in his book *Vom Ursprung und Ziel der Geschichte:*

> It is a prejudice (to believe) that where tradition is missing, the thing itself — history — could have existed or even would have necessarily existed. History is the past enlightened for man, at a given moment.[34]

[29] R. Aron, *Introduction à la philosophie de l'histoire* (Paris, 1938), p. 45.
[30] G. W. F. Hegel, *Sämtliche Werke* (edit. Glockner), Band XI, p. 37.
[31] *Ibid.,* p. 98.
[32] M. Heidegger, *Sein und Zeit* (Tübingen, 1949), p. 396.
[33] B. Croce, *Teoria e storia della storiografia* (Bari, 1927), p. 6.
[34] K. Jaspers, *Vom Ursprung und Ziel der Geschichte* (Zürich, 1949), p. 50.

Having been educated in the tradition of Kantian criticism — a development of Cartesian doubt — I respect all these critical scruples. But there is a limit beyond which this doubt should not go. Its ultimate usefulness, says Descartes, consists "in that it makes it impossible for us to have any longer any doubt about that which we shall discover afterwards to be true" (*ac denique efficiat, ut de iis, quae postea vera esse comperiemus, non amplius dubitare possimus*).[35] Such a reality about which we can no longer have any doubt is, in my opinion, historical reality.

I admit, with the thinkers quoted before, that historical reality can be grasped only in the form of historical knowledge. But this is true only as long as we limit history to the past. As soon as we admit a history of the present, the difference between history as knowledge and history as reality becomes obvious, and the latter detaches itself from the former as an independent entity. Whoever lived through World War II, whoever participated in the great battle of France in May and June 1940 or in the landing in Sicily, whoever entered Paris with the victorious allied armies, whoever was wounded or deported by the Germans and who reads now the history of World War II by Churchill, Eisenhower or de Gaulle will realize that there is such a thing as historical reality and that it cannot be confused with the history laid down in documents and written in books.

We gain this conviction of the existence of a historical reality by recourse to subjectivity, a kind of pathetic *cogito* which could be expressed in the following terms: *I am suffering from it, or I have suffered from it — consequently there is a historical reality.*

Historical reality is thus a reality subjectively *lived, suffered, experienced — truly* experienced, and not only *re*-experienced in the imagition of the historian, like Croce's so called "contemporary" history.

How is this reality experienced by common man? It presents itself as an exterior force coming from the past and rushing towards the future which, while passing through the present, invades his private sphere and drags him along with it. Thus, the man who experiences historical reality is prone to define it as the evolution of the *res publica*. The *res publica* is the affair or the totality of the affairs of the group to which a man belongs — a nation, a class, mankind.

It may be alleged that it has become rather difficult to distinguish between the *res publica* and the *res privata*, since the French sociological school of Durkheim has shown us the social origin of the greater part of

---

[35] Descartes, *Meditationes de prima philosophia*, 12.

our categories and even of our feelings. It is not only Freud's *super-ego* which now appears as a social product. The collective unconscious of Karl Mannheim, more solidly established than Jung's, suggests that even Freud's *"id"* does not represent a purely individual sphere. "The individuals *bathe* in a collective mentality to which they owe their own" — says Masson-Oursel — "except to the extent to which consciousness depends on the condition of the body."[36]

But where philosophers see insuperable difficulties impeding all distinctions, the common man distinguishes with perfect certitude. The young man who wishes to marry his girl friend, who desires to found a family and wishes to live the unheroic life of a modest clerk and who, suddenly, is called to active service in order to defend some grandiose idea recognizes clearly that this demand comes to him from the public sphere, while his project of matrimonial happiness constitutes his private sphere. Although the origin of our ideas and feelings is, to a large extent, social, as soon as these ideas and feelings are assimilated by us, they are ours and belong to our private sphere.

I well realize that, in defining historical reality as the evolution of the *res publica*, I determine it by categories and change it into history as knowledge. Nevertheless, there exists an epistemological difference between history as reality and history as knowledge which can hardly be overlooked, even if the former is changed into the latter. To be sure, Kant said that "besides our knowledge, we have nothing with which we could contrast this knowledge as a corresponding term."[37] I think, however, that, as far as history is concerned, we are able to distinguish between two kinds of knowledge: the one based on documents, the only one recognized as valid by the historians of the past, the other based on actual experience, personal experience, grammatically expressed in the first person singular. If the latter is a first-hand history, the former is only at second hand. One cannot affirm a second-hand history at the cost of one based on first-hand experience.

Even if, thanks to the application of certain logical categories, the historical reality I experienced is changed into historical knowledge, it remains definitely distinct from historical knowledge properly so called — the one I did not experience and which is only based on documents and written accounts.

Consequently, I shall call *historical reality* the events of the *res publica*, subjectively experienced and expressed in the first person, even if,

---

[36] P. Masson-Oursel, *La morale et l'histoire* (Paris, 1955), p. 106.
[37] I. Kant, *Kritik der reinen Vernunft*, p. 570.

thanks to the application of certain categories, this historical reality is converted into historical knowledge.

Historical knowledge properly so called — the knowledge based on transmitted documents — is that which I shall call historiography. Later on, I shall give a more detailed analysis of these two kinds of historical knowledge.

Thus, the existence of an historical reality is established in the form of personally experienced history, the history of the personal present. This history has a Janus head with two faces, one looking backward, to the past, the other forward, toward the future. In fact, all great conceptions of history refuse to imprison their object in the past and ascribe to it three dimensions: the past, the present, the future. This holds for Saint Augustine, Vico, Hegel, Marx, Spengler, Toynbee and others.

The *res publica,* whose development constitutes historical reality, is opposed to the *res privata,* which is not an object of history. If one accepts this distinction, it is no longer possible to speak of the history of the life of Mr. So and So, if he is not a public figure. I shall, for instance, not speak of the history of my life, because it is my private affair and does not influence the evolution of the *res publica.* Let us reserve the term "chronology" to designate the succession of the events of the *res privatae.*

However, if it is a question of a Descartes, a Newton, a Goethe, a Jefferson one can speak of the history of their lives. Since their works have become public property and are a part of the objective mind of mankind, of its collective inheritance, those men have become public figures. Having belonged to the historical reality of their times, they have become objects of history as knowledge.

The American historian Freeman defined history as "past politics".[38] By this definition he not only limited history to one single dimension of time — as is so often done — but also to one single object: politics. However, there is also a history of ideas, a history of philosophy, of civilizations, of sciences, languages, arts, literatures, religions, etc. If we define history as the evolution of the *res publica* from the past through the present towards the future, all those diverse domains find their place in it. For ideas, arts, languages, religions, etc. are public property. They are *res publicae,* they present themselves to the subjects as something objective, exerting on them that coercive force which, according to Durkheim, is the distinctive sign of every social fact. Since history is the development of the *res publica,* it is, of necessity, a social fact.

[38] J. E. W. Sterling, "Who is Clio?", *The Pacific Spectator* (Stanford, Cal.), Vol. II, Nr. 3, Summer 1947, p. 273.

We shall not, in this book, go into a detailed analysis of the history of nature. Its structure is too different from that of human history. One has tried for a long time to understand the history of man as a prolongation of the history of the earth and of the other species. Recently, Historical Materialism established a scheme according to which matter is in permanent evolution forming more and more complicated entities: electrons, atoms, molecules, living cells, plants, animals, men, societies. This evolution consists of a series of revolutions: small quantitative changes accumulate in everything, provoke a tension, a struggle between the old and the new elements. When the new element has become strong enough, it breaks the equilibrium and, with a leap, a new quality is born of purely quantitative changes. In social life, these leaps are called revolutions.

But, in spite of certain analogies between natural history and the history of man, one cannot deny the deep differences which separate them. For Herder, man was the last stage of physical evolution and the first stage of moral evolution. In my opinion, nature can be the object of history, while man is both its object and its subject. He is its subject not only because he is the creator of his own history, but also because he is conscious of this history, because he accumulates the past of his species in the form of memory and imagines its future in the form of collective projects.

Fichte reminded us that the mole has built its mound in the same way, for thousands of years, just as the bee has never changed the manner in which it forms its hives. But man, Franklin's and Bergson's "tool-making animal" always invents new ways and transmits his inventions to his posterity.

> Man has a history — says Professor Raymond Aron — because he is developing through time, because he creates works which outlive him, because he collects the monuments of the past. History as reality and history as science exist authentically from the moment in which men transmit to each other their common conquests and progress by this enchainment.[39]

One can hardly find a better formula.

What is the relationship between historical reality considered as the evolution of the *res publica* and politics? The latter is certainly a public affair. But does politics always constitute an integral part of the evolution of the *res publica* from the past toward the future, a necessary link

---

[39] R. Aron, *Introduction à la philosophie de l'histoire* (Paris, 1938), p. 37.

in this evolution? Not always, of course. There is the every-day small-time politicking which has nothing to do with the development in time of the true problems of a community. In a few weeks it will have lost its significance. Since it does not constitute an essential link in the evolution of the *res publica* from the past toward the future, this small-time politics of the lobbies is not a part of history.

But there is also "high politics". It constitutes a necessary link between the past and the future. The superior politician is the one who understands the deep needs of the group he represents. If, thanks to this comprehension, he succeeds in determining, to a certain extent, the evolution of his group toward the future, if he ends up by changing politics into history, then he is a great politician and becomes a historical figure, a true statesman.

But since the significance of the historical past is always only tentative, the place of a statesman in history is no more definitive than that of a philosopher, a poet, a writer, a scientist, a painter or a composer. The one who, now, seems to constitute a necessary link between the past and the future may be revealed later as a purely ephemeral phenomenon. At the end of the eighteenth century, Salieri was placed above Mozart and Pleyel on a par with Haydn.

In 1845, the German publisher Wigand announced, under the title *French Classics,* the translations he was at that time preparing for publication. This list included one work by Montesquieu, four by Voltaire, four by Rousseau, Thiers' *History of the French Revolution* and *twenty* novels by George Sand. George Sand as a French classic! At that time, the German writer Heinrich Laube, also highly thought of as a penetrating critic, declared that Eugène Sue was *the* novelist of Europe in 1840, as George Sand and Balzac had been in earlier years. One century later, George Sand's and Eugène Sue's works were completely forgotten, while Balzac's were more alive than ever.

These examples show to what extent the significance of history is tentative, and not only in the light of the new projects of its interpreters, as Sartre affirms. By correcting the errors of perspective committed by contemporaries from their lack of distance, history appears, in the long run, as the world's tribunal, although in a sense different from Hegel's.

The *res publica,* whose development constitutes history as reality, is collective. The *res privata* is personal. We may now define more precisely the historical sense of our epoch by saying that it is the realization that the *res privata* depends on the evolution of the res publica. Perhaps it was also familiar to other epochs of great historical events — to that of the American and the French revolutions, for example, or during

Napoleon's wars. In our epoch, however, after two world wars and under the menace of a third one, this historical sense manifests itself, for the first time, on a world-wide scale.

Today, more than ever, we have the clear consciousness that our personal destinies, our *res privatae*, depend, to a large extent, on the development of the *res publica*. We have seen and are seeing, how, with a dynamic impetus, the collective forces of history rush from the past towards the future, very often destroying the present of the individuals. Many people experience this sacrifice of their *res privata* to the *res publica* as a tragic loss. In my book, *Philosophie du rire et des pleurs*, I said: "A necessary loss of values is *sad,* an unnecessary loss of values, which occurs nonetheless, is *tragic.*"[40] The loss of an individual life or of the project which gives it meaning, so that the collective forces of history may triumph, is certainly a loss of a value, of an irreplaceable value. Knowing that the forces of history are still human forces which, as such, cannot entirely escape human control, man has the feeling that the sacrifice of his individual happiness at the altar of history is an unnecessary loss of values, which nevertheless occurs. Consequently, it is a tragic loss.

Why does this loss nevertheless occur, if the forces of history are human forces? The reason is that if history does not escape human control, since it is a product of man, it is not a product of individual man, but of man as a member of the human collectivity. The latter, however, is not a simple sum of individuals, but a specific entity with its own characteristics. Durkheim and Royce have shown this convincingly. Furthermore, history is not only the product of the contemporary collectivity but also of past collectivities of which we are the heirs. From all this arises the impotence of common man when confronted with the forces of history.

Rousseau established the difference between "general will" (*la volonté générale*) and "the will of everybody" (*la volonté de tous*)." The former" he says "is only concerned with common interest; the latter with private interest and is only a sum of particular wills".[41] While Rousseau still granted that "besides the public person, we have to consider the private persons who compose it and whose lives and liberties are, of course, independent of it,"[42] Hegel, the great advocate of the sovereignty of the State and of history, declared, straight out:

---

[40] A. Stern, *Philosophie du rire et des pleurs* (Paris, 1949), p. 252.
[41] *Oeuvres complètes de J. J. Rousseau* (Paris, 1828), t. II, p. 147.
[42] *Ibid.,* t. II, p. 149.

> What is required in a state is the practice of acting according
> to a general will and of adopting general purposes. Also in
> a crude state, there is the subjection of the will to another.
> This does not mean, however, that the individual does not
> have a will of his own, but that his particular will does not
> count. Fancies and lusts have no validity.[43]

In another passage, Hegel declares: "The particular is, most often, too
unimportant in comparison with the general: the individuals are sacrificed and abandoned."[44]

But, besides common men who prefer happiness to grandeur and
become objects and victims of history, there are the subjects of history,
those who push history forward and find their happiness only in
grandeur. Is this privileged minority more fortunate than the great
majority of the victims of history? Evidently, they are equally not
absolute masters of the historical forces. But having recognized the
general trends of these forces, their hidden exigencies and possibilities,
they are able to introduce themselves into the historical currents and
thus to direct them for a short while. By varying Bacon's dictum about
nature, one could say: *Historia non vincitur nisi parendo* — history is
not dominated unless one obeys it.

Finally, those heroes of history are likewise engulfed by its whirlpools.
"As soon as their mission is fulfilled" — says Hegel — "they fall down
as empty husks fall from a kernel. They die young, as Alexander, are
murdered, like Caesar, or deported to Saint Helena, like Napoleon."[45]
One could add that they are hanged by the feet on butchers' hooks like
Mussolini, soaked with gasoline and burned like Hitler, or downgraded
after death like Stalin.

Thus, it becomes obvious that, in the long run, neither the great actors
nor the unwilling supernumeraries of history can escape the dynamism
of its collective forces.

Many of our contemporaries feel the need for protecting the *res
privata* against the unchained floods of the *res publica,* those tidal waves
which tear us away from the present and drag us along towards an
uncertain future. There are even some who rebel against history, and
Albert Camus, the great French writer, was their most eloquent spokesman. For Camus' *L'homme révolté* (*The Rebel*) is, essentially, the man
who rebels against history, against the fact of being imprisoned by

---

[43] G. W. F. Hegel, *Die Vernunft in der Geschichte,* edit. G. Lasson (Leipzig, 1920),
p. 92.
[44] G. W. F. Hegel, *Sämtliche Werke,* edit. H. Glockner (Stuttgart, 1928), Band XI,
p. 63.
[45] *Ibid.,* XI, p. 61.

history. "Man in his rebellion" — writes Camus — "sets ... a limit to history. At that limit, the promise of a value is born."[46]

Later, we shall examine the question whether values truly escape history. Camus only postulates the independence of values from history, without even trying to prove it.

It is art which, according to Camus, teaches us that man is not just a summary of history.

> Art brings us back ... to the origins of revolt, to the extent to which it tries to give its form to a value which flees into a perpetual becoming but of which the artist has a presentiment and which he wants to ravish from history.[47]

Camus tries to demonstrate this thesis by explaining to us the significance of the work of Marcel Proust.

> His endeavour has been to create, starting from reality, ... a closed, irreplaceable world which belongs to him alone and marks his victory over the flight of things and over death,[48]

that is to say over history. According to Camus, Proust has shown us that the past is found again at the end of time in an "imperishable present". In this respect, Camus seems to agree with Ernst-Robert Curtius, according to whom the literary work escapes time and belongs to a "timeless present".

But is not all this rather a beautiful dream than a reality, an illusion nourished by many artists who, considering themselves as creators in the image of God, refuse to admit the perishable nature of their work? As far as I am concerned, I doubt whether in two thousand years the world will still be able to appreciate the beauty of Proust's work, that it will find pleasure in reading the description of the taste of a French cookie called "madeleine" which aunt Léonie offered the narrator every Sunday morning in Combray, after having dipped it into tea. In reading Goethe's *Werther* today, one no longer understands how, one hundred and eighty years ago, it could move the whole world so deeply.

I admit that the artist wants to ravish from history a value which flees into a perpetual becoming, but I am not sure that he can do it. On the contrary, the history of arts and literatures shows that the aesthetic conceptions vary with the historical epochs, that they too are *filiae temporum,* daughters of the times. Only a few of the greatest works of art have, up to now, been able to escape the action of historical

---

[46] A. Camus, *L'homme révolté* (Paris, 1951), p. 307.
[47] *Ibid.,* p. 319.
[48] *Ibid.,* p. 329.

time which, slowly but surely, dissolves the old values to make room for new ones. How long will these great works of art still resist those dissolving forces of history?

Besides artistic beauty there is natural beauty. "One can refuse all history" — says Camus — "and yet concur with the world of the stars and of the sea."[49] If this implies the idea that natural beauty escapes history, I cannot accept this opinion, because natural beauty is not entirely objective but supposes a subject capable of appreciating it. The sense of natural beauty is of most recent origin; it is a conquest of Romanticism, and thus a child of history. Medieval man was insensible to nature, and for primitive man it was and still is a mystical force full of the most anguishing imaginary dangers. Lucien Lévy-Bruhl showed this clearly.

In his *Rebel*, Camus devoted a whole chapter to the thought of Nietzsche, limiting himself, however, to its last period. Thus, Camus omitted to study the young Nietzsche's revolt against history which took place in 1873 and with which his own has so much in common. If Camus insists that *"becoming is nothing without being"* and that the world *"is movement and stability"*,[50] Nietzsche declared eighty years earlier:

> It is high time to attack ... the divagations of the historical sense, that exaggerated pleasure people feel toward the *process* at the expense of *being*. ...[51]

Like Camus, Nietzsche believed in "supra-historical forces" (*das Überhistorische*):

> I call supra-historical all the forces which deviate our attention from *becoming* toward that which gives existence the character of eternity ...: *art* and *religion*.[52]

Here, the analogy between the antihistorical revolutions of Camus and Nietzsche becomes still more evident. Both believed in supra-historical forces capable of stopping the perpetual flight of historical becoming. For young Nietzsche these "eternizing forces" were art and religion; for young Camus they were art and nature. Had Camus lived longer, he might also have added religion.

We have already insisted on the historical character of art. As for the

---

[49] *Ibid.*, p. 341.
[50] *Ibid.*, p. 365.
[51] *Nietzsches Gesammelte Werke*, "Vom Nutzen und Nachteil der Historie für das Leben" (München, 1922), Band VI, p. 309.
[52] *Ibid.*, p. 321.

historical character of religions, it is obvious. How could it escape the attention of the classical philologist Nietzsche? The fact that the great religions have conserved their names leads us into the error of believing that they have not changed in the course of history. Maintained by powerful institutions, the great religions we know have, however, not ceased to change their content, making more and more concessions to the *Zeitgeist*, the spirit of the age. What is believed by Christians nowadays is very different from what was believed by them in the time of Saint Paul. The social functions of the religions likewise change in the course of history. Today, many people consider religions only as a means to stop the progress of Communism.

There is, nevertheless, a difference between the antihistorical revolution of Nietzsche and that of Camus. Considering history as an affair of the past, Nietzsche rebelled especially against history as knowledge, against the exaggeration of historical culture in German education. To fight this "historical disease", he was thus able to recommend "the art and power of forgetting"[53] and of living unhistorically.

Camus' case was quite different. He was born on the eve of World War I. When his father was killed in 1914 during the battle of the Marne, he was not yet one year old. He was twenty when Hitler rose to power. For him, history has never been anything else than a *present* reality.

"I grew up with all the men of my age" — he wrote — "to the sound of the drums of World War I, and since that time our history has not ceased to be murder, injustice, or violence." Thus Camus knew "the crude and furious movement of history"[54] which drags us towards the future, trying to deprive us of our only certain possession: the present. If Nietzsche's antihistorical revolt was thus, above all (although not exclusively), directed against history as knowledge, Camus rebelled against history as reality. Against this, Nietzsche's "art of forgetting" would no longer serve as a remedy. Here, the intentional forgetfulness would only be a means of duping oneself.

However, the values with which Camus tried to oppose the onslaught of history would be suprahistorical only if two conditions applied: that of the existence of a human nature immutable across the ages, and that of a natural right implanted in it. Upon these two pillars philosophy rested for centuries. Making use of these two pillars as supports for his antihistorical rebellion, Camus returned to the thought of the seventeenth and eighteenth centuries:

[53] *Ibid.*, p. 321.
[54] A. Camus, *L'homme révolté* (Paris, 1951), p. 372.

> There is no justice in society without *natural or civil right* as its foundation.[55] ... Historical absolutism, in spite of its triumphs, has never ceased to come into collision with an invincible exigency of *human nature* of which the Mediterranean Sea, where intelligence is the sister of a hard light, keeps the secret.[56]

In another passage of his *L'homme révolté*, Camus declares that man's rebellion is

> the refusal to be treated as a thing and to be reduced to simple history. It is the affirmation of a *human nature common to all men* which escapes the world of power.[57]

However, as we shall show later, it was the dissolution of the concepts of *human nature* and *natural right* by modern Historicism and Existentialism which provoked the most serious crisis in contemporary philosophy of history. Far from refuting the arguments which brought about the abandonment of the concepts of human nature and natural right, Camus postulates them, in order to give his revolt a foundation. But a postulate does not guarantee the reality of the thing postulated. If one can escape history as *knowledge* by practising Nietzsche's art of forgetting, it is impossible to escape history as *reality*, for, as Heidegger rightly says, "the essence of existence is basically historical",[58] for the simple reason that it is temporal and finite. "History belongs to the essence of existence",[59] he adds. How could we then escape history without giving up existence?

Thus, Camus' antihistorical revolt remains a *beau geste* of a great writer without philosophical significance. It is almost as sterile as his "metaphysical revolt" against the human condition and "the whole creation", those unchangeable facts which philosophical wisdom requires us to accept.

As we said, Camus was the mouth-piece of those of our contemporaries who refuse to sacrifice their *res privatae* at the altar of history. Another group of our contemporaries, the Marxists, still insist more vigorously on the fact that the *res privata* depends on the evolution of the *res publica*. Thus, they have the historical sense which characterizes our time. But they have learned so totally to submit their *res privatae* to the *res publica* that their historical sense has no tragic character, because

---

[55] *Ibid.*, p. 359.
[56] *Ibid.*, p. 370.
[57] *Ibid.*, pp. 306—307.
[58] M. Heidegger, *Sein und Zeit* (Tübingen, 1949), p. 392.
[59] *Ibid.*, p.379.

it is free from the sentiment of a sacrifice of their *res privatae*. On the contrary, they are convinced that history, as the dialectical evolution of the *res publica* must, with an intrinsic necessity, lead to the triumph of everybody's *res privata*. Toward the end of the nineteenth century, Friedrich Engels, the friend and collaborator of Marx, wrote in his book *Socialism Utopian and Scientific:*

> The possibility of securing for every member of society, by means of socialized production, an existence not only fully sufficient materially ... but an existence guaranteeing to all the free development and exercise of their physical and mental faculties — this possibility is now here for the first time ...[60]

Those who do not consider this message an utopia believe, with Marx, that if men are formed by their social relationships, these social relationships are likewise formed by men. Integrated in their collectivity, the Marxists try to contribute, by solidarity of action, to the realization of that golden age which has been promised them. Acting together, they no longer feel impotent toward history, because they are no longer isolated individuals.

To be sure, for them too, history remains a dangerous adventure, full of unforeseeable ups and downs. But, even in this respect, Marx' and Engels' message allows them to anticipate a future paradise where history will have passed completely under human control. In this respect, Engels tells them:

> The extraneous objective forces that have hitherto governed history pass under the control of man himself. Only from that time will man himself, more and more consciously, *make his own history*, only from that time will the social causes set in movement by him have, ... the results intended by him. It is *the ascent of man* from the *kingdom of necessity to the kingdom of freedom.*[61]

Many of our contemporaries will answer, with Faust: "I hear the message, but I have no faith."[62] Others take that message literally, although it sounds more "utopian" than "scientific", and draw all the conclusions for the future of history. For instance, Pierre Naville, France's leading dialectical materialist, wrote, in 1952, under the title *"Y a-t-il une fin de l'histoire?"* ("Is there an End of History?"):

---

[60] F. Engels, *Socialism Utopian and Scientific* (New York, 1935), p. 72.
[61] *Ibid.*, p. 73.
[62] Goethes *Faust*, I, p. 37.

> If man ceases to be the product of his own product, in order
> to become simply his own product, that is, if he passes from
> alienation to enjoyment, if he succeeds in "jumping into the
> realm of true liberty", history will cease to be what it is still
> today: a tragic destiny. Then, we will be able to speak of
> annals, of chronology or adventure, but no longer of history.[63]

Will the pessimism of the one group or the optimism of the other be the
final winner? Let us await the verdict of history.

---

[63] P. Naville, "Y a-t-il une fin de l'histoire?", *L'homme et l'histoire* (Paris, 1952),
p. 314.

III. THE PHILOSOPHY OF HISTORY — ITS ORIGIN AND AIMS

The new historical sense which we have just characterized explains the reawakening of interest in philosophy of history. Having recognized that his individual destiny is intimately linked to the historical evolution of the group to which he belongs, man, in the middle of the twentieth century, seeks to understand history in its wholeness, the principles by which it is governed and the meaning it may conceal. The totality of the endeavors to understand history and to integrate it into the wholeness of human existence is what — according to a term coined by Voltaire — is called *philosophy of history*.

We have seen that it is by virtue of his sufferings that man grasps historical reality. "I am suffering from it or I have suffered from it; consequently there *is* a historical reality", says the man of our epoch to himself. Thus, he refutes the idea of certain theorists that all history is history of the past and that historical reality is comprehensible only in the form of historical knowledge. By the sufferings it imposes upon man, history reveals itself as a present reality, neatly distinct from the shadow it throws behind itself in the form of historical knowledge. Historical reality is experienced history.

The sufferings imposed upon individuals by the collective tragedies called "historical" have been, in all epochs, the main motives for the development of a philosophy of history. The first fully conscious attempt to create such a philosophy — Saint Augustine's *City of God* — was motivated by the conquest of Rome by Alaric's Visigoths. The triumph of these hordes, their atrocities and, especially, "the outrages suffered by Christian women on the part of the barbarian soldiers" — all these events concerning the collectivity posed a grave problem which, of necessity, aroused a philosophical mind like Saint Augustine's. What had that city, considered eternal, done to deserve such a cruel fate? Thus, the fall of the capital of the civilized world led Augustine to meditate on the caducity of secular civilizations and to seek the salvation of mankind in its supernatural vocation. The result of these meditations was the first great treatise on philosophy of history.

The intimate relation between Saint Augustine's philosophy of history and the pillage of Rome by the Goths in 410 A.D. becomes obvious from the beginning of the *City of God.* In its first book, the author rises up

> against the pagans who ascribed to the Christian religion, because it prohibits the worship of the gods, the disasters of the world and especially the recent pillage of Rome by the Goths (*maximeque Romanae urbis recentem a Gothis vastationem*).[1]

The invasions of Italy in the sixteenth century and the moral sufferings they imposed on his patriotism and national pride had a decisive influence on the philosophy of history of Niccolo Machiavelli. The final chapter of his *Prince* has the title *Esortazione a liberare l'Italia da barbari*,[2] Exhortation to liberate Italy from the Barbarians.

The greatest attempt at a philosophy of history in modern times — Hegel's — was partly conceived under the thunder of Napoleon's cannons. Hegel was a young professor in the University of Jena, when the victorious French troops took the city. The night before the battle of Jena, Hegel saw through the windows of his room the fires of the French battalions camping in the market place. During this historical night he revised the last pages of the manuscript of his *Phenomenology of the Spirit*. The next day the Prussian troops were beaten, and Hegel's apartment wrecked, so that the Minister of State, Goethe, had to grant him a subsidy.

On the eve of the battle of Jena Hegel saw Napoleon and wrote to a friend:

> I have seen the emperor — that world soul — riding on horseback through the city. . . . It is indeed a sublime feeling to see such an individual, who, concentrated on one point, on horseback, spreads over the world and dominates it.[3]

The whole of Hegel's philosophy of history was to bear the stamp of these individual experiences of a collective destiny. His ideas on the stabilization of history, on great statesmen as "managers" of the universal spirit, on their passions and sacrifices, on their right to place themselves above morals, etc. — all these were intimately linked with Hegel's

---

[1] Sancti Aurelii Augustini episcopi *De Civitate Dei contra Paganos*, Liber Primus.
[2] *Opere di Niccolò Machiavelli*, Tomo VI (MDCCXVII), Cap. 26, p. 356.
[3] K. Fischer, *Hegels Leben, Werke und Lehre* (Heidelberg, 1911), I, p. 70.

personal experience of the battle of Jena and its hero, Bonaparte, an experience at the same time distressing and sublime.

The most sensational book on philosophy of history in the twentieth century, Oswald Spengler's *Decline of the West*, was published in 1917, during the third year of World War I. In his preface, Spengler wrote: "This war is one of the conditions from which the ultimate features of the new image of the world could be conceived."[4]

Finally, the latest sensation in the domain of philosophy of history, Toynbee's *A Study of History*, underwent the influence of two world wars. Referring to the first of these disasters, Toynbee wrote: "... my mind was ... not yet set hard when history took my generation by the throat in 1914. ..."[5] Even the most static, antihistorical, supratemporal philosopher of our century — Edmund Husserl — had to re-interpret his doctrine in a new, historical sense, when the historical catastrophe of Hitler's so-called "national revolution" took him by the throat, almost in a literal sense.[6]

The new vigor of philosophy of history we have been noticing since the days of World War II is thus well explained by the personal sufferings of so many individuals, undergoing a cruel collective destiny which befell their time, their generation.

From the standpoint of their psychological motives, philosophical systems may be divided into "theorogone" and "pathogone". Theorogone philosophy is motivated by observing the world: the antique θεωρός was the observer who attended public games in an official capacity. On the contrary, pathogone philosophy is motivated by the sufferings, the πάθος, which our human existence imposes on us. If epistemology is, in general, theorogone, we may affirm that in most cases philosophy of history is pathogone.

In my book on the philosophical foundations of truth, reality and value, I outlined the differences between philosophy and science by stating: Philosophy examines the relationships between determining thought and the objects determined, that is between man as a subject and the world. The sciences, on the contrary, examine the mutual relationships among the objects determined which constitute the world.[7] Many people do not consider history as a science. What it has in common with science is, however, the characteristic feature of examining the

[4] O. Spengler, *Der Untergang des Abendlandes* (München, 1923), I, p. X.
[5] A. J. Toynbee, *Civilization on Trial* (New York, 1948), p. 3.
[6] Cf. E. Husserl, *Die Krisis der europäischen Wissenschaften und die transzendentale Phänomenologie* (Haag, 1956).
[7] A. Stern, *Die philosophischen Grundlagen von Wahrheit, Wirklichkeit, Wert* (München, 1932), p. 290.

mutual relationships among its objects. For history, these objects in a logical sense are very frequently psychological subjects. On the other hand, philosophy of history tries to find out how determining thought can determine the concept of history as distinct from the concept of nature; how it succeeds in determining the logical, epistemological, psychological and axiological conditions of historical knowledge; if and how it ends up by determining historical laws and by conceiving the concepts of meaning and value of history.

In the present volume, we are especially concerned with the axiological implications of history or, expressed in a more general way, with the relations between philosophy of history and philosophy of values or axiology. But before going deeper into this subject, we have to clarify a bit more the concept of philosophy of history by examining its origins and its aims.

Having determined the psychological origins and the logical character of philosophy of history, let us examine now its historical origins. What are these origins? The opinions answering this question vary. But, in general, the authors agree on the fact that the Greeks, although they were the creators of occidental philosophy and of historiography, did not develop a philosophy of history properly speaking. In spite of having produced men like Herodotus, Thucydides, Polybius and Plutarch, the Greeks were not very history-minded.[8] Greek methaphysics was composed of extra-temporal entities, without birth, development and decay — be it the uncreated, indestructible and immobile sphere of Parmenides, the Platonic ideas, Aristotle's forms or the natural laws of the Stoics. To be sure, in its immense wealth and variety, Greek philosophy also produced a Heraclitus who discovered the dynamic mobilism of our universe and the dialectical movement of all things. He showed us that "πόλεμος πάντων πατήρ ἐστι χαὶ βασιλεύς,"[9] that war, in the sense of the strife of opposites, is the father and king of all things.

By showing us that πάντα ῥεῖ (everything is flowing), that we cannot descend twice into the same river because new waters flow towards us; by showing that being is inseparable from this continuous movement of development and decay, from this endless alternation of

---

[8] In his *Timaeus* (22 A, B), Plato tells us the following about Solon's travel to Egypt: "Questioning such of their priests as were most versed in ancient lore about their early history, he discovered that neither he himself nor any other Greek knew anything at all, one might say, about such matters." Whereupon a very old Egyptian priest said: "O Solon, Solon, you Greeks are always children: there is not such a thing as an old Greek" (῍Ω Σόλων, Σόλων, ῞Ελληνες ἀεὶ παῖδές ἐστε, γέρων δέ ῞Ελλην οὐκ ἔστιν)

[9] Hippolytus, *Ref. hoer.* IX, 9.

creation and destruction, and that the opposites can maintain themselves only by the unity which envelops them and limits them mutually; by teaching us all this, Heraclitus gave modern philosophy of history its most precious ideas and impulses. Hegel and Marx were to draw from Heraclitus' teaching the essential elements of their philosophical interpretations of history: the dialectical laws. But this transformation of Heraclitus' thought into a philosophy of history was only achieved twenty-three centuries after his death.

In examining the reasons for the absence of a philosophy of history among the Greeks, many thinkers ascribe the blame to the idea of the cycle, which dominated Greek thought, even that of Heraclitus. According to an ancient tradition — Sumerian and Greek — there is a regularity in the changes of time which, after an always identical cycle, produces a recurrence of the same days, months, years and, with them, of the same events. This idea of an eternal return deprives events of their individual character. *"Aimez ce que jamais on ne verra deux fois"* said Alfred de Vigny — love that which one will never see twice. The Greek historian had this love, and, therefore, there was Greek history. But being under the domination of the idea of an eternal return, the Greek philosopher did not believe in events which one would never see twice. Therefore, he did not create a philosophy of history. The idea of an eternal return deprives history of all significance and transforms it into a mechanical, unchangeable repetition of confused images of that which really exists: the One and the Permanent which, as a typical feature of Greek thought, is even to be found in Heraclitus.

However, the idea of the cycle alone does not explain the absence of a philosophy of history among the Greeks, for that idea is to be found also in some philosophers of history of the Christian era and of modern times, such as Vico, Croce, Spengler, Toynbee. There is a difference between the Greeks, on the one hand, and the Christians and Moderns, on the other: for the majority of Greek thinkers, matter was eternal, uncreated, without beginning or end, and the universe was without progress. Thus, time was for them free from any direction, from any privileged dimension, from any evolution towards an end. All this changed with the adoption by medieval philosophers of the Hebrew genesis. For the Christian thinker, time is linear. It has a beginning: the creation of the world and Adam. It has a central date: the birth of Christ. It moves towards an end: the last Judgment. Since time is thus finite, all nations have to achieve their destiny between the creation of Adam and the last Judgment. With this, time acquires a one-way direction; it becomes irreversible and, therefore, precious, for, being finite, it must be used before it passes. With this idea of finiteness, the value of time is established — in other words, its historicity.

Lucius Annaeas Seneca, that great forerunner of Christianity, had already written to his friend Lucilius: *"Omnia, Lucili, aliena sunt, tempus tantum nostrum est. . . . Dum differtur, vita transcurrit. . . . Fac ergo, . . . quod facere te scribis, omnes horas conplectere."*[10] All things, Lucilius, are foreign; time alone belongs to us. . . . While you are postponing things, life flows away. . . . Therefore, do what you write you are doing: use every hour.

As for modern thinkers, it was Carnot-Clausius' second principle of thermodynamics which taught them the irreversibility of time. If entropy tends toward a maximum, if the amount of free energy diminishes constantly, there is a difference between "earlier" and "later", and the historicity of time likewise becomes obvious.

This argument has, however, sometimes been criticized. Some thinkers insisted that the second principle of thermodynamics is only valid for certain parts of the universe considered as closed systems. Consequently, it does not state anything about the unique character of the history of the world in its totality nor about the history of one of its parts, since neither of them is a closed system.[11]

It has also been objected that it is not possible to use the entropy law to define the forward direction of time, for, if we declare that, of two given entropy states, the state of greater entropy will be said to be "later" than the state of smaller entropy, then we have only stated a tautology.[12]

It would be wrong to suppose that modern science favors a linear conception of time which is opposed to the cyclic conception of the Greeks. Professor Gödel has shown that there exist solutions of Einstein's field equations which yield closed time-like world lines, thus making time cyclic in the large.[13]

A recent hypothesis seems to accentuate the cyclic character of cosmic time. According to this assumption, the universe is comparable to a breathing organism: the expanding universe in which we live would be followed by a phase of contraction, and this alternation of expansion

---

[10] *L. Annaei Senecae ad Lucilium Epistulae,* I, 3, 2.
[11] H. Rickert, *Kulturwissenschaft und Naturwissenschaft* (Tübingen, 1915), pp. 142—143.
[12] A. Grünbaum, "Time and Entropy", *American Scientist,* Vol. 43, No. 4, Oct. 1955, p. 52.
[13] K. Gödel, "Example of a New Type of Cosmological Solutions of Einstein's Field Equations of Gravitation" 2, *Review of Modern Physics* (Lancaster, Penn., 1949), Vol. 21, pp. 447—450.

and contraction would go on and on. Time would thus run in alternating cycles. But even if this hypothesis is valid — it is in fact, rejected by some leading astrophysicists — the cyclic character of cosmic time which it implies will not affect the linear character of our historical time. The reason is that our historical, telluric time will have ended long before the beginning of the hypothetical opposite time sector of a contracting universe. History means to us only the evolution of mankind on this earth or in its immediate neighborhood — if we take into account the possibility of space flight. According to recent computations, the end of this history must occur in about six billion years. At that time twelve percent of the sun's hydrogen supply will have been converted into helium, and astrophysicists know that beyond this limit a star must lose its stability. The sun will then expand, brighten, and drive the earth's temperature first above the boiling point of water, then beyond the melting point of lead, up to 800 degrees centigrade. At its maximum size, the ageing sun will have thirty times its present radius, burn up its fuel at a tremendous rate and rapidly exhaust its hydrogen supply. But, to man, this will be no longer of any practical consequence, because, a long time before, organic life will have ended on earth, the oceans will have boiled away, and our civilizations, with all their treasures, will have been turned into ashes.

This end of history will look quite different from the picture painted in Saint Augustine's description of the "eternal Sunday". It will much more resemble the Greek myth of Phaeton, son of Helios, who yoked his father's sun-chariot and, unable to drive it along the course taken by his father, scorched and burned up everything which was on the earth.[14]

Thus, contemporary astrophysics makes us realize the finiteness of our telluric, historical time, and its linear character.

To be sure, the irreversibility of thermodynamic processes which gives time its direction depends on an interpretation of statistics and, therefore, is in the realm of probability. It is only extremely probable that energy will run down toward a state of uniform temperature, and it is not impossible that, from a certain moment on, energy will run up again. Such a shift would also mean a change in the direction of time to the other way round. But, although this is a theoretical possibility, envisaged by Boltzmann, its probability is so small that the philosophy of history may ignore it. I think that the latter should only take into account the following rather elementary facts:

Whereas mechanical work can be entirely transformed into heat — by

---

[14] Plato, *Timaeus*, 22 C, and Ovid, *Metamorphoses*, i. 751ff.

friction or shock — it is impossible entirely to retransform heat into mechanical work, since a part of the heat passes over into cooler bodies. This empirically verifiable fact finds its expression in the second principle of thermodynamics. While, according to the first principle, the amount of energy in a closed system remains constant, the second principle states that the amount of free energy, that is of energy which can be changed into work, diminishes constantly. By determining all terrestrial processes in a unique irreversible sense, the second principle of thermodynamics gives a direction to our historical time.

In the world of classical mechanics, all systems can be restored to their initial states; but this world is only an abstraction, a simplification of facts — in short, a fictitious world. Admitting absolutely smooth planes, liquids without frictions and completely flexible ropes, that world does not take into account the real conditions of our physical bodies. The second principle of thermodynamics, however, no longer describes an ideal world but, rather, our physical world with its progressive and observable dissipation of free energy.

Wilhelm Ostwald, who, with Duhem, established the doctrine of Energism, considered the second principle of thermodynamics as the source of all values.[15] In the ideal fictitious world of classical mechanics, a person would be able to commit the greatest stupidities and the worst ignominies, to no real detriment. Since in such a world all events are supposed to be reversible, it would always be possible to repair the evil consequences of an act by restoring the initial state. In a world exclusively governed by the first principle of thermodynamics, there would not even be a reason for complaining about a loss of time, since time itself would be totally reversible. It would always be possible to restore a condition identical to the initial one. The inexorable dictum *facta infecta fieri nequeunt* — things done cannot be made undone — would no longer be valid, and life and history would, therefore, not be tragic.

According to Wilhelm Ostwald, a reversible world would, consequently, offer no possibility of distinguishing between a positive and a negative value. In such a world, the notion of value would be theoretically impossible.

With the possibility of directing the sequence of events in an opposite direction also, man living in a reversible world would have the possibility of eternal life. It would suffice to go at any moment in the opposite direction in order to become younger and to begin again a life which would not have any privileged direction.

15 W. Ostwald, *Die Philosophie der Werte* (Leipzig, 1913), p. 112.

Our historical world, however, is not this ideal fictitious world, and in it everything happens in a different way. The reason for this is the degradation of free energy which gives all terrestrial processes an irreversible one-way orientation and, thus, forces our time into one direction.

Whatever the statistical probability of an inversion of the law of entropy may be, it could be of interest only to the theoretical physicist, but not to the historian. The historical world has always been one in which events were irreversible, a world in which no damage could be completely repaired, a world where no individual and no nation could ever go through life more than once. In short, the historical world is and always was a one-way temporal world. This is the best proof for the validity of the second principle of thermodynamics, at least, for the world in which we live and where our history takes place — despite all objections.

This irreversible historical world is and always was one characterized by Bergson's "duration" (*durée*), with its individual and collective ageing and that prolongation of the past into the present which we call memory. If, in such a world, one conceives of historical cycles, they can no longer be considered identical, as they were in ancient philosophy. For Benedetto Croce, for example, the evolution of the spirit in four moments — from the aesthetic to the ethical activity, by passing through the logical and economic activities — certainly repeats in cycles, but none of them is identical to the other. For, as soon as the dialectical evolution of the spirit reaches its fourth degree, the dialectical movement starts a new cycle on a higher level, enriched by the experiences of the previous cycles.

As far as Spengler's historical cycles are concerned, there exists among them only a relation of "analogy" and in no way one of identity. If, as Spengler says, "every culture has its own civilization", it is evident that there must exist an analogy between Roman civilization, the conclusion of Greek culture, and American civilization, the conclusion of European culture. But the one is not a repetition of the other. On the contrary, Spengler declares "every culture has its new possibilities of expression which appear, ripen, wither and never recur (*nie wiederkehren*)".[16] Consequently, each of these cultures has its unique specific and irreplaceable character and, therefore, constitutes a value.

Thus, it is superficial to say — as is currently done — that Greek thought did not develop a philosophy of history because of its cyclic conception. Only if this cyclic conception is applied to a time without

[16] O. Spengler, *Der Untergang des Abendlandes,* I (München, 1923), p. 29.

privileged direction can these cycles become an eternal return which would deprive the different historical epochs of their unique character, their interest, their value. The only great modern philosopher who, lacking scientific knowledge, adopted the doctrine of eternal return — Nietzsche — rejected history and tried to heal modern man from his "historical sickness".

If, however, the idea of the cycle is applied to an irreversible time, such as that of modern physics or that of Bergson's *durée*, it is perfectly compatible with an historical conception, as our examples have shown. Because, then, the later cycle differs from the earlier by the increase of entropy, by the decrease of free energy, by biological ageing and by the survival and accumulation of the past in the form of memory. In an irreversible time, as that of our history, no later period can be identical with an earlier one, even if this time progresses in cycles. Each period has its specific character; each is unique in its historicity.

It is well known that, while maintaining cyclic conceptions, Plato also admitted creation, although not *ex nihilo*. This is, at least, the impression given by the myth of Timaeus. Plato's "time", as later that of Augustine, begins with the creation of the universe and with the movement of created things. It is only the measure of motion. Nevertheless, we must keep in mind that, even in his *Timaeus,* Plato insists on the difference between τὸ ὂν ἀεί, perpetual being, which is withous genesis, and τὸ γιγνόμενον ἀεί, the perpetual becoming, which is without being.[17] According to Plato, the temporal distinctions of past, present and future cannot be applied to that which *is* i.e. that which is uncreated.[18] And for Plato, as for the majority of Greek thinkers, becoming is inferior to being which is the only object of true knowledge. I believe that this *inferiority of becoming* in comparison with *being* is the main reason for the absence of a philosophy of history among the Greeks. For what is history, if not the *becoming* of mankind? I agree with Professor Felice Battaglia, the distinguished Italian philosopher, when he writes:

> The philosophies which exalt being and claim for it immutable perfection (although in different forms), are condemned to disregard history. Even when they propose to man's effort a liberating ascesis (the ascent toward eternal ideas in Plato) or the return to a primitive age of happiness (golden age, . . .), there is no true history in the sense that there is always beyond us or before us, in the hyperuranium or at the beginnings of time, something perfect, already achieved.[19]

[17] Plato, *Timaeus,* 27 D—28.
[18] *Ibid.,* 37 D, E, 38 A, B.
[19] F. Battaglia, *La valeur dans l'histoire* (Paris, 1955), p. 14.

What Plato and Aristotle created in their works about the State was not philosophy of history but political philosophy with purely practical aims. They were searching for the ὀρθή πολιτεία, the right constitution, which would guarantee the εὖ ζῆν, the good life; they did not, however, raise the philosophical problem of the meaning of history.

But, if the Greeks did not create an explicit philosophy of history, their myths about history contain a whole implicit philosophy. Let us examine the Hellenic myths about history, in order to elicit their lesson.

According to myth, Clio was the muse of history and, at the same time, the muse of epic poetry. This personal union of the two functions shows that the Greeks must have felt what we know today, thanks to an additional experience of twenty-five hundred years: namely that, in historiography, it is difficult to trace a neat demarcation line between historical truth and poetic fiction. History, inevitably, contains fictitious elements besides truth; it is a product of documentation *and* imagination. By entrusting Clio with the functions of the muse of history and of epic poetry, the Greeks repudiated in advance the historical realism of the nineteenth century which, in the words of the German historian Leopold von Ranke, imposed upon history the duty to tell us how things have happened "in reality" (*wie es eigentlich gewesen ist*).

For other modern philosophers and historians — I mention, at random, Renan, Cournot, Carlyle, Dilthey, Croce, Windelband, Simmel, Gibbon, Toynbee, Russell, Korn — the historian must also be an artist endowed with imagination. In this contemporary conception, we may see a triumph of the Greek myth of Clio, muse of history *and* of epic poetry.

By giving the muse of history the name Clio, the Greeks wished perhaps to say that history is not the simple inquiry suggested by the word ἱστορία but also an exaltation, a glorification of events; the word Clio comes from the verb κλείω, κλείειν, which signifies "to glorify", "to celebrate". This etymology shows that, for the Greeks, historiography implied an evaluation of the facts, a selection of events considered as great, marvellous, glorious. This selection presupposes a concept of value, a whole hierarchy of values in the historian's mind. The Greek historian applied this hierarchy consciously. Why did Herodotus, the father of historiography, write history? "In order that the memory of the past may not be blotted out from among men by time and that *great* and *marvellous* deeds done by Greeks and foreigners and especially the reason why they warred against each other may not lack renown."[20]

[20] Herodotus, *Book I*, A.

With these words, Herodotus entrusted history with three tasks: that of commemorating (Clio was indeed the daughter of Mnemosyne, goddess of memory), that of searching for causes and that of evaluating. For more than two thousand years, historians have done nothing else but carry out this program of their illustrious ancestor Herodotus, although, sometimes, in spite of themselves.

We have to conclude that, from its beginnings, historiography has been indissolubly linked with the domain of values, and, for this reason, it has often been blamed for being partial and for lacking scientific generality, since value judgments are subjective and variable. Up to our day, the philosophers of history have not ceased to struggle in order to get out of the epistemological difficulties of that somehow disreputable situation which, for the Greeks, was in no way reprehensible. On the contrary: Clio, crowned with laurels, and distributing glory and blame, fulfilled in their eyes a majestic function.

Let us further mention that the Greeks represented Clio with a clepsydra. This word, composed of the verb κλέπτειν, to steal, and the noun ὕδωρ, water, designated a kind of water clock which, in the Greek assemblies, measured the time granted to the different speakers by the running of a certain quantity of water. The latter passed "stealthily" through an orifice and dropped slowly from one vessel into another.

In my opinion, the clepsydra, as an attribute of Clio, not only symbolizes the temporality of history. It also reminds us that the time granted to the actors of that great drama called "history" — be they individuals, parties, nations, classes or whole continents — is measured. In the nineteenth century, this idea concealed in the Greek myth found its explicit expression in the philosophy of Hegel, who told us that each nation is the expression of a certain "moment" in the evolution of the "universal spirit". As soon as a nation has expressed the idea it represents, as soon as it has fulfilled its mission, it loses its rights and yields them to another nation.

We have seen, indeed, the appearance and disappearance of the great empires of the Babylonians, the Egyptians, the Greeks, the Romans, the Spaniards, the Germans. Spengler proclaimed the decline of the West; Europe had to yield a part of its power to America, and already we see Asia emerging as a new giant. Russia, a nation which is at the same time European and Asian, fulfils Nietzsche's prediction by becoming a first-rate world power. In a group of nations representing a billion people, the reigning working class has taken over the government from the capitalist class. All these events of modern history, unforeseeable for the

Greeks, justify their symbol of Clio's clepsydra, measuring and limiting the time granted to the actors of the historical drama.

Thus we see that the Greek myths of history concealed many fertile germs for times to come. Nevertheless, the Greeks themselves did not develop a philosophy of history properly speaking.

What is then the origin of philosophy of history? Referring to Herodotus, Vico seems to see this origin in the Egyptians who had divided all time past into three ages: the age of the gods, the age of the heroes, and the age of men, a division which he was to adopt himself and to apply to the history of all nations. Vico also refers to the Roman Marcus Terentius Varro who, "in that great book *Rerum divinarum et humanarum* of which the injury of time has deprived us, divided all past centuries into three periods: obscure time ..., fabulous time, ... and, finally, historical time, or the age of men."[21]

However, a simple division of time into historical periods still does not constitute a philosophy of history.

Ernest Renan insisted on the Jewish origin of philosophy of history. "The Jew" — he wrote — "thanks to a kind of prophetic sense which, at certain moments, makes the Semite admirably adept at envisaging the broad lines of the future, made history enter the domain of religion." Linking the destiny of mankind with that of their nation, the Jewish thinkers were the first who, according to Renan, were concerned with a general theory of the progress of our species. Renan considered the author of the book Daniel as the "true creator of philosophy of history".[22]

Besides the Jews, the Persians should also be mentioned, a fact which Renan did not omit to underline. In our day, Arnold Toynbee traces back philosophy of history to the same sources as Renan when he writes:

> In the vision seen by the Prophets of Israel, Judah and Iran, history is not a cyclic and not a mechanical process. It is the masterful and progressive execution, on the narrow stage of this world, of a divine plan which is revealed to us in this fragmentary glimpse, but which transcends our human power of vision and understanding. . . .[23]

In general, philosophy of history is considered a creation of Christianity and, especially, of Saint Augustine. According to this thinker, history is a perpetual struggle between two cities which, for the time being, are commingled: the earthly city — *civitas terrena,* and the heavenly city —

---

[21] G. Vico, *Principj di Scienza Nuova d'intorno alla Comune Natura delle Nazioni,* Seconda Edizione (1744), Libro Primo, p. 60.
[22] E. Renan, *La vie de Jésus* (Paris, 1861), p. 49.
[23] A. J. Toynbee, *Civilization on Trial* (New York, 1948), pp. 14—15.

civitas coelestis or *civitas Dei.* The earthly city, which belongs to the devil, is the community of the impious — *societas impiorum*,[24] the world of sinful mankind, corrupted by earthly joys and material interests. It is destined for eternal damnation. The city of God is the small community of the Saints and other righteous people, predestined to salvation and eternal felicity. They constitute the true eternal city, a spiritual Rome, which the arms of the barbarians will never be able to destroy. The first representatives of these two cities were Cain and Abel.

The whole history, which Saint Augustine divides into six periods, tends toward the final triumph of the City of God over the city of Satan. God wishes to save a part of mankind, in order to show his mercy; however, only the smaller part. The great majority of men are "predestined to go into eternal fire with the devil" (*praedestinati sunt in aeternum ignem ire cum diabolo*).[25] In this way, God will show what all men would deserve.[26]

History will culminate in the final triumph of the City of God over the city of Satan, the rising of all generations of the dead and the last Judgment, by which the elect and the reprobate will be irrevocably separated: the citizens of Satan will go to hell, while the righteous and blessed will live on in eternal felicity in the celestial city of God. With the realization of this kingdom of heaven, the drama of history will end.

However, according to the bishop of Hippo, this end of history will not be tantamount to the end of all things. It will be a kind of "endless eighth day, an eternal Sunday", *Dominicus dies velut octavus aeternus.*

What will happen then? Saint Augustine imagines it in the following way:

> *Ibi vacabimus, et videbimus. Videbimus, et amabimus; amabimus, et laudabimus. Ecce quod erit in fine sine fine. Nam quis alius noster est finis, nisi pervenire ad regnum, cujus nullus est finis?*[27] In English: Then we shall be at leisure and shall see; we shall see and shall love; we shall love and shall praise. That is what will be at the end without an end. For what other end can there be for us than to arrive at the kingdom which will never end?

Although this is supposed to be an end without an end, it is, nevertheless, no longer history. For, in that blessed city imagined by Saint Augustine, there will no longer be the "incentive of need" ... and "no one who is inferior will envy those placed above him. ... Thus, to the smallest gift

---

[24] Sancti Aurelii Augustini *De Civitate Dei*, XVI, 10, XIX, 24.
[25] *Ibid.*, XXI, 24.
[26] *Ibid.*, XXI, 12.
[27] *Ibid.*, XXII, 30.

a person has received that other gift will be added which consists in not desiring more."[28]

Evidently, a world without the incentive of need, without envy, without desire, will be a world without history; for — as Vico, Kant, Hegel and Marx showed us later — envies, passions and needs constitute the fuel, maintaining the march of history. We may, indeed, say that history is a continuous will to get out of a present considered as imperfect towards a future dreamt of as more perfect. History subsists on this opposition between real negative values and imagined positive values affirmed by groups. Since Saint Augustine's blessed city is supposed to be free from negative values — *ubi nullum erit malum*[29] — it will no longer contain any difference of values. And, without differences between values, there are no values at all. Thus, it becomes clear to what extent history as reality is linked with the concept of value. Later, we shall see that the same is true for history as knowledge.

Thus, with his description of the "eternal Sunday", Saint Augustine gave us, really, an idea of a world without history, and allied to this, the image of an end of our history.

At present, Saint Augustine's contribution to the philosophy of history is not always duly recognized. Speaking of him, of Eusebius and Hieronymus, the Protestant theologian Ernst Troeltsch, a well known philosopher of history, declares:

> They are called philosophers of history, but they are the contrary: compilators and dogmatics who sketch for every event a frame made up of miracles and the historical scholastic convention of antiquity.[30]

"These are symbols, not realities,"[31] says Karl Jaspers about the biblical interpretations of history, although he is not an unbeliever. Max Scheler, who, during his most fertile period, had been a fervent Catholic, likewise rejected theological interpretations of history such as they appear in the works of Saint Augustine and Bossuet. "It need hardly be said that this religious anthropology is in every respect completely insignificant (*bedeutungslos*) as an autonomous philosophy and science", declared Scheler.[32] And, in spite of his tradition as a former Spanish Catholic, the American philosopher George Santayana considered Saint Augustine's

---

[28] *Ibid.*, XXII, 30.
[29] *Ibid.*, XXII, 30.
[30] E. Troeltsch, *Der Historismus und seine Probleme* (Tübingen, 1922), p. 15.
[31] K. Jaspers, *Vom Ursprung und Ziel der Geschichte* (Zürich, 1949), p. 18.
[32] M. Scheler, *Mensch und Geschichte* (Zürich, 1929), p. 17.

interpretation of history "a myth ..., half innocent, half arrogant."[33]

Judging in a purely philosophical way, I cannot agree with those opinions. To be sure, nobody can deny what Saint Augustine owed not only to Plato and the Stoïcs but also to Zoroaster; for the Augustinian conflict between the City of God and the City of Satan overcome by the establishment of the eternal blessed city is the Christian counterpart of the struggle between the good spirit, Ahurô Mazdaô, and the spirit of evil, Angrô Mainyush, described in the Zend-Avesta and the Ghâtâs. With Zoroaster, as later with Saint Augustine, the final victory belongs to the divine principle, and the conflict ends with the establishment of a blessed city. But, in uniting Persian and Greek elements with the teachings of Judaism and Christianity, Saint Augustine sketched the image of a unilinear evolution of history towards an end. While giving us a glimpse of an eternity after the end of history — *in aeternitate autem nulla mutatio est* — Saint Augustine assigned to history a finite character which it has never lost in Western thought.

More than that: In interpreting history as the realization of a divine plan to assure the final salvation of mankind, Saint Augustine showed that the whole of human history can be interpreted and understood by a unitary idea. Thus he gave philosophy of history its decisive impulsion. Whether one accepts his interpretation or rejects it — and I reject it, of course — there remains the fact that, thanks to Saint Augustine, the Western world gained the conviction that the whole of history is interpretable. From this conviction sprang all our philosophy of history, which is basically a series of attempts to interpret the whole of human history.

In his book, *The Rise of Scientific Philosophy*, Hans Reichenbach reproaches philosophy with having given — by hasty and naïve generalizations — answers, when the time had not arrived for the giving of "correct answers", that is scientific ones.[34] I find this argument oversimplified. Not only is it psychologically impossible to say to men craving for philosophical answers: "Wait two thousand years until the time for right answers has come." It is also logically evident that without risking false answers no one will ever succeed in giving right ones. Only by giving wrong answers does man end up by giving right ones some day.

Thus, it would be ridiculous to reproach Saint Augustine with having answered the question of the significance of history in a naïve way. His answer was conceived in the intellectual style of his time, and one under-

[33] G. Santayana, *The Life of Reason* (New York, 1930), pp. 90—91.
[34] H. Reichenbach, *The Rise of Scientific Philosophy* (Berkeley and Los Angeles, 1951), p. 8.

stands that it could satisfy his time. Encouraged by his example, other epochs gave other answers which were less naïve.

Saint Augustine's philosophy of history certainly belongs to the stage which Auguste Comte called "theological", for its author imagined all events of history as products of a direct intervention of supernatural agents. Furthermore, Augustine's philosophy of history contains much more biblical history than history properly speaking.

Bossuet's *Discours sur l'histoire universelle* represents the theological state in a more attenuated form, although it, too, begins with "God creating heaven and earth by his word and making man in his image".[35] Bossuet considered religious myths as historical facts and mixed them with truly historical facts. Thus, he wrote:

> One must take hold of a small number of epochs, such as . . . Adam, or creation; Noah, or the deluge, the vocation of Abraham, or the beginning of the alliance between God and men. Moses, or the written law; the capture of Troy; Solomon, or the foundation of the temple; Romulus, or the building of Rome; Cyrus, or the deliverance of God's people from the Babylonian captivity, etc.[36]

But, although the permanent intervention of miracles was for Bossuet the most legitimate historical explanation — and he was always searching for a divine plan in man's actions — nevertheless, he also did good work as a historian by explaining certain events from their natural causes. If his philosophy of history still represents the theological stage of that discipline, it is, nevertheless, less absolute than with Saint Augustine.

In the eighteenth century, philosophy of history enters its modern phase. Who founded modern philosophy of history? According to the German Troeltsch, it was the Frenchman Voltaire; according to the Frenchman Michelet, it was the Italian Giambattista Vico. As for us, we are inclined to think that the foundation of philosophy of history in a modern sense was the work of these two geniuses, who complemented each other most happily. Vico had the priority. In 1725, he published his book *Principj di Scienza Nuova d'intorno alla comune Natura delle Nazioni* — Principles of a new science concerning the common nature of the nations. It constitutes the beginning of the secularization of philosophy of history. As Friedrich Meinecke rightly says, Vico's book is the *"novum organum"* of histoircal thought.[37]

On the one hand, the Italian thinker remained attached to the Chris-

---

[35] *Oeuvres de Bossuet* (Paris, 1856), tome X, p. 133.
[36] *Ibid.*, t. X, p. 132.
[37] F. Meinecke, *Die Entstehung des Historismus* (München, 1936), Band I, p. 56.

tian conception of history by accepting the fundamental positions of
Saint Augustine and Bossuet. For Vico, as for his predecessors, the first
man was Adam, created at the same time as the universe, and the
Hebrews were the first nation. In the "vain pretension" of several pagan
nations — the Chaldeans, Scythians, Egyptians and Chinese — to have
founded ancient civilization and in the wisdom of Israel, "that privileged
people", Vico saw "a strong proof of the truth of the Scriptures" (*una
gran prova della verità della Storia Sagra*).[38]

But these traditional ideas were only the starting point of Vico's
thought, the trend of which was completely opposed to tradition. For
what truly interested the Italian thinker was the search for the natural
laws of history, or, as he said, "the natural course of human things
themselves" (*il Natural Corso delle medesime cose umane*),[39] independently of supernatural interventions. It was Vico's great discovery that
"the social world has certainly been made by men; consequently, its
principles can and must be found in the modifications of our human
mind itself".[40]

By this discovery and the conclusions he drew from it, Vico inaugurated the secularization of philosophy of history and of historiography.
To be sure, Vico did not recant his Catholic faith and still considered
religion the only powerful means (*l'unico potente mezzo*) to restrain men
liberated from the bondage of human laws.[41] Nevertheless, he changed,
imperceptibly, the transcendent God of the Scriptures into an immanent
God, that is, into an abstract, metaphysical force. For Vico, history was
the evolution of the human species, governed by the legislative power of
Providence, thanks to which men themselves achieve, progressively, the
idea of their own nature, by virtue of their freedom.

In the development of history, Vico distinguished three periods: the
theocratic or divine age, the heroic age and the human or civilized age,
in which men enjoy "equality before the law". This drama in three acts,
first performed in antiquity, is repeated, according to Vico, in the history
of all nations. Their triadic evolution follows the laws immanent in
human nature. The latter, to be sure, is a divine creation, but, according
to Vico, God acts in history only indirectly, through the human nature
he has created.

After showing how human society converts the vices of ferocity,

---

[38] G. Vico, *Principj di Scienza Nuova d'intorno alla comune Natura delle Nazioni*,
Seconda Edizione (1744) (Milano, 1854), Libro Primo, III, p. 95.
[39] *Ibid.*, Libro Quinto, p. 537.
[40] *Ibid.*, Libro Primo, p. 136.
[41] *Ibid.*, Libro Primo, XXXI, p. 106.

avarice and ambition into the social virtues of courage, industry and civic activity, Vico concluded by writing:

> All this proves that there is a Divine Providence, a Divine Legislative Intelligence. Thanks to it, the passions of men, entirely devoted to private interests, because of which they would live like wild beasts in the deserts, these very passions have created the civic hierarchies by which men live in human society.[42]

While Vico's triad foreshadows Hegel's and Comte's philosophies of history, his idea that history puts men's passions at the service of goals unknown to them was later repeated in the historical conceptions of Kant, Hegel, Schopenhauer and others. Voltaire, Herder, Schiller and the majority of the philosophers of the enlightenment developed Vico's idea that man's rational nature is his true nature and that, thanks to the free play of human passions, history overcomes, progressively, barbarism and finishes up by realizing humanism and civilization. Even a germ of Spengler's doctrine of the morphological analogies between the diverse cycles of historical evolution can be found in Vico's theory, according to which history begins with each nation and follows a similar path. It was, indeed, almost no exaggeration when Jules Michelet wrote about Vico: "While the crowd either followed or combatted Descartes' reform, a solitary genius created the philosophy of history"[43]

With Voltaire, the modern era of historiography and philosophy of history was finally established. With his *Essai sur les moeurs et l'esprit des nations,* Voltaire provoked a revolution in the way of writing history as well as of interpreting it. As is known, the fifty-three paragraphs which form the Introduction to this work were published in 1765 under the title *Philosophie de l'histoire* — Philosophy of History. This expression coined by Voltaire soon gained permanent status in the fields of philosophy and history.

As far as historiography is concerned, the first of Voltaire's new ideas was to write the histories of civilizations and not of kings. "You finally want to overcome the disgust which modern history causes you. ... You seek in this immensity only that which *merits* to be known by you: the spirit, the habits, the usages of the principal nations. ...[44]

These words of Voltaire throw into relief his second new idea: that of a selective principle applied by the historian in full awareness and on

---

[42] *Ibid.,* Libro Primo, VII, p. 97.
[43] J. Michelet, *Discours sur le système et la vie de Vico* (Paris, 1827), p. 1.
[44] *Oeuvres complètes de Voltaire* (Paris, 1878), tome XI, "Essai sur les moeurs", I, p. 157.

purpose. While Descartes had seen in the necessity of such a selection one of the flaws of historiography[45], Voltaire considered it one of its strengths, namely a means of submitting the whole interpretation of history to a directive value, an ideal. He wrote about this: "In all these immense collections which one cannot embrace, one has to limit oneself and to *choose*. It is a vast storehouse where you will take what you can use."[46]

The directive value, the ideal by virtue of which Voltaire interpreted all history of mankind, was that of the philosophy of enlightenment: the ideal of the progress of mankind towards reason, liberty, tolerance, peace and the perfection of the mind in the domains of arts and sciences. In his book, *Le siècle de Louis XIV*, Voltaire wrote:

> Whoever thinks and — what is even rarer — whoever has good taste only counts four centuries in the history of the world. These four fortunate ages were those in which the arts have been perfected and which, serving as an epoch of the greatness of the human spirit, are the example for posterity.[47]

In another passage, Voltaire showed what constituted his selective principle for writing history:

> Not all that which has been done deserves to be written. In this history, we will rather concentrate on that which deserves the attention of all times, on that which can paint the genius and the habits of men, on that which can serve as a lesson and advise the love of virtue, of the arts and of the fatherland.[48]

With the other representatives of the doctrine of natural right Voltaire believed that "man, in general, has always been what he is"[49] and that "(human) nature being everywhere the same, men had, necessarily, to adopt the same truths".[50] Basing his thinking on these premises, Voltaire could admit the existence of value standards apparently independent of history and geography. Therefore, he could make the following statement: "Everything has changed on earth; virtue alone never changes."[51] But, in reality, Voltaire made of the values of his epoch the norm by which to measure those of the past and even the standard for the values

[45] R. Descartes, *Discours de la méthode* (Paris, 1898), I, p. 14.
[46] *Oeuvres complètes de Voltaire,* tome XI, "Essai ...", I, p. 158.
[47] *Ibid.,* tome XIV, I, p. 155.
[48] *Ibid.,* t. XIV, pp. 158—159.
[49] *Ibid.,* t. XI, I, p. 21.
[50] *Ibid.,* t. XI, I, p. 15.
[51] *Ibid.,* t. XI, I, p. 137.

of the future, since he wanted them to be *"l'exemple de la postérité"*,[52] the example for posterity.

After enumerating the first three great centuries of history — those of Pericles and Plato, of Caesar and Virgil, and that of the Medicis in Italy, Voltaire wrote: "The fourth century is called the century of Louis XIV, and of the four it is probably the one which comes closest to *perfection*."[53]

This century of Louis XIV absolutism appeared to him "the most enlightened century which ever was."[54] While warning us "against our custom of judging everything according to our usages",[55] Voltaire himself always violated this principle. Later, Historicism, with its thesis, *veritas filia temporis* — truth is a daughter of time — corrected Voltaire's axiological transhistorism.

Let us recall some of Voltaire's other basic contributions to historiography and philosophy of history: He wrote the history of the world and not only of the West. In our century, Oswald Spengler boasted of attributing to the histories of India, China, Arabia and Mexico the same importance as to that of the West. In this, as in so many other respects, he was imitated by Toynbee. However, Spengler, as well as Toynbee, only followed a path opened up by Voltaire. It was this French philosopher who replaced the "Ptolemaic system" of history by a "Copernican system", in spite of Spengler's claims to this achievement.[56]

Overcoming historical provincialism, Voltaire also made a decisive step toward a total secularization of history. In reproaching Bossuet for having written his history "uniquely in order to insinuate that everything in the world has been done for the Jewish nation",[57] and in insisting on the importance of pagan civilizations, Voltaire broke the monopoly of Hebrew-Christian ethics and showed that morality was possible also among pagans. While for Bossuet the recourse to divine Providence was the most legitimate explanation, Voltaire tried to explain all events — historical and natural — as necessary products of universal laws.

To be sure, sometimes he still referred to Providence. For instance in the following passage, where he said: "The Providence which put men into Norway also put them into America and into the Antarctic region, just as it planted trees there and made grass grow."[58]

However, Voltaire's Providence was no longer Bossuet's. One remem-

---

[52] *Ibid.*, t. XIV, I, p. 155.
[53] *Ibid.*, t. XIV, I, p. 156.
[54] *Ibid.*, t. XIV, I, p. 155.
[55] *Ibid.*, t. t. XI, I, p. 208.
[56] O. Spengler, *Der Untergang des Abendlandes* (München, 1923), I, pp. 23—24.
[57] *Oeuvres complètes de Voltaire*, t. XI, I, p. 208.
[58] *Ibid.*, t. XI, I, p. 7.

bers the ironical dialogue between *"la soeur Fessue"*, a nun, and the metaphysician in the article "Providence" in Voltaire's *Dictionnaire philosophique*. There, the metaphysician says:

> I believe, my dear sister, in the general Providence, from which the *law* which governs everything has eternally emanated, just as light gushes from the sun; but I do not at all believe that a special Providence changes the world's economy in favor of your sparrow or your cat.[59]

Voltaire adds that the laws of this Providence are "inmutable". With him, Providence lost its theological character and changed into a metaphysical force. That means that with Voltaire the philosophy of history passes from its theological to its metaphysical stage. Speaking of his law of the three stages, Auguste Comte wrote:

> In the metaphysical stage, which, basically, is only a simple, general modification of the first one (the theological stage), the supernatural agents are replaced by abstract forces ... inherent in the world's different beings and considered as capable of engendering *by themselves* all observed phenomena.[60]

This is what happens in Voltaire's philosophy of history, in spite of a terminology which sometimes still reminds us of the theological stage.

In his history of the theory of colors, Goethe suspected Voltaire of displaying his Deism, so that he would not seem to be an atheist. However, Voltaire needed the "author of nature" not only as the supreme engineer of the machinery called the universe, but also as a guarantor of the moral law. The latter seemed to him necessary to secure the survival of society, especially that refined society of the French salons in which he reveled. Friedrich Meinecke was right in saying that Voltaire's Supreme Being was "a God of bourgeois security".[61] He was hardly the God of the theologians.

With Condorcet, God disappeared from the philosophical interpretation of history, and the "indefinite progress" of mankind became an irresistible force. While Voltaire's Deism could not avoid contracting loans from that Christendom he hated so much, Condorcet rejected such transactions. "There is no religion which would not force its sectarians to swallow some physical absurdities," he said.[62]

One might, therefore, believe that with Condorcet, Turgot, Hume,

[59] *Ibid.*, t. XX, IV, p. 295.
[60] A. Comte, *Cours de philosophie positive* (Paris, 1930), t. I, p. 4.
[61] F. Meinecke, *Die Entstehung des Historismus* (München-Berlin, 1936), I, p. 85.
[62] Condorcet, *Tableau historique des progrès de l'esprit humain* (Paris, 1900), p. 66.

Gibbon, Buckle, Taine and Comte the philosophy of history reached its positive stage which, according to the last-named, was to constitute the final stage of mankind. Let us recall Comte's following reflection:

> Does not each of us remember, when contemplating his own history, that he has been, as far as his most important notions are concerned, successively a theologian in his childhood, a metaphysician in his youth and a physicist in his manhood?[63]

But while no man ever returns from his virility to his youth and child-hood, such retrogradations are rather frequent in the history of thought and especially in the history of philosophy of history. After having reached its positive stage with Condorcet and Hume, philosophy of history became metaphysical again with Hegel and, in our day, theological with Toynbee. One might even consider Hegel's philosophy of history as a return of this discipline to its theological stage. Did Hegel not write: "God governs the world: the contents of His government, the execution of His plan, is World History?"[64] For Hegel, history was "a theodicy, a justification of God".[65] When he defined world history as "the unfolding of the Spirit in time",[66] he considered this Spirit as divine. "For Hegel," says Ernst Cassirer in an excellent formulation, "God not only *has* history, he *is* history."[67] And, in a no less brilliant metaphor, the American philosopher Sidney Hook declared that for Hegel history was "the autobiography of God".[68]

Nevertheless, I believe that Hegel's philosophy of history represents the metaphysical stage of this discipline rather than the theological one. For Hegel's God is abstract; he is the Absolute or logical Idea which exists first as a system of precosmic concepts, dives into the unconscious sphere of nature, awakens in man to self-consciousness in the form of the subjective mind, realizes its contents in history as the objective mind by creating the States, social institutions, law, ethics, etc. Finally, the Absolute returns to itself, enriched and perfected as art, religion and philosophy. This whole evolution is subjected to the rigorous laws of dialectics: the law of strife, interpenetration and unity of the opposites, the law of the negation of negation and the law of the transformation of quantity into quality. It is here a question of metaphysical forces rather than of supernatural agents, and Hegel's terminology could be

[63] A. Comte, *Cours de philosophie positive* (Paris, 1830), I, p. 6.
[64] G. W. F. Hegel, *Sämtliche Werke* (ed. Glockner), Band XI, p. 67.
[65] *Ibid.*, XI, p. 42.
[66] *Ibid.*, XI, p. 111.
[67] E. Cassirer, *The Myth of the State* (Garden City, N.Y., 1955), p. 330.
[68] S. Hook, *From Hegel to Marx* (New York, 1950), p. 36.

considered a semantic concession to Lutheran orthodoxy, that powerful buttress of the Prussian monarchy, which the "philosopher of the Prussian State" tried to protect against the onslaught of Liberalism. The rather accidental character of his theological terminology is also revealed by the fact that, according to Hegel, the absolute Spirit reaches the supreme degree of self-consciousness in philosophy, and not in religion. To him, only philosophy was the "adequate" expression of the absolute Idea.

If, in this way, Hegel's philosophy of history constitutes a return of this discipline to the metaphysical stage, the philosophy of history of our contemporary, Arnold Toynbee, is tantamount to its total return to the theological stage. As a matter of fact, the celebrated British historian would be the last to deny this. He declares that in all his historical research he has been guided by the motto of the University of Oxford, *Dominus Illuminatio Mea,* the Lord is my light. For Toynbee, God is not only a historical fact, he is the supreme historical fact, and religion is the only subject worthy of the historian's attention. "The mundane history of the higher religions," he says, "is one aspect of the life of a Kingdom of Heaven of which this world is one province. So, history passes over into theology."[69] The transformation of history into theology is, indeed, the key to the whole of Toynbee's philosophy of history.

In an autobiographical sketch, this great scholar speaks about his fundamental "discoveries". The first was that nations were only arbitrarily insulated fragments of more complex wholes, of societies or civilizations. The latter constitute "the smallest intelligible fields of historical study".[70] His second discovery was that the histories of all civilizations were in some sense parallel and contemporary. However, one day, Toynbee had to realize that these doctrines were "discoveries" only to him but not to the general public, which had read them before in Oswald Spengler's *Untergang des Abendlandes.*[71]

Searching for another justification of his historico-philosophical enterprise, Toynbee declared himself dissatisfied with Spengler's answer to the question about the geneses of civilizations. It was in the *Prolog im Himmel* of Goethe's *Faust* that Toynbee found the explanatory principle of the history of civilizations. It is well known that, inspired by the story

---

[69] A. J. Toynbee, *Civilization on Trial* (New York, 1948), p. V.

[70] *Ibid.,* p. 9.

[71] We have already remarked that, in his "Copernican revolution", Spengler had been preceded by Voltaire. But Spengler and Toynbee had also another predecessor, Leo Tolstoy, who wrote: "... to depict the life, not of humanity, but merely of a single people, is an impossibility." (*The Complete Works of L. N. Tolstoy,* New York, 1899, "War and Peace", Vol. VI, p. 232).

of Job, the German poet suggests a kind of wager between God and the devil, who challenges the Supreme Being to give him a free hand to corrupt Faust, if he can do it. Thus, for Toynbee, history appears as a kind of wager between God and Mephisto, a struggle between good and evil and, above all, a relationship of "challenge-and-response". It is this latter which explains, according to the English historian, the geneses, growths, declines and disintegrations of civilizations.

Rejecting the idea of his compatriots, Gibbon and Frazer, that Christianity has been the destroyer of Graeco-Roman civilization, Toynbee first considered the hypothesis that Christianity has been a kind of chrysalis which has held and preserved the surviving germs of antique culture until they could break through in the form of a new secular civilization. But this hypothesis would degrade Christianity and religion in general to the role of civilization's humble servants — a role which would not agree with Toynbee's theological conception af history. Therefore, he proposes an alternative view, more satisfactory to him, which sees in civilization the means and in religion the end.

From this point of view "civilizations are the handmaids of religion," and the most useful function of Graeco-Roman civilization has been to give birth to Christianity, before disappearing. Comparing religion to a chariot, Toynbee thinks that "the wheels on which it mounts towards Heaven may be the periodic downfalls of civilizations on earth". Thus, he combines a cyclic view of the development of civilizations with a linear view of the evolution of religions. "The continuous upward movement of religion may be served and promoted by the cyclic movement of civilizations round the cycle of birth, death, birth."[72]

In this way, our secularized scientific technological civilization appears to Toynbee only "an almost meaningless repetition of something that the Greeks and Romans did before us".[73] After all, says he in his *Study of History*, what science has done from the close of the seventeenth century up till our day has only been "a series of socially and morally subversive intellectual discoveries".[74]

If modern civilization is brushed aside as "monotonous", "superfluous" and "subversive" — what is then the greatest event in history? It is still the "Crucifixion and its spiritual consequences". In this respect our contemporary, Toynbee, does not differ from his medieval predecessors. Like Saint Augustine and Bossuet, he admits as a historical fact that man has been created by God, that this God is love and that he loved mankind

[72] *Ibid.*, p. 236.
[73] *Ibid.*, p. 237.
[74] A. Toynbee, *A Study of History* (London, 1954), Vol. IX, p. 749.

so much that "He became incarnate in order to bring redemption to human souls during their life on earth".[75] In this *"theologia historici"*, as Toynbee himself calls it, civilizations appear only to be "stepping-stones to higher things on the religious plane", in a process tending towards "the revelation of ever deeper religious insight". What is then the role of democracy? Reflected in the distorting mirror of Toynbee's theological view of history, it appears as a page torn out, of the book of Christianity, but half emptied of meaning, because it has been secularized. Our civilization may perish; Christianity, however, especially in its Catholic form, not only will survive but grow in wisdom and stature, according to our British expert.

In the light of this medieval image sketched in the middle of the twentieth century, what constitutes historical progress and what is the meaning of history? Toynbee answers in the following passage:

> A conceivable kind of *progress* in these spiritual terms — a kind that would give *significance to history* and would, so to speak, justify God's love for this world and His incarnation in it — would be a cumulative increase in the means of Grace at the disposal of each soul in this world. ... The actual — and momentous — effect of a cumulative increase in the means of Grace at man's disposal in this world would be to make it possible for human souls, while still in this world, to come to know God better and come to love Him more nearly in His own way.[76]

I believe that one has to be a mystic to find meaning in what, to Toynbee, appears to be the supreme meaning of history.

Let us go on to mention the last prophecy of this strange theologian of history: in dying, he says, civilizations give birth to religions. For the future he foresees the coming of a universal religion which would constitute "a higher species of society", uniting Christianity, Hinduism, Islam and Buddhism. Of course, Christianity will constitute the "culminating" point in this hierarchy. Then, war and the class struggle will disappear and the State will be subordinate to the Church. All men will turn to God, and the communion of the Saints will be a reality on earth and in heaven, as Saint Augustine imagined fifteen hundred years ago. This view was propounded in the middle of the twentieth century by the modern historian, Arnold J. Toynbee. Incidentally, these are quotations; not a parody.

Toynbee is the most striking example of the return of philosophy of

---

[75] A. Toynbee, *Civilization on Trial* (New York, 1948), p. 259.
[76] *Ibid.*, pp. 262—263.

history to its theological stage, after having passed through its metaphysical and positive stages. Thus, it becomes obvious that, although offering us the possibility of classifying certain manifestations of philosophy of history, Comte's law of the three stages does not describe the evolution of this discipline. It cannot even classify all its manifestations, for dialectical Materialism is neither theological nor metaphysical nor positive. The same holds for Spengler's doctrine.

Let us give up all attempts to find a law describing the course of the philosophy of history, for, probably, such a law does not exist. As for the classifications, let us limit ourselves to dividing the philosophies of history into speculative and critical ones. The speculative systems try to establish a general doctrine of the evolution of history from its beginnings to its end, to find its laws, purpose, meaning, and value. These speculative systems are teleological and try to prophesy the course of historical events. Almost all the great systems of philosophy of history, from Saint Augustine to Hegel and Toynbee, belong to this speculative type.

The first people who protested against these universalistic pretensions were professional historians. One of the greatest of them — the Swiss Jakob Burckhardt — declared, in the second half of the nineteenth century: "We are not privy to the secrets of eternal Wisdom and do not know its aims. Those bold anticipations of a universal plan lead to errors, because they start from erroneous premises."[77]

In our day, Professor Karl R. Popper protested most vigorously against these speculative systems of history by branding them as "oracular philosophy,"[78] and Professor Marrou asked their authors the embarrassing question: *What* do you know of that history to which you appeal so willingly, and *how* do you know it?"[79]

The aims of a critical philosophy of history are much more modest: they are limited to determining the logical, epistemological and axiological conditions of history. As Professor Raymond Aron says, the critical analysis of historical knowledge is to traditional philosophy of history what Kant's critique was to dogmatic metaphysics.

Nevertheless, it was not Kant himself who created the critical philosophy of history. Kant's critique was limited to dogmatic metaphysics in the fields of knowledge and moral behavior, while his philosophy of history remained speculative, teleological, metaphysical. Kant wrote his famous essay on universal history in 1784, three years after publishing

[77] J. Burckhardt, *Weltgeschichtliche Betrachtungen* (Bern, 1941), p. 44.
[78] K. R. Popper, *The Open Society and its Enemies* (Londen, 1945), II, p. 212.
[79] H.-I. Marrou, *De la connaissance historique* (Paris, 1956), p. 17.

his *Critique of Pure Reason*. Nevertheless, that essay does not show any trace of philosophical criticism. Hitsory is for Kant the execution of a preestablished plan of a metaphysical force called "nature" or "Providence". It is endowed with wisdom (*Weisheit*), and, although men are unaware of its intentions, they fulfil them unconsciously. So far, Kant follows the road delineated by Vico. It is the contents of this plan which gives Kant's historical conception a specific character. Here is what he says: "The history of the human species as a whole may be regarded as the execution of a hidden plan of nature to accomplish a perfect civil constitution, as the sole condition in which it can fully develop all the potentialities of mankind."[80]

Having endowed man with reason and liberty, nature "wanted" everything in man which goes beyond his animal existence to be achieved by himself. The means used by nature to force man to develop all his potentialities is, according to Kant, antagonism. Like Heraclitus, Kant exalted discord among men, because without it they would become victims of their propensity to laziness. But, "fortunately", men are possessed by envy, vanity, greed and a will to power. Without these vices, says Kant, all of man's excellent potentialities would remain atrophic. 'Man wants concord, but nature knows better what is good for the species: it wants discord."[81] Driven to action by his greed, man learns how to use his reason and so he gradually develops all his potentialities.

But this same unsociability which drives man into a *bellum omnium contra omnes*, a war of all against all, forces him finally to create a perfect civil constitution, in which the freedom of the individual can coexist with the freedom of the group. By destructive wars and costly armaments, nature forces men and states to overcome their antagonisms, "to get out of the lawless condition of savages and to enter a league of nations",[82] which would guarantee even the security of the weakest countries. This is an idea which Kant was to develop later in his booklet on eternal peace.

Since the achievement of eternal peace by means of a supranational constitution was considered to be the secret aim of nature, Kant was able to give to his well known essay on history the title *Idee zu einer allgemeinen Geschichte in weltbürgerlicher Absicht* — Idea of a universal history with a cosmopolitan purpose. In concluding it, Kant stated:

[80] I. Kant's *Sämmtliche Werke*, VI (Leipzig, 1870), "Idee zu einer allgemeinen Geschichte in weltbürgerlicher Absicht", p. 14.
[81] *Ibid.*, p. 8.
[82] *Ibid.*, p. 11.

> This gives us the hope that after many a revolution of remodeling, the supreme purpose of nature will be accomplished in the establishment of a cosmopolitan state as the nursery in which all the original potentialities of the human species are to be developed.[83]

This is, to be sure, a noble conception, but is is far from representing a critical philosophy of history. By considering nature as a meta-empirical force hidden behind the phenomena, by giving it a will and a purpose, by endowing it with wisdom and by ascribing to it a plan governed by final causes, Kant changed nature into a metaphysical power which directs history teleologically. In sketching this plan, Kant presented a general doctrine of history from its beginnings, with an evaluation of its meaning and a prophecy of its future. Thus, Kant's philosophy of history is metaphysical, speculative, teleological, panoramic, oracular. It is not critical.

The neo-Kantian, Heinrich Rickert, distinguished three epochs in the philosophy of history: a dogmatic, a sceptical and a critical period, considering not only Kant's but also Hegel's and Fichte's historical doctrines as "critical".[84] But we have already seen that Hegel's doctrine is the prototype of a teleological, speculative, metaphysical, oracular approach to history and, thus, absolutely uncritical. The same holds for Fichte, who, in his *Grundzüge des gegenwärtigen Zeitalters,* presented history as an evolution towards an ultimate purpose: the synthesis of reason and freedom, after their antagonism during the Enlightenment. In my opinion, the critical philosophy of history is post-Kantian, post-Fichtean and post-Hegelian. It starts with Dilthey.

As we have said, a critical philosophy of history should limit itself to an examination of the logical, epistemological and axiological conditions of history. Although Kant did not create such a critical philosophy of history, he gave it its decisive direction. Having achieved the critique of pure reason, Kant suggested to posterity the idea of a critique of historical reason, based on the same principles.

The epoch of the great speculative systems of philosophy of history ended with Hegel and his disciples. Half a century after the death of that last metaphysician of history in the grand style, Wilhelm Dilthey inaugurated, in 1883, the period of a critical philosophy of history. It was he who propagated the concept and the expression of a "critique of historical reason". He even intended to give his main work the title

---

[83] *Ibid.,* pp. 16—17.
[84] H. Rickert, *Die Probleme der Geschichtsphilosophie* (Heidelberg, 1924), pp. 133—142.

Kritik der historischen Vernunft — Critique of Historical Reason, but published it later as *Einleitung in die Geisteswissenschaften* — Introduction to the Sciences of the Mind.

What Dilthey decried in the great speculative systems of philosophy of history was, above all, their ambition to determine the meaning and value of human history as a whole. Dilthey invited the philosophers of history to search for the roots of the concepts of meaning and value in their own consciousness, introspectively. Then they would discover that

> value and law exist only in relation to our systems of energies and that, without any relation to such a system, they have no longer any imaginable meaning. An arrangement of reality can never have a *value in itself,* but only a value in relation to a system of energies.[85]

According to Dilthey, every formula by which we express the meaning of history is only a reflection of our inner life. Even the idea of historical progress seems to reside less in the idea of an objective aim than in the *"Selbsterfahrung unseres ringenden Willens"* — that is, in the inner experience of our struggling will. We project this inner psychic experience into historical reality in the form of an image of general progress. "What a man, struggling with destiny, experiences in his lonely soul, in the depth of his conscience, exists for *him* not for the world process or for any organism of human society."[86]

By refuting meaning and value as entities in themselves and by affirming the relativity of the ideas of value, meaning and progress to definite systems of psychic energies, Dilthey cut through the metaphysical roots of speculative philosophy of history.

Although this German philosopher did not have the gift of directing the abundant flow of his ideas into the channels of a system but expressed them piecemeal — Ortega y Gasset called him *"este genial tartamudo",* that stuttering genius — they, nevertheless, opened up a new road to philosophy of history, toward a critique of its foundations.

The few modern attempts to explain historical evolution teleologically show how justified Dilthey's psychological critique of speculative philosophy of history has been. In his work on *The Birth of Tragedy,* Nietzsche had tried to interpret the whole history of Western civilization from the Greek tragedy to the end of the nineteenth century as aiming at the reunification of the "Apollonian" and "Dionysian" principles in

---

[85] *Wilhelm Diltheys Gesammelte Schriften* (Leipzig-Berlin, 1933), "Einleitung in die Geisteswissenschaften", I, p. 97.
[86] *Ibid.,* I, p. 100.

the musical drama of Richard Wagner. But several years later, after breaking with Wagner, Nietzsche recognized the purely subjective and ephemeral motives of his teleological interpretation of history. He even scoffed then at his juvenile tendency of surrounding his idols with "a halo of world history".[87]

In our century, Edmund Husserl, whose whole work had been a defiance of history, toward the end of his days propounded a new speculative, teleological, panoramic philosophy of history. He wanted to develop the "historico-philosophical idea or the teleological meaning of European man".[88] The motives of this enterprise were rather personal: the situation of Husserl, for decades the admired leader of German philosophy, in Nazi Germany, which rejected him as a Jew. Professor Ricoeur characterized this situation very well, when he wrote:

> Old Husserl could not fail to discover that mind has a history important for the whole of history, that mind can be sick, that history is for the mind the place of danger, of possible loss.[89]

In this "teleology of European history", Husserl tried to show that European man was born in Greece, between the seventh and the sixth centuries B.C., with the idea of "infinite tasks". This idea characterizes occidental philosophy and its science. With Greek philosophy, the European changed from a purely biological into a spiritual being, representing a "humanity with infinite tasks" (*Menschentum unendlicher Aufgaben*).[90]

To be sure, philosophy with its sciences is only a partial aspect of European civilization, but it is its brain; and on the normal function of this brain depends the European mind's health. Thus, the crisis of the European mind was for Husserl a crisis of its philosophy. The latter had allowed the sciences to devote themselves to an extreme "Objectivism", to a Naturalism which forgot the subjective roots of all sciences. "For true nature, in its scientific meaning, is a product of the scientific mind (*Erzeugnis des naturforschenden Geistes*) and, thus, presupposes the science of the mind."[91]

According to Husserl, only "transcendental phenomenology" — that

---

[87] F. Nietzsche, *Gesammelte Werke* (München, 1928), Band XXI, "Ecce homo", p. 241.
[88] E. Husserl, *Die Krisis der europäischen Wissenschaften und die transzendentale Phänomenologie* (Haag, 1954), p. 314.
[89] P. Ricoeur, "Husserl et le sens de l'histoire", *Revue de Métaphysique et de Morale*, Paris, juillet-octobre 1949, p. 281.
[90] E. Husserl, *op. cit.*, p. 325.
[91] *Ibid.*, p. 345.

is, his own philosophy — is able to overcome the objectivism of the modern scientific mind and, with it, the crisis of Western civilization. It is able to do so by a restoration of the primacy of the subject, that is of the mind, as the source of all science, including natural science. In that new science of the mind which Husserl called transcendental phenomenology, the mind "is not in or with nature, but nature itself enters the mental sphere".[92]

It seems evident to me that this Husserlian interpretation of the history of the European mind, from the early Greek philosophers to transcendental phenomenology, is the result of a very personal perspective related to that attitude which Dilthey called "the inner experience of the struggling will". That "teleology of European history", which Husserl elaborated on the eve of World War II, was intimately linked with his "system of energies" struggling with an adverse historical world. As for Hegel, the whole evolution of the universal Mind in history had aimed at its self-recognition in Hegel's own philosophy, so, for Husserl, the whole evolution of the European mind aimed at the restoration of its subjectivity in Husserl's own transcendental phenomenology.

This kind of teleological, speculative philosophy of history tends to perpetuate the personal perspectives of philosophers which are often ephemeral and a result of momentary interests or emotions and to present them as objective aims of the entire historical evolution. How could such tendencies avoid philosophical provincialisms? A critical philosophy of history has the task of unmasking such illusions.

[92] *Ibid.*, p. 346.

IV. HISTORICAL KNOWLEDGE

As we have said earlier, critical philosophy of history tries to determine the logical, epistemological and axiological conditions of historical knowledge. Since the main subject of our present investigation is that of the relations between history and values, we shall try to clarify, above all, the axiological conditions of historiography. However, the realization of this plan presupposes an inquiry into the logical and epistemological structure of that discipline.

Often the problem of historical knowledge has been considered less difficult than that of the knowledge of nature. Giambattista Vico expressed the profound idea that man can truly know only what he has created. Since nature has been created by God, it can, according to Vico, be known only by its august author. The case of the social, historical world is different. It is man's most authentic creation, and, therefore, the Italian thinker was convinced that it could be known by man.[1]

Half a century later, Immanuel Kant confirmed Vico's idea that man can only know what he has created; he demonstrated, however, that nature is not entirely beyond that realm. For the thinker of Königsberg showed us that it is our understanding (*Verstand*) which, by virtue of its categories and its pure forms of perception (*reine Anschauungsformen*), constructs the object of knowledge of nature and recognizes it, therefore, to the extent to which he has constructed it. What is behind his construction — the thing in itself — remains hidden to human understanding.

As for history, however, thinkers continued, in the post-Kantian period, to consider it as knowable in an absolute way, as it is in itself. *"Geschichte ist die Wirklichkeit selber"* — history is reality itself, declared, in complete naïveté, the famous German historian Leopold von Ranke. Bacon's formula, *scientia est veritatis imago*, science is the

[1] G. Vico, *Principj di Scienza Nuova d'intorno alla Comune Natura delle Nazioni,* Seconda Edizione (1744) (Milano, 1854), Libro Primo, III, p. 136.

image of truth, was replaced by the principle, *historia est veritatis imago*
— history is the image of truth. The temptation of this naïve Realism
was especially powerful in view of the fact that historical knowledge
refers to human beings, their actions, their desires, their motives, their
creations. Nothing was more natural than to suppose that man is capable
of knowing man.

All these suppositions were destroyed by the investigations of certain
thinkers of neo-Kantian lineage, among which one must mention
Wilhelm Dilthey, Wilhelm Windelband, Heinrich Rickert, Georg Simmel, Max Weber, and others. Their critical job was done with such
efficiency that, in 1921, Theodor Lessing ended up by declaring that
historical reality is just as "fictitious" as the reality of the physical
sciences with their atoms, electrons, and mathematical formulas. "The
one is no truer and no more real than the other,"[2] declared Lessing.
According to this philosopher, history is historiography; and the latter
is the positing of causal connections, the invention of an evolution, the
creation of a meaning. This thinker who, in 1933, became a victim of
history — he was assassinated by Hitler's agents — described the situation of history in the following way: "History is a tapestry-worker; she
has patterns of categories, traced beforehand, into which she must weave
all the strings of reality."[3]

I think that the problem of critical philosophy of history was raised
by Descartes, in the following passage of his *Discours de la méthode:*

> . . . even the most faithful histories, if they neither change
> nor increase the value of things in order to make them more
> worthy of being read, at least omit almost always the lowest
> and the least illustrious circumstances, with the result that
> the remainder does not appear as it is. . . .[4]

This omission of a great number of circumstances — and not only of
those which Descartes called *"les plus basses et moins illustres"* (the
lowest and least illustrious) is an unavoidable necessity for historiography. The historian who, for example, wants to write the history of
Julius Caesar must omit a thousand circumstances of his hero's life —
to begin with, all those for which no documentary evidence is available.
But even of the circumstances known by documents the historian must
eliminate a great number: in the first place, all the permanent circumstances which his hero shares with all other men, such as the organic

[2] Th. Lessing, *Geschichte als Sinngebung des Sinnlosen* (München, 1921), p. 16.
[3] *Ibid.*, p. 8.
[4] R. Descartes, *Discours de la Méthode* (Paris, 1898), I, p. 14.

functions of his body, or his every-day life. The historian can take interest only in the traits which are peculiar to his hero, those which he does not share with everybody and which distinguish him from the great mass of non-historic beings. Historical evolution is something other than the totality of a human life, and not all that which a historic personage does belongs to history. In my opinion, Voltaire's definition of history as "the account of the facts given as true"[5] is too wide, because many facts are true without being "historical". It is true that I am typing this manuscript. Nevertheless, this true fact is not an historical fact. To be sure, I am not an historical figure. But let us take Hannibal or Molière: Even if certain documents were to establish beyond doubt the composition of Hannibal's menu on the evening after the battle of Cannae or the cost of the pens with which Molière wrote his *Tartuffe,* these would not be truly historical facts. The Argentine philosopher, Alejandro Korn, remarks that of the innumerable children born on August 15, 1769, only one is interesting to history: Napoleon Bonaparte.[6] All these facts show that to be "historical" a fact must have a certain "value". Later, we shall try to determine the specific character of this value which bestows upon a fact the epithet "historical". The historian passes the facts verified as authentic through a sieve, retaining only those which have that specific value.

The fact that history as knowledge is something other than the totality of a human life becomes evident when we realize that a man's life, such as Plato's, lasted eighty years, while the history of his life — even a very detailed one — must be read within several days. The historian detaches certain facts from their organic connections with other facts, isolates them and links together those isolated facts. The outcome is a fictitious construction such as never existed nor could exist. Descartes was certainly right in saying that, if one omits certain circumstances, "the remainder does not appear as it is" or rather was. Instead of complaining, the historian and the philosopher should admit, with Georg Simmel, that "history as knowledge cannot be a copy of reality".[7] Rickert even sees a logical contradiction in the postulate that history should be a copy of reality. Neither historical nor natural reality can be presented such as it is independently of our concepts, since all knowledge is a transformation and schematization of reality, a means of organizing and thinking it. In order to be able to form his concepts

[5] *Oeuvres complètes de Voltaire* (Paris, 1879), tome XIX, "Dictionnaire philosophique", III, p. 346.
[6] A. Korn, *Sistema filosófico* (Buenos Aires, 1959), p. 59.
[7] G. Simmel, *Die Probleme der Geschichtsphilosophie* (Leipzig, 1907), p. 51.

and to offer us knowledge, the historian must replace the continuous
flow of historical events by a conceptual discontinuity.

The selective principles according to which the historian detaches
certain facts and reconnects them with others depends on the categories
he uses, on the standards of value he adopts and, in the last analysis
— on his historiographical project.

Speaking of the categories used by the historian in order to shape his
raw material, one must, in my opinion, distinguish two kinds:

1. The *general* categories of thought.
2. The *specific* categories of *historical* thought.

The general categories are the widest conceptual types by means of
which the relations between phenomena can be contemplated. By specific categories of history, I mean the widest conceptual types by means
of which historical phenomena can be contemplated.

Aristotle's and Kant's categories are general categories of thought.
In Aristotle, we find such categories as substance, quantity, quality,
relation, place, time, position, modality, passivity, activity. Kant divided
quality into reality, negation and limitation; quantity into unity, plurality, totality; modality into possibility and impossibility, existence
and non-existence, necessity and contingency; relation into subsistence
and inherence, causality and dependence and reciprocal action (community). Evidently, the historian, as every other thinking being, uses
these general categories of thought and some others, of more recent
origin.

However, besides these general categories of thought, the historian
uses special categories, by means of which he conceives the specific
relations between historical phenomena. Let us mention some of these
categories: friend, enemy, peace, war, evolution, revolution, majority,
minority, right, might, oligarchy, aristocracy, democracy, plutocracy,
feudalism, dictatorship, class struggle, imperialism, etc., etc.

A considerable number of these historical categories constitute what
Max Weber called *"Idealtypen"* — ideal types. The ideal type, says
Max Weber, is not a representation of reality but rather its idealization,
a "utopia", useful for research and for the communication of its results.
One of the great advantages of these ideal types is that they allow more
precise definitions than the real phenomena.[8] Historical research must
discover in each concrete case the distance between the ideal type and
reality. Weber insisted that concepts like "mercantilism", "individual-

[8] M. Weber, *Gesammelte Aufsätze zur Wissenschaftslehre* (Tübingen, 1922), pp. 190,
191.

ism", "imperialism", "feudalism", etc. are not descriptions of realities but ideal types. He warned us not to confuse ideal types with historical reality and insisted that ideal concepts are only "means for the knowledge of connections important from individual points of view". They express only the "directing axiological ideas" (*die leitenden Wertideen*)[9] of an epoch. We shall take up this subject again when discussing the relations between historical knowledge and values.

The facts transmitted to the historian and verified by the modern methods of criticism of sources can be synthesized by means of a great variety of posisble historical categories. To give an example, I should say that a certain epoch could be described as a struggle between good and evil, or between reason and unreason, or between right and might, invidual and mass, tyranny and freedom, nationalism and humanism, state and church, or as a class struggle between labor and capital.

In order to create these diverse historical images, the historian must sift the verified facts and select those which can be brought under the headings of the categories he has chosen for his specific historiographical project.

Political history can be one of nations or one of civilizations, one of customs, of ideas, of economic principles or of classes. As Simmel said, each unitary image of history is achieved thanks to a unilateral construction. Therefore, this thinker was opposed to the illusion of certain historians who believe in the possibility of a "precise" historical description, "according to reality". All a historian can offer us is a "stylized" construction adapted to the requirements of the categories chosen by him.

But this is not to say that the choice of the categories depends on the caprice of the historians. We only affirm that the same historical facts can be grouped and mutually connected from different standpoints. The choice of the categories to be applied in a concrete case will depend on the theory adopted by the historian. As Professor Raymond Aron says — "theory precedes history".[10] The fact that the history of a certain epoch is written and rewritten again an again, although no new sources have been discovered, shows clearly that it is a question of new theories, trying to give more satisfactory interpretations of the same facts. Just as the modern chemical theories no longer use the categories of alchemy, so modern historians no longer apply the historical categories used by medieval or antique historians. Every theory — scientific or historical — exhibits the impress of its epoch.

---

[9] *Ibid.*, pp. 208—209.
[10] R. Aron, *Introduction à la philosophie de l'histoire* (Paris, 1938), p. 93.

Plutarch reported that Philip of Macedonia found a serpent lying by his wife Olympias as she slept. But, "in reality", this serpent was the god Ammon. With other antique historians, Plutarch derives from this "fact" the divine origin of Alexander the Great. He also reports that King Philip was told by the oracle of Delphi that he should one day lose the eye with which he presumed to peep through a chink of the door, when he saw the god, in the form of a serpent, in the company of his wife.

Evidently, we are here in the presence of mythical categories which carry the seal of their time. Where a medieval historian saw a struggle between the principles of salvation and damnation, a contemporary historian sees perhaps a combat between different economic interests. It is here a question of different theories, each of which reflects the predominant tendencies of its epoch. Certain modern historians use psychoanalytic categories in order to explain the character of Nero — a theoretical principle which one would hardly find in Gibbon's or Mommsen's works.

In this respect, history is, however, not in a more disadvantageous situation than natural science. For the latter, too, experiences the effects of the historical evolution of the categories on which the theories are based. The categories of Cartesian mechanics were no longer those of Aristotelian scholastic physics. Newton no longer used Descartes' categories, and the categories of Einstein's physics or of quantum mechanics are different from Newton's. Likewise, the categories of evolutionary and genetic botany are no longer those of Linné's static botany.

But, although the variability of the categories and theories is a well established and universally accepted fact in the realm of the history of sciences, it is far from being generally admitted as far as the history of historiography is concerned.

One of the deepest divisions in contemporary philosophy is that which exists between the supporters and the opponents of the doctrine of the invariability of reason and its categories. Rationalism affirms it; Historicism denies it. The consequences of Historicism would be serious — not only for philosophy of history, but for philosophy as such and for human knowledge. For, if all the categories of mind are products of history, then we have no supra-historical standards capable of measuring the truth or falsehood of the conceptions of a given historical period. Historicism not only implies the thesis *veritas filia temporis* — truth is a daughter of time, but also the principle *virtus filia temporis* — value is a daughter of time. Therefore, we will delve into the problems of Historicism only after having analyzed the problem of values. The latter will be taken up in the next chapter.

The plurality of systems of historical interpretation is, however, not only due to the changes which our categories experience in the course of history but, also, to individual variations among the historians living at the same epoch. Professor Raymond Aron formulated this problem in the following way:

> The human event, as it takes place in the conciousnesses, is inaccessible. After the event, we reconstruct the inner experience (*le vécu*). What are the uncertainties or ambiguities of this reconstruction? To what extent is it separable from the situation and the intention of the historian or capable of universal validity?[11]

Using his rich experience as a historian and a student of critical philosophy, Professor Marrou answered these questions by ascertaining "a massive intrusion of the historian's personality", whose thought, categories and intentions "shape historical knowledge and give it form and countenance".[12] As Paul Valéry once said, history is inseparable from the historian.[13] Against the unrealizable ideal of an historical knowledge valid for everybody, says Professor Marrou, "I shall set that of a truth valid *for myself*, and I shall see in it a guarantee of seriousness, exigency and rigor."[14]

Logically speaking, the study of every historical epoch can suggest an infinity of questions and answers, so that historical certitude is never more than probability. Let us recall some of the answers offered successively by historians to Gibbon's question about the causes of the decline and ruin of the Roman Empire: For Gibbon himself, the cause was the triumph of Christianity and barbarism; for Seeck, it was the extermination of the Roman élite; for Kaphahn, physical decline; for T. Frank, racial degeneracy; for Huntington, a climatic crises and drought; for Liebig and Vassiliev, the degradation of the soil; for Max Weber, the decline of slavery and the return to natural economy; for Rostovtzeff, a class struggle between the peasant-soldiers and bourgeois townspeople; for Piganiol, the barbarian invasions; and, finally, for Toynbee the danger from abroad and the desertion by the masses.

In looking at this survey, which is far from being complete, we ask ourselves where Professor Mandelbaum found the empirical facts capable

---

[11] *Ibid.*, p. 90.
[12] H.-I. Marrou, *De la connaissance historique* (Paris, 1956), p. 187.
[13] P. Valéry, "Discours de l'histoire", *Variété IV* (Paris, 1938), p. 132.
[14] H.-I. Marrou, *op. cit.*, p. 221.

of supporting his thesis that historical knowledge is independent of the opinions and evaluations of the historians.[15]

When, in December 1933, the American historian Charles A. Beard delivered before the American Historical Association his presidential address entitled "Written History as an Act of Faith",[16] he provoked a storm of indignation among the majority of his colleagues. He was accused of attacking "the noble dream" of an objectively true history and almost created a split among American historians.[17] Today, the French historian Marrou takes up the thesis of his American colleague by declaring that historical knowledge "rests definitely on an act of faith" (acte de foi), for "we know of the past what we believe to be true of what we have understood of what the documents have preserved".[18] But, today, this judgment no longer provokes such indignation. Twenty additional years of critical philosophy of history have prepared more minds to the acceptance of certain facts which, before, had been considered humiliating.

Among the pioneers of critical philosophy of history, is was Georg Simmel who showed most convincingly that historical truth, just as scientific truth, is not a simple reproduction of data but the product of a rational activity which changes its raw material into something which it was not before. A political historian, for example, will not deal with the personal joys and griefs of his hero. They were his private affairs. The historian rather constructs an unreal being, the carrier of certain political ideas, the continuity of whose existence skips all the events of his non-political life, as if it had not existed. The political historian deals with his hero as if he had been an exclusively political being, a homo politicus.

Several years before the publication of Vaihinger's Philosophy of the As-If, Simmel discovered in the "as-if", in fictitious constructs, one of the fundamental principles of historiography. According to him, Historical Materialism interprets events "as if" people were dominated by economic motives.[19] This leading idea and those of any other historical

[15] M. Mandelbaum, The Problem of Historical Knowledge (New York, 1938), pp. 190, 202, etc.
[16] C. A. Beard, "Written History as an Act of Faith", The American Historical Review, Vol. XXXIX, Num. 2, Jan. 1934, pp. 219—229.
[17] Ibid., Vol. XL (1934), pp. 439—449, and XLI (1936), pp. 74—87.
[18] H.-I. Marrou, op. cit., pp. 133—134.
[19] G. Simmel, Die Probleme der Geschichtsphilosophie (Leipzig, 1907), p. 156. — Let us not forget the way in which Engels limited this principle by writing in a letter to Bloch, in December 1890: "According to the materialist conception of history, the determining element in history is ultimately production and reproduction in real life. More than this neither Marx nor I have ever asserted. If, therefore, someone twists

conception are not constitutive principles of history but regulative principles in Kant's sense — that is, heuristic maxims of historiography.

If Simmel showed that history is no more the reproduction of human reality than physics is the copy of nature, if he made us understand that the historian constructs his object just as the physicist constructs his, the conclusions this penetrating mind drew from these insights are, nevertheless, not acceptable to me. The philosophical value of Kant's answer to the question "How is nature possible?" resides, according to Simmel, in the "freedom" regained by the Ego towards nature. Simmel believed that he himself had regained the same kind of freedom towards history.

Since the Ego "produces nature as his idea" and since the general laws which shape nature are (according to Kant) only forms of our understanding, Simmel concluded that "the existence of nature is subject to the sovereign Ego".[20] Thus, he adds, of the two violations which threaten modern man — nature and history — one is eliminated. By establishing the autonomy of the mind which prescribes its laws to nature, Kant has, according to Simmel, "liberated" the Ego from the grip of nature.

However, history, that supra-personal power which invades the private sphere of the individual, constitutes no less a violation of the Ego than nature. Camus knew it, and Simmel likewise understood it. Now, just as Kant had liberated us from naturalism by showing that nature is the result of the sovereign activity of our mind and its categories, so Simmel believed he could liberate us from the oppression of history by showing us that it, too, is a product of the sovereign activity of our mind and its categories.[21]

In rejecting this conclusion of Simmel's, I must, first of all, deny that Kant liberated the Ego from the grip of nature, for the Kantian Ego which prescribes its laws to nature is not the psycho-physiological Ego of the individuals but the transcendental Ego which does not belong to any real human being. It is, however, the real, psycho-physiological Ego which suffers from the pressure of nature, and the autonomy of the transcendental Ego with respect to nature does not relieve the psycho-physiological Ego when it suffers from tooth-ache or is dying from cancer.

In fact, after Kant, just as before him, we are subject to nature, its

---

this into the statement that the economic element is the only determining one, he transforms it into a meaningless, abstract and absurd sentence." (*Correspondence 1846—1895*, p. 475).

[20] G. Simmel, *op. cit.*, p. VIII.

[21] *Ibid.*, pp. VIII, IX.

forces, the diseases it sends us and the death it imposes upon us.

As for Simmel's hope to liberate the individual from the grip of history by the demonstration that it is the work of the sovereign mind and its categories, it derives from another equivocation: that misleading confusion between history as knowledge and history as reality. To be sure, both are man's creation. However, history as reality is not created by individual man but by collective man: by Rousseau's *"volonté géné-rale"* (general will), by Herder's *"Volksgeist"* (national mind) and Hegel's *"Weltgeist"* (universal mind), by Renan's "nation", Durkheim's and Royce's "collective soul", by Le Bon's "masses" *(foules)*, or by Marx's "classes". Whatever the name we are choosing to designate that force which creates history as reality, it is different from the individual Ego; it is a force which comes from outside and invades the private sphere of the individual. This collective force exerts on the individual that coercive influence which, according to Durkheim, is the distinctive criterion of every social phenomenon. History is imposed on the individual as a Sartrian *"situation"* or *"facticité"*, as a Marxian *"Klassenlage"* (class-situation) or as a *"circunstancia"* in the sense of Ortega y Gasset.

To be sure, the individual is free to react, but he is "forcibly free" *(por fuerza libre)*,[22] as Ortega says, or "condemned to be free" *(condamné à être libre)*, as Sartre said later.[23] This freedom of the individual is imprisoned in the narrow limits of historical situations and circumstances into which he was "cast" *(geworfen)*, as Heidegger says, without having created or chosen them. All this is far removed from Simmel's freedom of the Ego as a sovereign creator of history and its categories. If history as reality is a creation of man's freedom, it is, nevertheless, not a creation of his freedom as an individual.

As for history as knowledge, Simmel demonstrated convincingly that it is truly the work of both the psychological and the transcendental Ego. To this thinker, history as knowledge is a "transformation" *(Umbildung)* of the data of the past, and he admits that the portrait painted by the historian is at the same time a portrait of the painter. With the same documents before their eyes and endowed with the same degree of intelligence, two historians with different characters will present different histories of Caesar, Gregory VII, or Mirabeau. For Simmel, the postulate that the historian should also be an artist is not limited to the form but extends to its contents. Empathy *(Einfühlung)* is to him an indispensible element of all historiography.

[22] J. Ortega y Gasset, *Obras completas* (Madrid, 1950—1952), tomo VI, p. 34.
[23] J. P. Sartre, *L'être et le néant* (Paris, 1943), p. 515, and *L'âge de raison* (Paris, 1945), p. 249.

The possibility of historical knowledge depends, therefore, according to Simmel, to a large extent on the individuality of the historian and presupposes it. Here, it is truly the psychological Ego of the historian, his individuality, which possesses a certain sovereignty in modeling the historical raw material; it is no longer exclusively Kant's transcendental Ego. However, that relative sovereignty of the historian, limited by documents, does not help us in the least if we wish to free ourselves from that which Simmel called the Ego's "violation" by history. For, evidently, the Ego does not suffer from the pressure of history as knowledge but from the impact of history as reality, i. e., not from historiography but from history properly speaking. It was certainly not Konrad Heiden's history of Hitler nor Francis T. Miller's *History of World War II* which cost humanity twenty-six million dead and tons of blood and tears. It was history as reality made by Hitler, by Germany's heavy industry, by the German people and its *Wehrmacht* which imposed upon us those sufferings. Evidently, the ambiguity of the term history led Simmel into error.

The majority of the thinkers interested in what Rickert called "logic of history" (*Logik der Geschichtswissenschaft*) were interested in past history. Their problem was the reconstruction of a connected history out of the data transmitted in documents. However, the construction of history as knowledge out of the data of experienced historical reality appears to me a problem of no less epistemological interest. In my opinion, it has been somehow neglected by the philosophers of history. In his book *The Idea of History*, the British philosopher Collingwood characterizes history as "a science whose business is to study events not accessible to our observation and to study these events inferentially".[24] In my opinion, this definition is correct as long as it refers to history of the past. But there is also contemporary history, and this is certainly not covered by the foregoing definition, for it is accessible to our observation. As one recalls, the ancients and Hegel appreciated it very much. For Collingwood, this history accessible to our direct observation seems without value. Astronomers and meteorologists will make long journeys to places where they can observe for themselves certain phenomena in which they are interested. Historians, however, will not travel to countries where wars or revolutions are going on, for, as Collingwood says, the events they could observe on the spot would not teach them anything they want to know. If natural scientists want to observe for themselves the phenomena they are studying, it is "because

[24] R. G. Collingwood, *The Idea of History* (Oxford, 1946), p. 251.

their standard of observation is such that they cannot be satisfied with descriptions by inexpert witnesses".[25]

By implication, this statement suggests that the historian can be satisfied with descriptions by inexpert witnesses. Of course he can, when he must — thanks to the modern methods of historical criticism. To the true historian, not even expert witnesses are authorities as long as he has not discovered the grounds on which their statements are based. Then, the historian's acceptance of a testimony is no longer based on authority but on evidence. By critical treatment of the statements contained in his sources, the historian may elicit from them information which in their original statement they have withheld. The critical historian can discover and correct errors and falsifications in his sources as well as reject parts of their testimony as contradictory and substitute more cogent explanations.[25a] He may interpolate between the statements of the witnesses and sources other statements implied by them etc., etc. Finally, he can use as evidence some perceived facts — even unwritten sources — which historians have, up to that moment, found useless or which he himself had considered unimportant. I gladly admit all this and concede to Collingwood that it is in this way that the idea of history comes into being, "the idea of an imaginary picture of the past".[26] And yet, I still believe that the historian can also be a very valuable first-hand witness. The services rendered by our rich literature of memoirs show it clearly.

I think that, besides this well known problem of historical criticism, the transformation of experienced history into history as knowledge also offers an important epistemological problem which has not been sufficiently clarified. As I said before, I call historical reality the evolution of the *res publica*, subjectively experienced and expressed in the first person. It is obviously a question here of the singular of the first person, for, although often modified by the psychology of the masses, an experience is always lived by an individual consciousness. The experience is localized in an individual space, and its time is of individual duration. How can these individual historic experiences be transformed into a supra-individual intersubjective history? How are the individual durations changed into an intersubjective historical time, and the individual spaces of the historical experiences transformed into an objective space, the location of the historical events?

[25] *Ibid.*, p. 250.
[25a] A posthumous publication by Marc Bloch, *Apologie pour l'histoire ou Métier d'historien* (Paris, 1961), presents excellent examples of the working of historical criticism.
[26] *Ibid.*, p. 248.

In his posthumous book, *La mémoire collective*, Maurice Halbwachs says that our memory is based on history experienced rather than learned. He also admits the existence of "collective space and time and a collective history" which envelop the individual minds.[27] I agree with this view, but I ask myself how this collective time, space and history is formed when we start from individual historical experiences confined to subjective durations and individual spaces. I shall try to explain this process by drawing on my own experience.

Like all people of my age, I have experienced much history. In particular I have lived through those dramatic epochs of history called wars. In World War I, I was a lieutenant in the Austro-Hungarian army and in World War II, a private in the French army. I can recount what I experienced in those two wars. Even if I recounted everything I experienced in those wars, without omitting anything, without changing or embellishing anything, it would still be only a very limited personal experience. The events occurred within the very restricted sphere of my individual perspective and survive in my narrow personal memory.

But, of the millions of other soldiers who went through the same wars, in the same armies or in those of the opposite camps, each had his individual perspective and all these historical perspectives complement each other and form together an intersubjective picture. Theoretically, this intersubjetcive picture created by mutual complementation, by the synthesis and integration of the diverse individual perspectives of the events of the *res publica,* constitutes the collective, intersubjective, military history of the two world wars.

Even the historiographies of a Caesar, a Foch, a Churchill or an Eisenhower are only subjective perspectives, although much wider ones, since their authors saw the events from much higher standpoints and directed them in part. But many perspectives, even of that superior kind, will be necessary to construct, for example, the image of World War II as known history. Although World War II is finished as real history, it is still not finished as known history, for many individual perspectives laid down in documents have not yet been critically examined and integrated into the whole of the other perspectives.

I believe that, theoretically, history as knowledge could be defined as the verbalized, critically examined and integrated ensemble of the individual perspectives of history as reality. As for the latter, we defined it as the experience in the first person singular of the evolution of the *res publica.* This would mean that historical reality exists only at the

[27] M. Halbwachs, *La mémoire collective* (Paris, 1950), pp. 43—45.

subjective, individual level. To be sure, as Gustave Le Bon showed, individual experiences are greatly influenced by the group of which the individual is a part. This influence is particularly strong in such collective events as wars, where emotions and passions rule supreme. But, although the events of a war are experienced by a multitude dominated by collective feelings and collective ideas, each member of this crowd has an individual experience of those collective events, ideas and feelings. The individual sees and can see an event only as a single Ego in a unique perspective. Thus, history as reality only truly exists at the subjective level, while intersubjective history only exists as historical knowledge.

One might object that it is possible to integrate the individually experienced perspectives, after critical examination, in order to construct historical reality as an intersubjective, collective evolution. This is, indeed, always attempted. But the result of these attempts is no longer historical reality but historical knowledge, a theoretical construction articulated by the categories chosen by the different historians in their work of the critique of the sources, of integration and synthesis. All that can be said of an "objective" historical reality is that it is this which makes subjective historical perspectives possible.

We said that the integration of the subjective perspectives of historical reality is "verbalized" in historical knowledge. This verbalization is, indeed, a constitutive part of historical knowledge and raises all kinds of semantic problems to which our attention was drawn by the French historian, Marc Bloch. By the connotations of the words chosen in the writing of history the historian can smuggle in all kinds of hidden moral and political attitudes. Furthermore, the meaning of words changes in the course of history. In asking the question as to whether the economy of the sixteenth century was "capitalistic", one has to realize that, in relation to the Renaissance, the word capitalism has another meaning than it has with respect to Saint-Simonism and to the industrial revolution.

Let us now try to answer the question as to how the multitude of spatio-temporal orders of individual historical perspectives can be converted into the unique spatio-temporal order of historical knowledge. I believe that one can, in this case, apply to the domain of history the procedure used by Kant to distinguish the objective order of the natural events from the subjective order of our impressions of these events.

The reader will remember Kant's example of the stone heated by the sun. I may, for example, first perceive the hot stone and then the shining sun. This would be the subjective, psychological succession of the events. But by applying the categories of substance and inherence, causality and dependence, our understanding succeeds in establishing the objective succession of the physical events expressed in the statement: The sun heats the stone. This statement is a description of objective empirical nature, since it connects my perceptions and determines their objective order in time independently of the subjective succession of my sensations. For considered, conceptually, as the objective cause of the stone's rising temperature, the shining of the sun must have preceded the heating of the stone, even though, subjectively, I may have perceived the hot stone before noticing the shining sun. If the latter succession is psychological, the former represents the physical sequence of events.

By this ingenious example, Kant showed that, even for an idealist, the empirical world is not necessarily a subjective, psychic dream world, as in Berkeley and, later, in Schopenhauer, but that the empirical world of phenomena is subject to objective physical laws different from the psychological order of our impressions of those events. Thus, Kant showed that the physical world can be known, even if it is only an empirical world and not a thing in itself.

I believe that we are able, in an analogous way, to distinguish objective historical events from the subjective order in which these events succeed one another in our individual perspectives. Let us give an example: On May 10, 1940, at five seventeen in the morning, the people of Brussels were rudely awakened by the violent explosions of aerial bombs. Soon they saw flames blazing from different buildings and columns of black smoke rising up into the sky. At the same time, they heard the anti-aircraft guns firing in a desperate rhythm.

What had happened? After all, Belgium was a neutral in the war which had been going on beyond its frontiers for eight months between France and Great Britain on the one hand and Germany on the other. A few hours after the event, the people of Brussels were told by radio that the bombardment of their city had been the second act in a tragedy which had started at four o'clock in the morning with a savage attack by the German airforce on the Belgian airfields and with the dropping of Nazi parachutists over the Albert Canal and the Eben-Emael fortress. They, also, were told that at half past eight on this tragic morning, after Belgium had lost half of her airforce on the ground, the German ambassador had come to tell Mr. Spaak that the Reich had invaded Belgium. In violating this country's neutrality, Germany pretended that it was "protecting" it against a possible violation on the part of France and England. The German ambassador called upon Belgium not to resist the Reich's armed force under pain of total destruction and loss of her independence.

By complementing their individual experience of the capital's bombardment, this second-hand information allowed the people of Brussels to reconstruct the objective order of the historical events as they had taken place independently of the subjective order in which these events had succeeded each other in their individual experiences. For, in the latter, the attack on the Albert Canal and on the airfields had appeared after the bombardment of Brussels, while in reality, it had occurred before this event. In the same way, the inhabitants of Brussels were by now able to interpret the bombardment of their town as a vain German attempt to break Belgian resistance.

In spite of the fact that historical reality is only subjectively experienced in individual perspectives, history as knowledge is capable of disengaging, by means of second-hand information and of logical inferences, an objective historical order of events different from the subjective orders of the individual perspectives of these events.

What is the spatial aspect of the individual historical perspectives? By looking through the window of his apartment in the Avenue des Arts an inhabitant of Brussels could see the conflagration of a building in the Chaussée de Louvain; but he could not see the blaze in the Schaerbeek barracks visible only to the inhabitants of that suburb. Nevertheless, for history as knowledge of World War II, it is an established fact that, during the first bombardment of Brussels on May 10, 1940, there were big fires on the Chaussée de Louvain as well as in the suburb of Schaerbeek. But historical reality, just as physical reality, is broken up into innumerable subjective facets or individual perspectives, each of which is determined by the spatio-temporal circumstances of the spectator. In his *Monadologie,* Leibniz wrote:

> As a city looked at from different sides appears quite differently (*tout autre*) and is, as if it were, perspectively multiplied, it likewise happens that, by the infinite multitude of simple substances, there appear to be as many different universes, which are, nevertheless, only the perspectives of one single universe, according to the different points of view of each monad.[28]

This perspectivism of Leibniz reappeared in a modified way in Husserl's doctrine of the "*Abschattungen*".[29] If we apply it to history, we see that historical reality is, likewise, "perspectively multiplied". The unitary system of history as knowledge is constructed by the integration of mil-

---

[28] *Oeuvres de Leibniz,* 2è série "La Monadologie", p. 399 (Paris, 1842).
[29] E. Husserl, *Ideen zu einer reinen Phänomenologie* (Haag, 1950), I, pp. 91—95.

lions of individual historical perspectives which co-exist or succeed each other in time.

José Ortega Gasset, who adopted Leibniz's perspectivism and developed it by applying it to life, once mentioned the example of the Sierra del Guadarrama, which one sees in a certain way from the side of the Escorial, while an inhabitant of Segovia sees this same mountain range quite differently, for he perceives its opposite slope. Would it be meaningful to quarrel over the question as to which of these views is the right one? Ortega answers: *"Ambas lo son ciertamente, y ciertamente por ser distintas"* — both perspectives are correct and precisely because they are different.[30]

I believe that the same can be said about historical perspectives. Two histories of the battle of Verdun, the one written by a French general, the other by a German general, will necessarily be different, even if they are conceived with the same impartiality and the same preoccupation with historical truth. From the standpoint of historical perspectivism, this fact appears to be quite natural. Observing and experiencing the battle of Verdun from the French perspective, the French historian had to see it in a way which differs from that of his German colleague, who saw it from the other side of the barrier.

Theoretically speaking, none of the innumerable individual historical perspectives exhausts reality, and, in spite of their diversity, they do not exclude each other. On the contrary, each requires the other as its complement, and all individual perspectives together build up the idea of an objective historical reality, as it is reflected in the ideal system of historical knowledge.

If we, thus, arrive at the idea of an "objective" history, as the critically examined, integrated system of subjective historical perspectives, it is, in my opinion, only an intersubjective reality but not an absolute one. Kant has shown that nature is a synthesis of our categories and the pure forms of perception (space and time) applied to our subjective sense data; therefore, the objectivity of nature does not entail its absolute metaphysical but only its empirical reality. I should say that, in a similar way, the objectivity of history as a synthesis, integration and categorical articulation of subjective historical perspectives is not tantamount to an absolute metaphysical reality of history but only to its empirical reality. Both nature and history represent only phenomenal realities. In both, we are able to distinguish between the subjective order of our impressions and the objective order of the phenomena,

[30] J. Ortega y Gasset, *Obras completas* (Madrid, 1950—1952), t. II, p. 19.

thanks to the application of categories, of spatio-temporal conceptions and logical inferences. That is all. But the total synthesis of all the relative perspectives which would build up absolute entities is beyond our reach, in history as well as in nature. In order to be conceivable, inter-subjective history and objective nature need the assumption of a transcendental Ego, in relation to which they are "relative"; and this excludes their "absolute" character. Absolute history, like absolute nature, is a noumenon.

Defined as the critically examined, verbalized and integrated ensemble of the individual perspectives of history as reality, history as knowledge is at an ideal, potential level. In reality, this ensemble is integrated only by the syntheses of the historians. As we said, these syntheses are carried out not only by means of the general categories of thought but, also, by virtue of the specific categories of historic thought. These categories represent a wide variety from which the synthesizing historians may choose, when linking together the data of the diverse historical perspectives offered in the documents. When we take into account the great variety of possible general and special categories applicable to the same historical data, we realize that the syntheses of the historians are themselves split up into a variety of perspectives. If we designate as primary the perspectives of the witnesses of an historical event, the unifying perpectives of those primary perspectives may be called secondary. They are the work of the historians. Thus, the idea of history as knowledge is achieved in the form of a multiplicity of secondary perspectives of a multiplicity of primary perspectives.

We have shown the epistemological processes by virtue of which an objective order of historical events detaches itself from the subjective individual perspectives of these events. But, besides these epistemological conditions, both the primary and secondary perspectives are also subject to certain psychological and sociological conditions which limit them to a large extent. Let us first speak of the former: In his famous story, *Crainquebille*, Anatole France tells us an anecdote about Sir Walter Raleigh. One day, when this great British warrior, statesman and historian was working in the Tower of London on the second part of his *History of the World*, a riot started below his window. He looked at the people who were quarreling and believed that he had observed them well. But, the next day, when he spoke to a friend who had participated in the riot, he was contradicted in every detail. Reflecting then on the difficulty of knowing the truth about events which took place far away and in the past, if it was even possible to misapprehend those which had just happened under his very eyes, he threw the second part of his manuscript of the *History of the World* into the fire. This is, at least, what Anatole France recounts.

One may doubt the authenticity of this anecdote, which is in contradiction to the reports of Raleigh's biographers such as Winstanley and, especially, Edward Edwards, the most reliable of them. Psychologically, however, the story could be true, for William Stern's psychology of the testimony (*Psychologie der Aussage*) and certain of Edouard Claparède's experiments confirm, if not the historical facts mentioned, at least the psychological facts. Many people look at their watches several times every day. But, when asked whether the figures on their dial-plate are Roman or Arabic or whether some of the figures are replaced by points, they commit errors.

As for the raw material for their syntheses, the majority of historians depend on the written or oral testimony of those who experienced the historical reality they are studying. This testimony is psychologically limited not only by the natural inaccuracy of observations and depositions, but also by the specific interests of the witness or of the group to which he belongs, and by the degree of his intelligence. But, even if the witness were a kind of fact-registering machine, free from all psychological hazards, which would report nothing but the authentic facts of historical reality, not all of these facts would be useful for history as knowledge. According to Simmel, there exists a "threshold" (*Schwelle*) of historical consciousness below which events lose their historical interest, although they remain above the threshold of perception. It is, therefore, a mere question of quantity. If an historical event is to conserve its individuality, it must not become too small. Simmel gives the example of the fight between an Austrian and a Prussian soldier during the battle of Kunersdorf. Although this fight might have taken place during that battle just as it was reported, it is of no interest to historical knowledge; it is below the threshold of historical consciousness. History as knowledge is not interested in such details but in higher synthetic units such as "the battle of Kunersdorf". "From a certain point on," Simmel writes, "the quantitative accumulation of elements changes into a qualitative modification of the effect."[31] This is certainly an example illustrating Hegel's dialectical law of the transformation of quantity into quality.

However, the witness of historical reality is never an objective fact-registering apparatus but a human being with all his individual and social

---

[31] G. Simmel, *Die Probleme der Geschichtsphilosophie* (Leipzig, 1907), p. 144, and *Das Problem der historischen Zeit* (Berlin, 1916), p. 29.

limitations. Of the factors responsible for the distance between the idea
of historical knowledge and its realization in the diverse historiographies,
the most important is the social, ideological factor. It manifests itself in
the influence of the group on the historical perspectives of the individuals
who belong to it.

The discovery of this influence was made in different stages. During
the Renaissance, Machiavelli ascertained that one does not think the
same way in the palaces as on public squares. A little later, Sir Francis
Bacon established his thesis of the four idols by which our minds are
obsessed: the *idola theatri* which consist in our tendency to rely on
authorities rather than on the strength of our own thought; the *idola
fori* which induce us to take words for things; the *idola specus,* or
personal prejudices, which often prevent us from recognizing the facts
as they are, and the *idola tribus,* such as the illusions of our senses or our
inclination toward anthropomorphisms. These latter idols are a common
heritage of mankind.[32] Obviously, all these idols set narrow limits to the
objectivity of historiography.

The modern concept of *ideology* was born in France during the epoch
of Napoleon I. It is intimately linked with the name of the philosopher
Destutt de Tracy, author of *Éléments d'Idéologie,* friend of Jefferson
and head of the ideological school. The latter was opposed to Bonaparte's imperial ambitions and to his restoration of religion. Napoleon made
the ideologists responsible for all of France's misfortunes. It was in the
emperor's mouth that the word "ideology" finally acquired its deroga-
tory meaning of a falsified idea divorced from practical reality — a
meaning it has retained until our day.

But it was Marxism which gave the term ideology its definitive
character. In their book, *Die deutsche Ideologie* — German Ideology —,
the complete publication of which took place as late as 1932, Marx and
Engels established the concept of ideology in the following way: *"Das
Bewusstsein ist ein gesellschaftliches Produkt"*[33] — consciousness is a
social product. Furthermore, they wrote:

> The ideas of the ruling class are, in each epoch, the ruling
> ideas; that means that the class which is the ruling *material*
> power in society is, at the same time, its ruling *spiritual*
> power. .... The ruling ideas are nothing but the ideological
> expression of the ruling material conditions; they are these
> ruling material conditions conveiced as ideas.[34]

---

[32] F. Bacon, *Novum Organum,* par. 38.
[33] K. Marx, F. Engels, *Die deutsche Ideologie* (Berlin, 1953), p. 27.
[34] *Ibid.,* p. 44.

By "ideologists", Marx and Engels referred to the members of the ruling class who, by virtue of the division of labor, devote themselves to the job of building up "the illusion of that class about itself". Marx and Engels declared, furthermore, that each new class which replaces a ruling class is compelled to present its interest as the common interest of all members of a society and to present its own ideas as "the only ones which are sensible and universally valid".[35]

These statements by Marx and Engels allow us to define the concept of ideology as an ensemble of ideas, falsified by the interests of the group which dominates a society, but presented to this society as an expression of absolute truth. An ideology is a group of ideas refracted through the prism of interest. Ideologies are more or less conscious disguises of the true character of certain social situations, the acknowledgment of which would be contrary to the interests of those who propagate them. Those falsifications may be conscious lies or half-conscious concealments.

In Marx's and Engels' writings, ideology appears as a phenomenon limited to the bourgeois class. On the contrary, the revolutionary class appears as "the representative of the whole society" (*als Vertreterin der ganzen Gesellschaft*),[36] since its interest is — at least at the beginning of its appearance — identical with that of all non-ruling classes. Marx and Engels also insisted that ideologies disappear in the classless society, for then it is no longer necessary to present "a particular interest as general interest".[37]

The Marxists use this doctrine as an intellectual weapon to discredit their opponents' opinions, by unmasking the "ideological" character of these opinions. They do this by showing that the ideas they are fighting are mere functions of their opponents' social positions and economic interests. But, nowadays, the socialists no longer have a monopoly of that weapon, for now all parties are able to interpret their opponents' ideas in ideological terms. Nothing is to prevent anti-Marxists from availing themselves of the weapon forged by their enemies, turning it against its inventors.

Some non-socialistic thinkers like Max Weber, Werner Sombart, Ernst Troeltsch, Max Scheler, and Karl Mannheim, generalized the doctrine of ideology. Mannheim, especially, tried to show that, in a general way, social ideas expressed by individuals are functions of the life-situations in which these individuals exist, of their social habitat. "The specific character and life-situation of the subject influence his opinions, percep-

[35] *Ibid.*, p. 45.
[36] *Ibid.*, p. 45.
[37] *Ibid.*, p. 46.

tions and interpretations,"[38] said Mannheim. In a similar way, Max Scheler declared: "All knowledge is ... determined by the society and its structure. ..." And, in line with the French school of sociology (Durkheim, Lévy-Bruhl), he added: "There is no *Ego* without a *We;* genetically, the *We* was supplied with a content before the *Ego.*"[39]

Guided by these convictions, Scheler and Mannheim started a new discipline called *Soziologie des Wissens* or *Wissenssoziologie* — sociology of knowledge. The German term was coined by Wilhelm Jerusalem, an Austrian philosopher. In France, this discipline had its most brilliant precursors in men like Condorcet, Saint-Simon, Comte, Durkheim, Lévy-Bruhl. In Italy and in the United States, it is linked with the famous names of Vilfredo Pareto and Pitirim A. Sorokin. The latter — of whom we shall speak later — tried to detach sociology of knowledge from its Marxian roots. As a search for the social sources responsible for the distortion of our historical and sociological knowledge, sociology of knowledge was especially developed by the Hungarian scholar, Karl Mannheim, who declared: "The principal thesis of the sociology of knowledge is that there are modes of thought which cannot be adequately understood as long as their social origins are obscured."[40]

In contradistinction to the political ideologist, the sociologist of knowledge renounces the intention to expose or unmask ideas with which he is in disagreement. He simply tries to show the general interrelationships between the intellectual point of view held and the social position occupied — in whatever camp it may be. But, if such a relationship exists as a general fact, the influence of socially conditioned ideologies on historiography becomes evident. In this respect, Mannheim writes:

> A modern theory of knowledge which takes account of the relational ... character of all historical knowledge must start with the assumption that there are spheres of thought in which it is impossible to conceive of absolute truth existing independently of the values and position of the subject and unrelated to the social context. Even a god could not formulate a proposition on historical subjects like $2 \times 2 = 4$, for what is intelligible in history can be formulated only with reference to problems and conceptual constructions which themselves arise in the flux of historical experience.[41]

While the physical sciences are able to make statements which are

[38] K. Mannheim, *Ideology and Utopia* (New York and London, 1936), p. 50.
[39] M. Scheler, *Die Wissensformen und die Gesellschaft* (Leipzig, 1926), p. 48.
[40] K. Mannheim, *op. cit.*, p. 2.
[41] *Ibid.*, pp. 70—71.

independent of the knowing subject's historical and social surroundings and of his evaluations, Mannheim believed that the situation of historical, political and social knowledge was quite different. It constitutes an existentially conditioned knowledge.

In my opinion, the fact that natural sciences are capable of findings the validity of which is independent of the finder's social milieu does not mean that all natural scientists make use of this possibility. Let us consider for a moment the present-day controversies around such purely scientific questions as the causal relations between cigarette smoking and the development of lung cancer, the causes of air-pollution or the detectability of nuclear tests from the underground and the dangers resulting for human life and health from radio-active fallout. The statements made on these and related subjects by the representatives of the most "exact" sciences are so contradictory and, obviously, so strongly coloured by the scientists' respective social habitat and their political ideas that one might doubt the privileged character of the natural sciences in comparison with social-historical disciplines. Recently, two American biochemists declared that from the results of certain research projects, as published in their professional journals, they can infer the names of the corporations sponsoring those projects.

Two hundred years ago, Voltaire described in his fantastic story, *Micromégas,* a trip to earth of two giants — one from Sirius, the other from Saturn. Asking our earthly scholars several scientific questions, the stellar visitors are impressed by the unanimity and precision of their answers. But, asking them several philosophical questions, the visiting giants are appalled by the contradictory answers given by our scholars. If Voltaire's giants visited us today, I believe that they would find no more harmony in our philosophical ideas, but certainly much less unanimity in our scientific views. "There is scarcely any scientific principle that is not nowadays challenged by somebody" — declared Max Planck in 1931,[42] and today this statement is valid to a much larger extent. I think that at least a part of this lack of unanimity among exact scientists could be ascribed to the influence of their different social habitats and the present historical situation. For their disagreement is strongest in the interpretation of scientific data involving social issues with possible historical consequences.

Sociology of knowledge tries to understand thought in the concrete setting of an historical, social situation. Individually differentiated thought emerges only gradually out of social-historical situations. It is

---

[42] M. Planck, *Positivismus und reale Aussenwelt* (Leipzig, 1931), p. 1.

not isolated individuals who think. The situation in modern society is rather similar to that described in primitive societies by Lévy-Bruhl, for civilized thought patterns also arise from groups which have developed particular "styles of thought". The latter result from long series of responses by the members of given groups to certain typical situations which characterize their common position in society.

Another phenomenon which the sociology of knowledge tries to take into account is the influence of collective action on thought. Men belonging to the same social group endeavour, according to the character and the social situation of that group, to change their natural and social surroundings or to maintain them in a given condition. It is the direction of that collective will to transform or to conserve, accompanied by appropriate collective actions, which produces the concepts and patterns of thought characterizing the members of a given group.

In this domain, one of Mannheim's most interesting discoveries was what he called the "collective unconscious". This sociological concept has nothing in common with the rather mystical notion of the same name in C. G. Jung's psychology. The political struggles in modern democracies revealed the unconscious motives which determine the thought orientation of the members of diverse social groups, representing either the ruling or the revolutionary classes. In each of these classes, the collective unconscious is manifested in a different way. Mannheim characterized these basic differences by the words "ideology" and "utopia". Here are his definitions:

> The concept "ideology" reflects the one discovery ... that ruling groups can, in their thinking, become so intensively interest-bound to a situation that they are simply no longer able to see certain facts which would undermine their sense of domination. There is implicit in the word 'ideology' the insight that, in certain situations, the collective unconscious of certain groups obscures the real condition of society, both to itself and to others, and thereby stabilizes it.[43]

An examination of international policy since the end of World War II would certainly offer many examples illustrating the doctrine of the collective unconscious, which Mannheim developed more than thirty years ago. It seems to me that one of its typical effects was revealed during the psychological crisis following the launching of the Sputniks. The distinguished American physicist, Dr. Lee A. DuBridge, President of California Institute of Technology, characterized this crisis by declaring:

[43] K. Mannheim, op. cit., p. 36.

> Now that the Sputnik has made us look at Russia more
> closely, we see very plainly — what we could have easily
> seen long ago — that for 30 years Russia has been systemati-
> cally building an educational system that would give rigid
> technical training to a large number of scientists and
> engineers, who, under the communist system, would then be
> available to serve the needs of the state.[44]

If we ask ourselves *why* Americans did not see plainly what, according
to Professor DuBridge, they "could have easily seen long ago", the
answer is, in my opinion: that the American ideology, shaped by the
collective unconscious, was so strongly interest-bound to the situation of
Russia's scientific and technological inferiority that it prevented the
majority of people in this country from seeing the facts which contradicted that situation. The rude awakening of American public opinion
after the launching of the Sputniks revealed all the dangers for the
survival of a nation too strongly governed by the collective unconscious
and the ideologies it sustains.

The ascendancy of such ideologies over individuals was revealed to
me several years ago, when an educated American lady, a graduate from
a great university, told me, during a conversation: "The Russians have
always cheated white people." When I drew her attention to the fact
that the Russians are just as white as the Americans and even as blond,
she looked at me in astonishment. At this moment, she rediscovered,
reluctantly, an obvious fact which the collective unconscious of her
group had blocked out of her mind.

But let us now consider the concept of "Utopian thinking" as defined
by Mannheim. It reflects the opposite discovery which emerged from
political struggle, namely,

> that certain oppressed groups are intellectually so strongly
> interested in the destruction and transformation of a given
> condition of society that they unwittingly see only those
> elements in the situation which tend to negate it. Their
> thought is never a diagnosis of the situation; it can be used
> only as a direction for action. In the Utopian mentality, the
> collective unconscious, guided by whisful representation and
> the will to action, hides certain aspects of reality. It turns its
> back on everything which would shake its belief or paralyse
> its desire to change things.[45]

In contemporary history, examples of "Utopian thinking" could perhaps

[44] L. A. DuBridge, "The Challenge of Sputnik", *Engineering and Science*, Vol. XXI,
No. 5 (Pasadena, Calif., February 1958), p. 16.
[45] K. Mannheim, *op. cit.*, p. 36.

be found in the attitude of many communist workers in such Western countries as France or Italy, who see only those elements in the situation of their respective countries which tend to negate it. They turn their backs on the obvious fact that the change they are seeking by their intended revolutionary action would deprive them of such basic liberties as the right to strike. Since a clear recognition of this consequence might shake the revolutionists' beliefs or paralyze their desire to change things, it is repressed by their collective unconscious.

Professor Karl R. Popper's objections to the sociology of knowledge and the facts on which it is based seem only partly valid to me. Of course, he is right in insisting that we "are only largely dependent on our upbringing — not totally",[46] for we are indeed capable of self-criticism. He is also right when he attacks the vain belief of certain representatives of sociology of knowledge that, belonging to a "freely poised intelligentsia" only "loosely anchored" in tradition, they themselves are capable of avoiding the pitfalls of ideologies. They also believe that they can reach higher degrees of objectivity by sociological self-analysis. One may, indeed, suspect in this attitude a hidden expression of the class interest of that particular social stratum to which most representatives of sociology of knowledge belong. We may recall here Gotthold Ephraim Lessing's wise remark: *"Der Aberglauben schlimmster ist, den seinen für den erträglichern zu halten"*[47] — the worst superstition is to consider one's own (superstition) a more tolerable sort.

Professor Popper's remedy against ideologies is the inter-subjectivity of scientific method, an idea he shares with other logical positivists. According to this school, "observation statements" are true when they are in agreement with those of the other scientists of the same epoch. Does this criterion truly offer a guarantee against ideologies? It would, if ideologies were due only to individual unconscious complexes. But, as we have seen, there exist also collective unconscious complexes, and, against them, the intersubjectivity of science, its public character, is not a sufficient protection. It is a typical feature of the collective unconscious that it infects large groups, including scientists. When it changes their ideas into ideologies, they consider only those phenomena which are in agreement with their collective prejudices. This fact was obvious among Russian biologists in the controversy concerning the inheritance of acquired characteristics. It was obvious again among American scientists in the controversies mentioned earlier, especially in

---

[46] K. R. Popper, *The Open Society And Its Enemies* (London, 1947), II, p. 197.
[47] G. E. Lessing, *Nathan der Weise*, IV. Aufzug, 4. Auftritt, p. 155.

that which concerns the detectability of nuclear tests and their possible harm to human health and life.

To be sure, natural science *is* intersubjective, in that it can subject nature to certain tests verifiable by any scientist under like conditions. Unfortunately, the interpretation of these testable data is not always free from ideologies or Utopias and, therefore, not intersubjective in an absolute sense. It seems to me that Professor Popper is overlooking this fact.

But, even if intersubjective agreement among the scientists of a given period were a perfect criterion of scientific truth, it would only compensate for the influences of their individual prejudices and their different social milieus and, thus, only eliminate Psychologism and Sociologism. It would not, however, refute Historicism, that is, the thesis that truth is a product of a given historical period and, therefore, valid only for that period. Since the scientists, whose agreement on a given question is considered a criterion of truth, live in the same historical period, their intersubjective consensus appears to me to be even a confirmation of Historicism.

As a logical positivist, Professor Popper believes in the unity of science and does not admit basic differences between natural and social sciences. To escape the pitfalls of ideologies, he recommends that social scientists should imitate natural sciences by using "the methods of trial and error, of inventing hypotheses which can be practically tested, and of submitting them to practical tests". He thinks that "a social technology is needed whose results can be tested by social engineering".[48] I do not believe in this possibility, for social sciences are *observational*, and not *experimental*, sciences and, therefore, exclude "tests". As Claude Bernard said, "observation is the investigation of a natural phenomenon; experimentation is the investigation of a phenomenon modified by the investigator".[49] Now, the objects of the social sciences are groups of people, and their behaviour cannot be modified by social scientists or social techniques. Societies are no guinea-pigs.

Obviously, the influences of the social habitat and its collective unconscious on the historian is much stronger than on the natural scientist. Max Scheler thought that only "the selection of the objects of knowledge" and their "forms" are sociologically conditioned by the interests of the group to which we belong, while the contents and the

---

[48] K. R. Popper, *op. cit.*, Vol. II, p. 210. See also Popper's *The Poverty of Historicism* (London, 1957), esp. pp. 42ff, 58ff, 64ff, etc.
[49] C. Bernard, *Introduction à l'étude de la médecine expérimentale* (Paris, 1926), I, p. 36.

validity of our knowledge are determined by the realm of "supra-
temporal", absolute essences in which this phenomenologist believed.
However, a sociologist could hardly accept that metaphysical limitation of social determinism. In commenting on the doctrines of
Troeltsch, Mannheim says that "no statement about history is possible
without the historico-philosophical preconceptions of the observing
subject entering into its *content*".[50] Indeed, any specialist who examines
a work of historiography is able to infer the epoch when it was written,
the nation and social class of its author, the philosophical standpoint
from which he conceived his subject, the cultural tendencies by which
he was guided. What Troeltsch called the *"Standort"*, i.e. the historical,
social, cultural and philosophical locus occupied by the historian not
only determines his value judgments but also his selective principles, his
categories, the significance of these categories and all his synthetic ideal
types. The hopes and fears concerning the future, which, in the form of
the collective unconscious, direct the thought of the group to which the
historian belongs, are also manifested in the way he interprets the past.
As a mode of existence, says Heidegger, historiography always depends
on the *"herrschende Weltanschauung"*,[51] the predominating philosophical conception of a period, of a society.

Nowadays, the existential and social determination of our historical
thought is recognized by many historians. Thus, Charles A. Beard
declared straight out that "each historian ... is a product of his age
and that his work reflects the spirit of his times, of a nation, race, group,
class, or section".[52] And Beard adds that no modern historian really
believes that Bossuet, Gibbon, Mommsen or Bancroft could be dupli-
cated today. Any selection and arrangement of facts is controlled
"inexorably" by the frames of reference in the historian's mind.
Therefore, the famous American historian invited his colleagues to
examine their own frames of reference. Recognizing the existence
of a "personal equation" for each historian comparable to that of each
astronomer, Professor Marrou goes so far as to propose a new "existential psycho-analysis" of the historiographer. In a kind of auto-analysis,
the author of an historical work should display before the reader all his
existential data likely to influence his interpretation of history. But this
penetrating historian and philosopher does not hide from himself the

[50] K. Mannheim, "Historicism", *Essays on the Sociology of Knowledge* (London,
1952), p. 101.
[51] M. Heidegger, *Sein und Zeit* (Tübingen, 1949), p. 392.
[52] Charles A. Beard, "Written History as an Act of Faith", *The American Historical
Review*, Vol. XXXIX, No. 2, Jan. 1934, p. 220.

obstacles of such an enterprise which he designates as *"en partie insur-montables"*[53] — partly insurmountable. The fundamental postulates, the basic options are too deeply rooted in his being to allow an author a judgment of himself. Of these elements resisting any self-analysis, the collective unconscious is probably one of the most stubborn.

Applying the results of all these investigations to our problem of historical knowledge, we come to the following conclusion: If, according to our epistemological theory of history, the different critically exami-ned historical perspectives do not exclude each other but, on the con-trary, require and complement one another, we, nonetheless, have to admit that, in psychological, existential, and sociological practice, the diverse perspectives of the historians are often less complementary than mutually exclusive.

Of the factors which determine the historians' perspectives the most important ones are the evaluations. While physical sciences are, in principle, exempt from values, we shall see that the concept of value enters the very definition of the historical object. This is one of the criteria which distinguish historical from scientific perspectives. The geometrical perspective, that is, the angle from which Philip II of Spain in 1570 saw the Sierra del Guadarrama from the Escorial, was the same from which the Spanish philosopher Ortega y Gasset saw it in 1954. But the way in which these two men saw an historical fact such as, for example, the Inquisition, was quite different. For the historical event is not only seen but, at the same time, judged, that is, evaluated. Theodor Lessing compared the historical connections to a cobweb in which the historian always occupies the place of the spider. Like the spider, the historian is always the center and the source of all the threads of the web. We could add that the majority of these threads are made up of the historian's evaluations. With the establishment of this relation, the problem of historical knowledge joins that of values, which we will study in the next chapter.

---

[53] H.-I. Marrou, *De la connaissance historique* (Paris, 1956), p. 241.

V. HISTORICAL KNOWLEDGE AND VALUES

Philosophy of values is one of the most fertile domains of philosophy. Inaugurated in the second half of the nineteenth century by the German, Hermann Lotze, and the Austrians, Franz Brentano, Alexius von Meinong and Christian von Ehrenfels — after Nietzsche had prepared its ground —, philosophy of values made remarkable strides in Central Europe, France, the Anglo-Saxon countries, Italy, and in the Spanish-American world. To be sure, Plato, Aristotle and other great philosophers who investigated the domains of ethics, aesthetics, economics, etc. dealt with values *factually*, but without realizing that goodness, beauty, utility, etc. have certain features in common which could be studied in a specific discipline. It is the latter which, today, is called philosophy of values or axiology (from the Greek ἄξιος, valuable, worthy).

This field has become so vast that, in the present volume, I can only study those of its aspects which exert some influence on philosophy of history and experience its influence. Moreover, I have already devoted a considerable number of studies to this subject.[1] In order to understand the axiological implications of philosophy of history, it is, however, necessary to outline at least the main features of the concept of value.

The individual is confronted with a world whose physical and mental elements are in a state of inequality of rank. In referring to this inequal-

---

[1] A. Stern, *Die philosophischen Grundlagen von Wahrheit, Wirklichkeit, Wert* (München, 1932), 432 pp.; *La philosophie des valeurs* (Cours libre professé à la Sorbonne) (Paris, 1936), 2 fasc., 132 pp.; *La filosofía de los valores* (Centro de Estudios Filosóficos de la Universidad Nacional de Mexico) (1944), 215 pp.; second, enlarged edition (Buenos Aires, 1960); *Philosophie du rire et des pleurs* (Paris, 1949), 256 pp.; *Filosofía de la risa y del llanto* (Buenos Aires, 1950), 272 pp.; *La filosofía de la política* (Mexico, 1943), 132 pp.; "The Current Crisis in the Realm of Values", *The Personalist*, Los Angeles, Summer 1950, pp. 245—259; "Society and Values", *The Personalist*, Summer 1948, pp. 242—251; "La philosophie des valeurs", *Thalès* (Paris, 1938); "Le problème de l'absolutisme et du relativisme axiologiques et la philosophie allemande", *Revue Internationale de Philosophie*, 4, Bruxelles, juillet 1939, pp. 703—742, etc.

ity of rank, man speaks of "values". Another individual is also confronted with this world, but he perceives the inequality of rank among the same elements in a different way. Consequently, he has a different world of values. The hierarchies of things and ideas conceived by men are intimately linked with their actions. In order to avoid having everybody thwart the actions of everybody else, men and groups of men try to impose upon others the hierarchies in which they themselves believe. From this spring the ideological, political and even the military struggles which characterize human history.

It is obvious that the inequality of rank among things and ideas does not come only from the objects themselves but is conditioned by the relation of the objects to the appreciating subjects. There would not be any values, if there were no subjective preferences. Values have been defined in various ways. There are thinkers who consider the values as Platonic ideas, as ideal essences which exist independently of our desires. According to this view, values are absolute metaphysical entities which do not even require the existence of appreciating subjects. Other philosophers regard values as expressions of an ideal ought-to-be, valid but not real. There are thinkers who see in values qualities of the objects or relations among the objects; and, on the contrary, there are those who see in values nothing but purely subjective creations. However, since a value always implies a reaction of a feeling subject towards a real or ideal object, I believe in a bi-polar character of values. Therefore, I define value as a relation between objects and appreciating subjects.

Values are rooted in the psychic components which are bound to any object by its relation to the subject. By this relation, the object receives its emotional tonality which is the foundation of its value. But this origin of all values in our subjectivity should not blind us against the objective factors involved in every evaluation. Even the most stalwart axiological subjectivist would not go so far as to affirm that the beauty and kindness of his beloved reside only in his eyes and in his judgment, without having anything to do with the objective features of her face, her figure, her character. If he were to go so far, the living object of his admiration would probably teach him a wholesome lesson.

Of course, the objective features appreciated by the subject vary from one historical period to another, from one civilization to another. The objective features of a Victorian apartment no longer correspond to our ideal of beauty. Other objective features have replaced them. If the objective features corresponding to our moral judgments vary less in the course of history than those corresponding to our aesthetic judgments, the reason resides probably in the fact that a society cannot survive without appreciating positively certain objective conditions of it survival.

The value of a thing has been defined as its property of being desirable. However, the subjective feelings which lay the foundation of a value are much more complex. The emotional foundations of our evaluations are desires, needs and their satisfactions, preferences, interests, attentions, pleasures, feelings of love or hate, of approval and reprobation, of admiration or disdain, and of relief from tensions; finally they are the feelings of boredom, displeasure, of aversion, of dissatisfaction, frustration and suffering, and other emotional reactions called forth by things, events and ideas.

However, the fact that something arouses in us one of these feelings does not yet constitute an evaluation but only a partial phenomenon of it, namely its emotional foundation. The evaluation and, with it, the value of an object are only constituted when the feelings mentioned are followed by a special act: the positing of a value.

The positing of a value results when our whole personality and, especially, our faculty of judgment adopts an attitude towards the different feelings inspired by things and ideas. In adopting such an attitude, the personality can approve of his own feelings or disapprove of them. From this springs the positing of a positive or a negative value.

Our primary emotional reactions, our desires, preferences, repugnances, etc. are of a volitional character. On the contrary, the secondary attitude of our personality towards our volitions often takes the character of an ought-to-be, a norm. If we were to try to determine the psychological sources of our values, we would perhaps find that their emotional part, the value feelings, come from the region which Freud called the unconscious "id", while our attitude towards our feelings, which is the source of our value judgments, proceeds mostly from our "super-ego". The latter reflects, to a large extent, the influences of our parents, our teachers and the ideals and coercive forces of the social surroundings in which we have grown up. From this springs the double character of values which are manifested either as personal tastes or as supra-individual, normative obligations.

Our "ego", which represents, especially, our intellectual forces, tries to reconcile the instinctive evaluations of our unconscious "id" with the moral impositions of our "super-ego" and the demands of the external world. If the normative impositions of the "super-ego" and the demands of the external reality become too domineering, so that the "ego" has to repress too large a portion of the instinctive evaluations of the "id", the result may be neurosis or crime.

Let us add a few more elementary characteristics of values. Positive as well as negative values are subject to gradations: according to their superiority or inferiority in relation to one another, they form orders of rank or hierarchies. One distinguishes different classes of values, the most important of which are: intellectual values, moral values, aesthetic, social, religious, economic and vital values.

From another point of view, a distinction between intrinsic and instrumental values is made. It is to be found already in Plato's *Republic* and in Aristotle's *Nicomachean Ethics*.[2] Although John Dewey rejects this distinction,[3] I think that it has to be maintained. The reasons for this necessity will appear later on. It is accepted that intrinsic values are appreciated for their own sake, as ends in themselves. Instrumental values, in their turn, are appreciated only as means fit for the realization of other values and, finally, of intrinsic values. Instrumental values are only deduced values. If, for example, health is appreciated as an intrinsic value, hygiene, as a means to preserve it, is an instrumental value. Later on, we shall distinguish another class of values called radiated values (*Strahlwerte*).

Values have no independent existence but always need a concrete carrier. Beauty must be reflected from a human face, a landscape, or a work of art, to be a felt value. Otherwise, beauty would be nothing but an abstract value idea. Valuable things are called "goods". But even goods have not always perceptual reality. Sometimes, their reality is only a picture in our minds. The external reality of a thing does not always guarantee its value; the value of a thing does not guarantee its external reality.

Logically speaking, the positive or negative value of an action, an idea, or a thing depends on its conformity or non-conformity with a postulated norm. Only this norm can confer validity on a given value judgment. As soon as a certain norm of the good, the beautiful, or the true, is postulated, it serves as a standard to determine the positive or negative character of a given concrete value and to measure its degree. A value consistent with the postulated norm will be positive; a value inconsistent with this norm will be negative.

Obviously, the postulated norm is itself a value. If we call the norms "values of the first degree", then the values for which they serve as standards may be called "values of the second degree". I think that one of the essential problems of philosophy of values is to determine the

[2] Plato, *The Republic*, II, 357; Aristotle, *Nichomachean Ethics*, I, 1094a.
[3] J. Dewey, *Reconstruction in Philosophy* (New York, 1950), pp. 137—138, and "The Field of Values", *Value* (New York, 1949), p.p. 69, 70, etc.

source of the norms which serve as standards for the values of the second degree. Do those norms arise from history or are they trans-historical? Later on, we shall try to answer this question.

What is the attitude of science toward values? As we said, values are rooted in the psychic components which are bound to any object by its relation to the subject. But, systematically and in principle, scientific thought has to disregard the subject-relation of its contents and to restrict itself so the examination of the mutual relationships between the determined objects. Only in this way can science constitute an objective world and construct the concept of an independent nature. But, by disregarding methodically any subject-relation of its objects, science is unable to take into account the psychic component which, included in the subject-relation, confers its value on each object. Thus, for science, the cattle are no more valuable than the cattle fly. Biology studies both with equal care. For scientific reflection, values are nothing but empirical facts without any value.

Considering — for methodological reasons — the world as an object in itself, and disregarding systematically its necessarry relations to the subject — to the perceiving and thinking subject as well as to the appreciating subject — the world of science is a world without values and without hierarchies. *Nihil in natura fit, quod ipsius vitio possit tribui,* said Spinoza[4] — nothing happens in nature which could be attributed to a vice in it. In nature, there is neither good nor evil, and the same is true of natural science. Science is free from values. But, if this is the case, then history cannot be considered a science, for it cannot be free from values. As we shall see, the concept of value enters the very definition of history.

We do not wish to discuss here the doctrine now so fashionable that value judgments are "meaningless". This doctrine only results from the narrow way in which logical Positivism defines the concepts of "meaningful" and "meaningless". These definitions are themselves based on a value judgment, because they are the result of a choice. By implication, many logical Positivists say: "We choose or decide to consider meaningful only such statements as are either empirically and operationally verifiable or tautological, because we think that this is a useful choice." This is, however, a practical decision and not a theoretical demonstration. Other people, who do not share their value judgment, still consider meaningful many statements which are neither observational nor tautological. To me and to millions of people around the

---

[4] Spinoza, *Ethica ordine geometrico demonstrata,* Pars Tertia, p. 242.

earth, value judgments are meaningful; they belong to the most meaningful of all statements.

In spite of being a logical Positivist, Professor Viktor Kraft does not consider value judgments as "meaningless" but rightly sees in them ways of summoning other people to take certain attitudes towards things and events. While Professor A. J. Ayer rejects the statement "stealing money is wrong" as "meaningless",[5] Professor V. Kraft recognizes that it means "stealing money should provoke shame".[6] Although such a statement cannot be qualified as "true" or "false", it can be declared as "valid", as a necessary condition of organized society, which we all affirm.

Since the days of ancient Greece, many scholars have realized that there exist some basic differences between natural science and history. Aristotle distinguished between science which analyzes the constants and φρόνησις, a kind of practical wisdom, which is interested in the contingent elements of life and history. The latter was considered by the Stagirite as a mass of documents, in contradistinction to the sciences, which are engaged in explaining and systematizing.

To the schoolmen, *historia significat singulorum notitiam, vel expositionem seu descriptionem* τοῦ ὅτι *rei*,[7] that is, history means the knowledge of single events, or the development and description of the "because" of a thing. Francis Bacon shared this view but insisted that history determines also the time and space of individual events. In the nineteenth century, the French philosopher, Cournot, stressed Aristotle's antithesis by distinguishing the historical disciplines from theoretical science and from practical, technical knowledge. Finally came Wilhelm Dilthey with his distinction between natural sciences and sciences of the mind (*Geisteswissenschaften*), defining the latter as "the totality of sciences, the object of which is the historical, social reality".[8]

This notion of sciences of the mind has been attacked from various quarters. Wilhelm Windelband reproached it with being unable to assign a satisfactory place to psychology, which, according to its subject matter, is a science of the mind — and is even the basic one — while its method is that of a natural science. What psychology shares with natural sciences is the feature of ascertaining and gathering facts, in order to draw general laws from them. History, on the contrary, tries to

[5] A. J. Ayer, *Language, Truth and Logic*, pp. 106-107.
[6] V. Kraft, *Die Grundlagen einer wissenschaftlichen Wertlehre* (Wien, 1937), p. 164 etc.
[7] Goclenius, Ve. 626 B.
[8] *Wilhelm Diltheys Gesammelte Schriften*, I. Band (Leipzig, 1933), "Einleitung in die Geisteswissenschaften", p. 4.

describe and to understand individual facts in their singularity. In other words: the natural sciences are interested in everything which, in the flow of the phenomena, is repeated in a uniform way. History, however, is interested, above all, in that "which one will never see twice", to use a phrase of Vigny already quoted.

This fact may constitute another reason for denying to history the character of a science. For, if one accepts Aristotle's famous doctrine that "all science is of the universal" (τὸ δὲ τὴν ἐπιστήμην εἶναι καθόλου πᾶσαν)[9] then a discipline wich, like history, is limited to the study of individual facts cannot claim to be a science. To be sure, Aristotle later restricted this principle by admitting that the particular could be an object of science as far as it is an instance of the universal. But even this affirmation cannot be made about all historical events. As Bergson showed us convincingly, science is only concerned with the aspect of repetition and will always manage to analyze a whole into elements which are approximately a reproduction of the past. Science can only work on what is supposed to repeat itself and which is thus withdrawn from the action of historical time. Now, if history is, according to Paul Valéry's definition, *la science des choses qui ne se répètent pas*[10] — the science of things which do not repeat themselves, then the term "science" attached to history cannot have the same meaning we usually give it when we speak of physical sciences. If history is to be regarded as a science, then it is necessary to redefine the word "science", perhaps in that very wide and liberal way in which it was proposed by the British philosopher Collingwood: "Science means any organized body of knowledge."[11] If we accept this definition, then we can regard history as a science, for, in spite of its relation to values and its lack of generality, it is an organized body of knowledge.

But what kind of science is history? Is it an empirical or a deductive one? I think that Windelband made an overstatement when he declared: "What natural science and history have in common is their character as empirical sciences" (*Erfahrungswissenschaft*)[12]; for, without certain restrictions, history can hardly be designated as an empirical science. We have already referred to Claude Bernard's pertinent division of empirical sciences into observational and experimental sciences: *"L'observation est l'investigation d'un phénomène naturel, et l'expérience est*

---

[9] Aristotle, *Metaphysics*, 1087 a.
[10] P. Valéry, "Discours de l'histoire", *Variété*, IV (Paris, 1938), p. 139.
[11] R. G. Collingwood, *The Idea of History* (Oxford, 1946), p. 249.
[12] W. Windelband, "Geschichte und Naturwissenschaft", *Präludien* (Tübingen, 1911), 2. Band, p. 148.

l'investigation d'un phénomène modifié par l'investigateur"[13] — observation is the investigation of a natural phenomenon; experimentation
is the investigation of a phenomenon modified by the investigator. It is
evident that, unlike the physicist, the historian cannot modify the conditions under which phenomena occur, for those which he studies are
far beyond the reach of his action. Consequently, history is not an
experimental science. Some historians have attempted to perform
"mental experiments" to replace the laboratory experiments denied to
them, but since mental experiments are purely fictitious, the conclusions
have had little weight.

But, if history is not an experimental science, perhaps it is an observational discipline. Unfortunately, this cannot be affirmed without
reservation either, for only the history of the present can be an object
of direct observation. However, the present is short and the past is long,
so that observable history represents only a small section of the historian's subject matter. For the greater part of history we have to accept
Collingwood's thesis that "history ... is a science whose business is to
study events not accessible to our observation and to study these events
inferentially ...".[14]

Thus, if history is not an experimental science and — as far as its
major part is concerned — not an observational science, we have to ask
ourselves in which sense its designation as an "empirical science" can be
upheld. The only thing which could be affirmed in this respect is that,
in principle, the subject matter studied by history belongs to the observable, empirical world. *Factually*, however, only one of its sections —
the history of the present — is truly accessible to human observation.

The majority of empirical sciences are interested only in the relations
between the phenomena which, while repeating themselves, remain
identical. These relations are the general laws, the search for which is
the main purpose of the natural sciences. According to a famous term
coined by Windelband, these law-seeking sciences are called nomothetic,
from the Greek νομο-θέτης, or lawgiver. Other empirical disciplines
are mainly interested in the individual content of the phenomena,
which is not repeated. These are the historical disciplines, which Windelband characterized with the epithet idiographic,[15] from the Greek words
ἴδιος, own, peculiar, distinct, and γράφω, to write, to describe.

For the nomothetic sciences, the individual phenomenon is of interest

---

[13] C. Bernard, *Introduction à l'étude de la médecine expérimentale* (Paris, 1926),
I, p. 36.
[14] R. G. Collingwood, *The Idea of History* (Oxford, 1946), p. 251.
[15] W. Windelband, *op. cit.*, II, p. 145.

only as an example fit to serve as an illustration for a general law. For the idiographic, or historical disciplines, the phenomenon is of interest for what it represents in itself, for its particular content. Natural laws are invariable and extra-temporal, while historical events are variable and confined to a definite point of time. Certain facts are comprehensible only because they occur at a certain moment of history. Thus, for example, the Baroque style could develop only after the Renaissance had exhausted all its possibilities. Only by its emergence at that definite 'moment does the Baroque become comprehensible as an historical phenomenon.

Windelband's characterization of natural sciences as nomothetic and of historical disciplines as idiographic was likewise attacked. The famous mathematician and positivistic philosopher, Richard von Mises, for instance, drew attention to the fact that, if the establishment of general laws were the specific criterion of natural sciences, then linguistics and political economy would have to be considered as natural sciences, which would, evidently, not be a very appropriate classification. On the other hand, palaeontology and the theory of evolution would be historical sciences, although their objects belong to nature. Mises thought that the distinction between generalizing, nomothetic sciences and individualizing, idiographic ones covers only the extreme cases of theoretical physics — a purely nomothetic science — and history properly speaking, which is predominantly idiographic.[16]

I believe, however, that these marginal cases justify Windelband's distinction. Besides, the latter is flexible enough to take care of the double character of palaeontology, geology and Darwin's theory both as historical and as natural sciences. Windelband himself admitted the possibility of submitting the same phenomena to an historical and to a systematic investigation, for the character of "singularity" is relative. A phenomenon which, for long periods, does not undergo any change and can, therefore, be treated nomothetically may reveal itself in the long run as a single, unique phenomenon. The disappearance of a star or sea can be the object of nomothetic research and constitute, at the same time, a single event of natural history. As a systematic science, biology is nomothetic, as history of organic evolution, it is an idiographic, individualizing science.

As for the fallacy of considering linguistics or political economy as natural sciences, it only follows from the wrong premise that all natural sciences are nomothetic and all historical disciplines are exclusively

---

[16] R. von Mises, *Positivism* (Cambridge, 1951), pp. 210-211.

idiographic. I would rather say that, in natural sciences, nomothetic methods prevail over idiographic ones, while, in historical disciplines, idiographic methods prevail over nomothetic ones. This view implies the possibility of idiographic methods in natural sciences and of nomothetic procedures in historial disciplines.

The first of these theses is generally admitted, for one can hardly deny the existence of natural history. The famous historian Ernest Renan insisted vehemently on the historical aspect of exact sciences. In 1863, he wrote to the great chemist Marcellin Berthelot: "What is chemistry in this conception? The history of the world's most ancient period, the history of the formation of the molecule."[17] By the new methods of determining the age of the earth by virtue of the residues of radioactive elements in rocks — especially of lead 206 — chemistry in our day has truly become, in part, an historical science.

As for the second thesis mentioned, that, although basically idiographic and individualizing, history could also establish certain general laws, it is one of the most controversial in modern philosophy of history. To mention only a few typical attitudes in this dispute, I would say that Rickert denied totally the existence of historical laws while admitting causal research in history. Spengler was more radical in denying both historical laws and historical causality. "There are only physical laws", he wrote, "the law ... is anti-historical. ... Nature should be treated scientifically, one should make poems about history. ..."[18] One has, indeed, the impression that some of Spengler's historical affirmations belong to the realm of poetry. Now, poetry is an art, and, in itself, there is nothing wrong with art is history. Even a philosopher so deeply rooted in science as Bertrand Russell declares that history is and should be both an art and a science.[19] But, by art, he means only the historian's gift to present the characters of a given period "with lively fancy and not merely with the cold desire to chronicle known facts".[20] He praises Gibbon for having had "his feelings" about the historical persons he described, so that they came to life before the reader's mind. Nevertheless, Russell insists that history must remain scientific, in that "the historian does his utmost to preserve fidelity to the facts".[21] Thus far, poetry is excluded from history.

[17] E. Renan, *Les sciences de la nature et les sciences historiques* (Princeton, 1944), p. 8.
[18] O. Spengler, *Der Untergang des Abendlandes* (München, 1923), I, pp. 129, 131.
[19] B. Russell, *History As An Art* (Ashford, Kent, 1951), p. 2.
[20] *Ibid.*, p. 13.
[21] *Ibid.*, p. 3.

In his tendency to overstress the dualism between history and natural science, Spengler declared that mathematics and the principle of causality belong to the natural order, while the historical order of phenomena is characterized by chronology and governed by the idea of destiny (*Schicksalsidee*).[22] Now, the concept of "destiny" obviously belongs to the realm of pseudo-explanations, which never have any possibility of being confirmed or refuted by concrete facts. Evidently, there is causality in history, since every historical event can be derived from another event. And, if history is governed by the relation between causes and effects it is also governed by general laws. As Professor Hempel correctly pointed out, "a set of events can be said to have caused the event to be explained only if general laws can be indicated which connect 'causes' and 'effects'."[23] So far, it can be affirmed that causality and the concept of general law are inseparable — in natural science as well as in history, although it should be admitted, with Professor Mario Bunge, that sociohistorical events have also some non-causal features (dialectical, teleological, statistical etc.).[24] The objections raised by Professor William Dray against Hempel-Popper's "covering law model" do not seem to me basic enough to require the abandonment of causal explanation in history. The "loosening-up" of this model, as attempted by Professor P. L. Gardiner, may suffice. However, most of the general laws usually advanced to prove the presence of laws in history are physical, biological, psychological, meteorological, sociological or economical laws, and, rarely, specifically historical laws. Concerning their existence, Professor Hempel declares himself "neutral". As a logical positivist, he is only interested in the unity of scientific method in all branches of human knowledge. The historian and the philosopher of history, however, are interested in the specific structure of their discipline and, therefore, cannot be neutral with respect to the question of the validity or non-validity of specific historical laws. But they will concede that only such historical laws could be regarded as valid as do not contradict well-established natural laws.

Spengler not only saw an opposition between scientific "causes" and historical "destiny" but, also, between scientific "law" and historical *"Gestalt"*. One could, however, question whether the distance between

---

[22] O. Spengler, *op. cit.*, I, p. 10.
[23] K. Hempel, "The Function of General Laws in History", *Journal of Philosophy*, Vol. 39 (Jan. 1942), p. 37.
[24] M. Bunge, *Causality* (Cambridge, 1959), p. 274ff. For a more detailed discussion of these problems see P. L. Gardiner, *The Nature of Historical Explanation* (Oxford, 1952), and W. Dray, *Laws and Explanation in History* (Oxford, 1957).

Spengler's historical morphology and historical law is really as great as he supposed it to be. There are cycles within Spengler's cultures, cycles which Toynbee calls laws. Dit not Spengler himself establish an historical law, when he affirmed categorically: "Every culture has *its own* civilization. . . . Civilization is the inevitable *destiny* of a culture. . . . Civilizations are . . . a conclusion; they succeed the evolution process as the thing evolved; they succeed life as death; they succeed evolution as petrification?"[25]

Recently, Arnold Toynbee started a war against the "anti-nomianism of modern historians". A long chapter in the ninth volume of his *Study of History* is devoted to this polemic. Toynbee reproaches his colleagues for denying what he calls in an archaic term "the working of laws of Nature in history", although, in general, it is not the validity of natural laws in history which is denied but the validity of specifically historical laws. It is almost an euphemism to say that Toynbee "reproaches" his colleagues for denying laws in history. What Toynbee does is to accuse them of "hybris" and "heresy", for, according to this modern Savonarola, the natural law of history is "the law of God".[26]

Thus, Toynbee reopens the question of historical laws and presents one with his principle of "challenge and response" in the growth and disintegration of civilizations. He sees in this law a "cyclically rhythmic movement" and finds no reason "why this process should not repeat itself *ad infinitum*".[27] It is interesting to note that, here, Toynbee presents a cyclical movement as a law, while Spengler replaced laws by cycles. These facts suggest the possibility that the affirmation or negation of historical laws may be, in part, a semantic problem.

I believe it to be unnecessary to revive the Inquisition in order to fight those who deny any historical law, for the question is not *aut Caesar, aut nihil*. It seems rather that, at their beginnings, all sciences — even the physical ones — are idiographic, individualizing, for, before being able to establish general laws, every science must describe each single phenomenon with the greatest care, as if it were a question of a purely individual case. Before he is able to establish general laws, the investigator does not know what, in the phenomena observed, is general and what is individual. Only later, when this distinction has become possible, can sciences become nomothetic.

The case of history is more complex. It remains attached to the

---

[25] O. Spengler, *op. cit.*, I, p. 42.
[26] A. Toynbee, *A Study of History* (London, New York, Toronto, 1954), vol. IX, pp. 173-219.
[27] *Ibid.*, vol. IX, p. 291.

idiographic, individualizing method and advances only hesitatingly towards generalizations. In fact, those who search for historical laws are mostly not historians but philosophers or sociologists. The reserved attitude of history towards nomothetic research is due to several factors. The main one is that, in history, facts are of interest to us, in the first place, for what is specific and individual in them and only, in the second place, for what they may have in common with other facts. The reason for this is that the historical fact is the carrier of a specific value absent in the natural facts which repeat themselves. It is this value which we shall try to determine in the present chapter.

Let us mention a few historical laws more or less accepted today by some schools of thought. The simplest and least discussed is probably the one which states that a victorious war strengthens the government and weakens the opposition, while a lost war strengthens the opposition and weakens the government. Some people would also accept the political law expressed by Plato, when he stated that tyranny naturally arises out of democracy and the most extreme forms of tyranny out of the most extreme excesses of liberty.[28]

Another historical law proclaims that, when, in primitive times, one nation invades another and merges with it, the nation representing the lower level of civilization adopts the language and customs of the nation representing the higher level of civilization — no matter who is the victor and who the vanquished. This law was verified in the case of the invasion of Gaul by the Romans, by the Germanic tribes, and by the Normans. In the first case, the victors represented the higher level of civilization and the vanquished adopted their language and customs. In the second and third cases, the victors represented the lower level of civilization and adopted the language and customs of the vanquished.

Another historical law is the one according to which, in all civilizations, the first men who create states are not agriculturists but cattle raisers. Riding on horseback, dominating the animals and counting them, they represent the lordly and rationalistic type of men able to create a state. This thesis, suggested by Father W. Schmidt, was developed by Alfred Weber.[29]

Let us also mention Comte's law of the three stages and Hegel's dialectical laws, which are supposed to be laws of logic and of historical

---

[28] Plato, *The Republic*, Book VIII, 564. Earlier, we said that the Greeks have not created a philosophy of history. It must, however, be admitted that, with their *political* theories, Plato and Aristotle prepared the ground for later philosophical doctrines concerning history.

[29] A. Weber, *Kulturgeschichte als Kultursoziologie* (Leiden, 1935), pp. 27, 28.

evolution, the latter being considered a logic in action. As is well known, these Hegelian laws are those of strife, interpenetration and unity of the opposites, the law of the negation of the negation and the law of the transformation of quantity into quality. According to this conception of Hegel's and some of his disciples, historical evolution follows a triadic movement, proceeding from the thesis by way of the antithesis to a synthesis which, in its turn, is the thesis of a new triad. In Croce's philosophy, these dialectics of the triad are replaced by a cyclical movement in four steps.

The Marxists maintain Hegel's triadic dialectics but give them a new content. Nowadays, the laws of historical materialism are recognized by a considerable number of historians. According to Marx, the inter-human relationships are determined by the methods of production in a given society. Thus, the philosophy, art, law and scientific doctrines of a society are only 'ideological superstructures" of its economic system. While the means of production are developing constantly, the forms of distribution fail to keep up with these changes and come into conflict with the new technological and social conditions. This conflict takes the form of an antagonism of two classes which represent, respectively, the old form struggling to maintain itself and the new form which is attempting to supersede it. According to a fundamental law of dialectical materialism, historical changes are brought about by these class struggles which terminate regularly in the oppressed class overthrowing by means of revolution the old ruling class and by establishing a new social order.

Recently, Professor James C. Davis declared that social revolutions are likely to occur when a period of economic growth is followed by a sharp reversal, creating an intolerable gap between the expected need satisfaction and the actual one. As for Fascist revolutions I think that they become probable, whenever the democratic system of universal suffrage threatens to impair the supremacy of the capitalistic class.

Some years ago, the American historian, Edward P. Cheyney, declared he had discovered the following six historical laws: first, the law of continuity, which states that everything in history is the outcome of something preceding it. "Thunderbolts do not come from a clear sky."[30] The immediate, sudden appearance of something is unknown in history. Second, the law of mutability, which states that, unless nations can change as the times change, they must die; third, the law of interdependence of individuals, classes, tribes and nations, which states that none of these entities can, in the long run, live at the expense of another

[30] E. P. Cheyney, *Law in History and Other Essays* (New York, 1927), p. 11.

one; fourth, the law of democracy, a tendency for all government to come under the control of all the people; fifth, the law of free consent, which states that men cannot be compelled permanently; sixth and last, the law of "moral progress", based on the assumption that "moral influences in human affairs have become stronger and more widely extended than material influences".[31]

While the first five of these laws are fairly well grounded in historical realities, the last one rather expresses the wishful thoughts of a gentle, noble-minded democrat. In claiming for these six statements the character of "natural laws" comparable to "the laws of gravitation, or of chemical affinity, or of evolution",[32] Cheyney certainly went too far. If there are historical laws, they never have the rigorous character of natural laws and never allow us to calculate or predict future developments with an accuracy comparable to that of natural laws. "In order to perceive the irreversible or cyclical rhythm of development or a certain direction," writes Professor Raymond Aron, "a simplicity, regularity and continuity would be necessary which are excluded by the accidents and the complexity of social events."[33] Professor Aron concludes that nomothetic thought in history results only in rather hazardous generalizations, in more or less partial laws, in constructed and probable formulas which the faith and passion of partisans elevate to the rank of fatalities.

Earlier, we came to the conclusion that, since no historical event occurs magically, without a cause, but is always the outcome of another event, there is causality in history. And since causality implies general laws connecting causes and effects, we had to admit that there are general laws in history. As specifically "historical", we may designate those of these general laws which allow us to explain historical events, after they have occurred, as effects of other historical events, considered as their causes. However, these "historical laws" never allow us to predict concrete historical events but, at best, will make it possible to foresee, with some probability and a large margin of uncertainty, the general trend of future developments. Minds trained in the exact physical sciences sometimes have difficulty in understanding these limitations of historical prognoses. By virtue of his calculations based on the general laws of celestial mechanics, the French astronomer Leverrier deduced, in 1846, the existence of the hitherto unknown planet Neptune and designated exactly the spot in the sky where his German colleague Galle

---

[31] *Ibid.*, p. 22.
[32] *Ibid.*, pp. 24-25.
[33] R. Aron, *Introduction à la philosophie de l'histoire* (Paris, 1938), p. 245.

was to observe the new body a few days later. If historical laws never allow us such precise predictions, it is not only because of the complexity of the factors involved in historical evolution. It is also — and mainly — because of the preeminence of the human factor in history. For, in spite of all the progress in genetics, psychology and sociology, this human factor remains, to a large extent, unpredictable. Sir Charles Galton Darwin, who ventured to write the history of "the next million years", had to admit that the same century which witnessed the tremendous acclaim of Malthus' *Essay on Population* refuted the latter's prediction that the growth of the earth's population will outgrow agricultural production. The reasons were the "unforeseeable" developments in agricultural chemistry, the fantastic economic evolution of America, the worldwide establishment of railroads and steamships to carry America's surplus products to the old world, etc. etc. The result was that, in contrast to Malthus' predictions, our planet's agricultural production increased at a rate greater than the population.

As a physicist, Professor Darwin establishes a parallel between human beings and gas molecules. It is well known that statistical mechanics can calculate the average behaviour of gas molecules, even without invoking many of the properties of the individual molecules. In the same way, Sir Charles believes it possible "to find the Boyle's Law which controls the behavior of those very complicated molecules, the members of the human race ... and to predict something of man's future".[34] However, Professor Darwin seems to forget that there are no single gas molecules which, suddenly, can change the behavior of millions of other molecules, while there have always been human beings who changed the course of history and forced their fellow citizens to change their behavior. Even a collectivistic approach to history can hardly deny that the course of events would have been quite different without such personalities as Moses, Buddha, Christ, Mohamet, Luther, and Calvin, or Alexander the Great, Caesar, Napoleon, Jefferson, Marx, Lenin, or without Galileo, Newton, Lavoisier, Volta, Ampère, Pasteur, Robert Fulton, George Stephenson, Graham Bell, the Curies, Marconi, and Einstein. By outstanding personalities like these, the average behaviour of human beings has been greatly influenced and modified in directions hardly foreseeable even by "specialists". Thus, the analogy between human beings and gas molecules is rather shaky.

There are, of course, certain trends in the evolution of societies which allow us to foresee certain events with some probability, but their exact

[34] C. G. Darwin, *The Next Million Years* (London, 1953), p. 20.

timing and specific, concrete realization is always determined by the appearance of some unpredictable, outstanding personalities. Whoever had read Georg Gottfried Gervinus, Ernst Moritz Arndt, and certain writings of Heinrich Heine — especially his *L'Allemagne depuis Luther* (1834), published later as *Zur Geschichte der Religion und Philosophie in Deutschland* (1852) — could foresee, a century ago, that some day German racialist nationalism would run wild and sever all the links of the German people with Western civilization. It was also foreseeable that this event would involve Germany in a war with the world's civilized nations which would end in her defeat. And yet, nobody could calculate the exact date of these events, nor foresee the diabolic, technologically implemented cruelty which Hitler's morbid personality was to impart to Germany's racialist uprising against mankind.

The Russian revolution of 1917 was foreseeable for many decades and had been foreseen, in some of its features, by Dostoevski and others. Unforeseeable and incalculable, however, was the personality of Stalin, whose individual character changed a proletarian mass movement into an authoritarian regime characterized by despotism and hero worship. The emergence of a given personality at a certain historical moment and his or her specific individual characteristics and influences cannot be computed in advance in the way Leverrier calculated the appearance and characteristics of the planet Neptune. The main reason is that we do not possess all the biological, psychological and sociological data which produce such personalities nor the laws which connect these causative data with their effects.

Since the third decade of our century, any student of modern physics has been able to foresee that some day it would be possible to produce atomic bombs, the destructive power of which would surpass anything hitherto achieved in the technique of weapons. I myself foresaw it. When, in January 1945, I had an interview with Einstein, I asked him "whether the disintegration of atoms would not soon be able to release the tremendous atomic energies for warfare". Einstein answered: "Unhappily, such a possibility is not entirely in the Utopian domain. When military art is able to utilize nuclear atomic energies, it will not be houses or blocks of houses that will be destroyed in a few seconds — it will be entire cities." Seven months after this conversation and two months after its publication in English,[35] Hiroshima and Nagasaki disappeared from the earth within a few seconds.

[35] A. Stern, "Interview with Einstein", *Contemporary Jewish Record* (New York), vol. VIII, Nr. 3 (June, 1945), p. 246. A Spanish version of this article appeared four months earlier in several Latin American newspapers.

And yet, none of the scientists who worked on the development of the atomic bomb was able to foresee all the tremendous political changes and international conflicts this invention was to bring about as soon as it left the laboratory and became an instrument of man's lust for power. In science and technology, man is mainly involved as a rational being, and, therefore, certain results of these disciplines can, to a certain extent, be foreseen, although, even in these fields the flash of genius of outstanding personalities, time and again, brings about totally unsuspected innovations. In political history, on the contrary, man is involved with his interests, feelings, desires and passions, and, here, his irrational components predominate. And, by definition, the irrational is unpredictable, incalculable. This is, in my opinion, one of the reasons why historical laws do not allow us to predict more than vague generalities. They are mainly devices for the classification and explanation of historical events which have already occurred, followed by some hazardous generalizations referring to a possible future. As explanations of past historical events, these laws are based on inferences from effects to previous causes, and, since a given effect may have resulted from many different causes, all such inferences offer only some degrees of probality. Historical laws are only statistical laws which always involve a large element of chance. I would not go as far as Professor K. R. Popper, who denies historical laws and the necessity on which they are based. "The future depends on ourselves, and we do not depend on any historical necessity,"[36] he says. I am not convinced by this argument. The spontaneity of our individual actions does not exclude the fact that these actions are subject to psychological laws. In the same way, I think that the spontaneity of our collective actions would not exclude the possibility that these actions may be subject to historical laws. But just as the knowledge of psychological laws does not allow us to predict the future course of an individual's life, the knowledge of some historical laws does not allow us to predict the future course of collective life (i.e., of history), except for some vague generalities.

However, I do accept Professor Popper's argument by which he refutes large-scale historical predictions. The course of human history, he says, is strongly influenced by the growth of human knowledge. But "no scientific predictor — whether a human scientist or a calculating machine — can possibly predict, by scientific methods, its own future results."[37] Hence, we cannot truly predict the future course of history.

[36] K. R. Popper, *The Open Society and Its Enemies* (London, 1947), vol. I, p. 3.
[37] K. R. Popper, *The Poverty of Historicism* (London, 1957), p. X.

It is also obvious that some historical predictions may bring about or prevent the predicted event. In the latter case, they would refute themselves.

Within all these limitations, we may admit the usefulness of the search for historical laws and consider them, in Georg Simmel's sense, as "provisional syntheses of the *typical* phenomena of history".[38] However, what a historian considers as "typical" depends on his standard of values. With this, we return to our main problem: that of values in history.

We have seen that the nomothetic, natural sciences collect individual facts only in order to draw general laws from them. They retain of these facts only those features which are repeated uniformly in all of them. On the contrary, the idiographic, historical sciences are interested in single facts mainly for the sake of what is particular, individual and unique in them and which is not repeated. Windelband insisted that all value feelings are linked to the singular and unique; hence, the haunting character of the idea of the "double", the "second self", be it our own or that of a person dear to us. Kant showed that only things replaceable by other things which render the same service have a price, while those which are irreplaceable by others have value.

We may conclude that the experiment of a physicist or a chemist has a price. It costs money and time, but it can be repeated under similar conditions and can be replaced by any other experiment which allows us to derive the same general law. On the contrary, an historical fact discovered by a historian, has a value, thanks to its unique character; since it is not repeated, it cannot be replaced by another fact.

However, it is not said that this specific value which results from the unique and irreplaceable character of the historical fact is a positive moral value. Hitler's rôle in modern history does certainly not constitute a positive moral value. Nevertheless, every fact concerning Hitler's historical activity constitutes a positive value for the historian.

In order to clarify the question as to what is the specific value of the historical object, we must glance at the way in which Heinrich Rickert tried to determine the relation between the historical object and value. Although we cannot accept Rickert's conclusions, his errors may help us to find a better solution.

Rickert accepted Windelband's distinction between nomothetic and idiographic sciences but used a different terminology. Here is what he wrote:

[38] G. Simmel, *Die Probleme der Geschichtsphilosophie* (Leipzig, 1907), p. 95.

> Reality becomes nature, when we consider it with respect to
> the general, it becomes history, when we consider it with
> respect to the particular and individual; therefore, I shall
> contrast the *individualizing* method of *history* with the
> *generalizing* method of *natural science*.[39]

One must, however, not interpret this methodological individualism of
Rickert's, in a political sense, as opposed to collectivism. When describing the attitude of the crowds during the French revolution or the
reactions of the English during the *"Blitz"*, the historian refers to
individual collectivities different from those which functioned in other
places and other periods. Rickert's methodological individualism should
not be confused with Hyppolite Taine's historiographical principle:
*"Rien n'existe que par l'individu; c'est l'individu lui-même qu'il faut
connaître"*[40] — nothing exists except by the individual; it is the
individual himself whom one must know. This principle may be justified
within the limited domain of the history of literature but cannot be
generalized in an absolute way. Carlyle's "hero worship" which identified history with the lives of great men is still farther removed from
the individualizing method of the anti-romantic neo-Kantian Rickert.

A legitimate criticism of Rickert's classification would, however, insist
on the fact that it traces too rigid a demarcation line between natural
sciences and history. Not only did Rickert banish the individualizing
method from the sciences, but he also excluded the possibility of a
generalizing history. Now, the great Swiss historian, Jacob Burckhardt,
insisted several times on the importance of generalizing methods in
history — especially in the history of civilizations — and he applied
these methods. "General facts ... like those of the history of civilizations
(*Kulturgeschichte*) may, on average, be more important than the special
ones; that which repeats may be more important than the unique,"[41] he
wrote. Burckhardt thought that the "constant" and "typical" was the true
content of antiquity and he granted to great men only the modest
function of serving as "illustrations" and "testimony" (*Zeugnis*) of
general, spiritual trends. This is *mutatis mutandis,* the rôle which
Rickert and Windelband granted to singular facts in natural sciences:
that of serving as "illustrations" of general laws.

In his *Weltgeschichtliche Betrachtungen,* Burckhardt demands no less
strongly the application of the methods of natural science to history,

---

[39] H. Rickert, *Kulturwissenschaft und Naturwissenschaft* (Tübingen, 1915), p. 60.
See also H. Rickert, *Grenzen der naturwissenschaftlichen Begriffsbildung* (Tübingen,
1913), p. 224.
[40] H. Taine, *Introduction à l'histoire de la littérature anglaise* (Princeton, 1944), p. 2.
[41] J. Burckhardt, *Griechische Kulturgeschichte* (Berlin, 1898), I, p. 4.

when he writes: *"Wir betrachten das sich Wiederholende, Konstante, Typische"*[42] — we (that is to say, the historians) consider that which repeats, the constant, the typical. Consequently, the division between history and the sciences is less rigid than it appears in Windelband's and Rickert's classifications. All that can be said is that the individualizing method prevails in the historical disciplines, but the latter do not exclude the generalizing approach.

One of the most important problems concerning the relations between historiography and the realm of values is that of the selection of the essential. We have already mentioned the insufficiency of Voltaire's definition of history as "the account of the facts given as true"; this definition is too wide, for many facts are true without being "historical". Or — in order to be more precise: there are facts which are "historical" from the standpoint of history as reality which, nevertheless, are of no interest to history as knowledge. In this respect, we mentioned the composition of Bonaparte's meal on the evening of the battle of Austerlitz, the cost of the pens with which Molière wrote his *Tartuffe*, and the struggle between an Austrian and a Prussian soldier in the battle of Kunersdorf. Confronted with the multiplicity of documented details of the diverse perspectives, the historian must make a choice, and he makes it — whether consciously or unconsciously. It is a choice of the essential, and, in order to be able to distinguish essential from nonessential events, the historian must have a standard of values. The related facts must be evaluated with respect to their importance. An importance with respect to what? We shall try to answer this question.

The scientist's attitude differs from the historian's. For the scientist, the essential coincides with the general, i.e. with what is uniformly repeated in all phenomena of a certain class. The logical ideal, says Rickert, is that the scientific investigator takes no other interest in his objects than that of understanding them in a generalizing way. Then, each of them becomes for him an indifferent specimen of a species.

The particular, on the contrary, which interests the historian, can become "essential" only with respect to a value; without such a relation to a value, the particular would lose all its historical interest and would be nothing but an indifferent element of reality. While the generalizing method of natural sciences is exempt from values, the individualizing method of history is only possible thanks to an evaluating approach to the objects. Thus, the relation to values is revealed as the constitutive principle of the historical object which distinguishes the latter from all

---

[42] J. Burckhardt, *Weltgeschichtliche Betrachtungen* (Bern, 1941), p. 45.

the other real objects. History as knowledge exists only for an evaluating being.

Rickert tried to show that the constitutive value of the historical object is that of culture. What is culture? By which criteria is culture different from nature? To take the simplest example, we may say that the products of nature are those which grow freely on the earth. On the contrary, the products of culture are those which the field produces only after having been "cultivated" by man. With nature, which develops without man's intervention one contrasts culture, produced or "cultivated" by man because of certain values which he attaches to it. Thus, every product of culture embodies a value for the sake of which man created or cultivated it, and it is by this value that the product of culture is distinguished from the product of nature. The latter is transformed into an object of culture as soon as man cultivates it for the sake of the values he attaches to it. As bearers of values, the objects of culture are goods, cultural goods.

Now, Rickert insists that cultural goods are not only appreciated because of an individual appetite, but because we feel ourselves obligated to appreciate them for the sake of the human community to which we belong. Rickert circumscribes this domain of culture by stating:

> Religion, church, law, the state, customs, science, language, literature, art, economy and also the technical means necessary for their management are ... cultural objects or goods, precisely in the sense that the values bound up with them are either recognized as valid by all members of a community or that this recognition is expected of them.[43]

Thus, it becomes clear why Rickert substituted the expression *"Kulturwissenschaft"* or science of culture for the term *"Geisteswissenschaft"* or science of the mind used by Dilthey and Wundt.

We see that, according to this conception, value becomes indispensable for the definition of the very object of history, for it is the concept of cultural value which constitutes the selective principle of the historian. He will choose as essential all the events of the *res publica* related to cultural values — whether they contribute to the evolution of these values, to their conservation, their delay or their regression. Having greatly contributed to the regression of the cultural values of our epoch, Hitler is certainly an essential phenomenon of modern history and a precious object of historical study. But this does not mean that the historian admires or loves him.

---

[43] H. Rickert, *Kulturwissenschaft und Naturwissenschaft* (Tübingen, 1915), p. 21.

It is one of the essential traits of Rickert's conception that, although considering values as constitutive principles of the historical objects, he insists on the "objective" character of historiography, its independence from the historians' subjective, individual evaluations. Here is what he says:

> It is the *universality of cultural values* which eliminates the arbitrariness in the formation of historical concepts and which is the basis of their objectivity. What is historically essential must not only be essential for this or for that individual, it must be *important for all*.[44]

I do not believe that this conception constitutes the protection against historical relativism which Rickert considers it. For who are those he calls "all"? They are the members of a cultural community confined to a certain space and a certain time. Perhaps it is the German cultural community of his epoch, perhaps the European or Occidental cultural community of the twentieth century. It certainly does not include that of the Renaissance nor those of the middle-ages or antiquity, for those communities had quite different cultural values. Nor does Rickert's "all" include the cultural communities of the Chinese, the Hindoos or the Arabs. The cultural values of Communist Russia of 1962 are very different from those of Dostoevski's Tsarist Russia. Since they are themselves products of history, cultural values cannot escape historical relativity.

In order to secure the objectivity of history in spite of its axiological orientation, Rickert also sought to establish the subtle distinction between "practical evaluations" and "the theoretical relation to values" — a distinction which was adopted by Croce for history and by Max Weber for all social sciences. The historian, says Rickert, does not evaluate "practically", but "finds" certain values such as state, art, religion as "empirically ascertainable facts".[45] For Rickert, history is a science related to values — to cultural values — but not an evaluating science. It ascertains for example that, in the course of evolution, certain values were appreciated by certain nations, but it does not judge these values; that is to say, the historian does not examine whether or to what extent these evaluations were justified. Rickert gave the following example:

> The historian — in his capacity as a historian — cannot decide whether the French Revolution has been useful or detrimental to France or Europe. This would be an evalua-

[44] *Ibid.*, p. 107.
[45] H. Rickert, *Die Probleme der Geschichtsphilosophie* (Heidelberg, 1924), p. 61.

tion. However, no historian will doubt that the events combined under that name have been *significant* and *important* for the cultural evolution of France and Europe and that they must, therefore be ... included as *essential* in the presentation of European history. This is not a practical evaluation but a theoretical relation to values. In short, evaluating must always be *praise* or *blame*. To relate to values is *neither* of the two.[46]

I agree with Rickert's contention that the historian does not have the right to praise and to blame — in his capacity as a historian, for, to do so, he would need a standard of values the validity of which cannot be admitted *a priori*. This does not prevent many historians from violating Rickert's rule. Convinced of the universal validity of his Puritan ethics, Thomas Carlyle wrote history as a judge. "Carlyle never could simply 'write' history. He had to canonize or anathematize,"[47] says Ernst Cassirer. Benedetto Croce strongly rejected the "symptoms of detestation" obvious in the history of Spinoza's life written by a contemporary Lutheran parson, teeming with words such as "abominable", "wretched", "poisonous", "devilish", "though the historical narrative is sufficiently objective to give internal evidence of Spinoza's lofty mind, sincere spirit and ascetically saintly life".[48]

In rejecting procedures like these, Rickert is on firm philosophical ground. This is no longer true when he tries to hide the fact — admitted by him on other occasions — that the judgment which determines what is "essential" and "important" in history expresses an evaluation. And Rickert is, likewise, in error, when he affirms that evaluating means necessarily "praise" or "blame". In my opinion, "to praise" and "to blame" only constitute moral and aesthetic evaluations, and I believe that those must, indeed, be avoided by the historian. However, the epithets "essential" and "non-essential", "important" and "unimportant" are also evaluations, but, in my opinion, they are not moral evaluations; rather, in the historian's case, historical evaluations. For, if the historian decides that an event is "essential" or "important", it means that it is so for the subsequent historical evolution.

To be sure, when the historian reconstitutes the history of — let us say — Islam, he will not examine the metaphysical, religious or moral validity of the values inspiring this movement. It will be enough for him to know that these values have been and still are vigorously

---

[46] H. Rickert, *Kulturwissenschaft und Naturwissenschaft*, p. 98.
[47] E. Cassirer, *The Myth of the State* (Garden City, N.Y., 1955), pp. 275-276.
[48] B. Croce, *My Philosophy* (London, 1949), p. 177.

affirmed by the devotion of millions of men. In this sense, Rickert was right in declaring that the historian has to accept these values as empirically ascertainable facts. Nevertheless, unlike Rickert, I think that the historian evaluates the events which constitute the history of Islam. His evaluation must, however, be neither religious nor methaphysical, nor moral and not even political — as far as this is possible — but simply *historical:* he will evaluate the importance of Islam for the subsequent evolution of the Orient and the Occident.

I, thus, affirm that, besides moral, political, social, methaphysical, and other evaluations, there are specifically historical evaluations. The historian evaluates, but his evaluations are related to another frame of reference than that of the historical agent. If the evaluations of the latter are political, social, moral, religious, or methaphysical, the historian's evaluations will be — at least, in ideal conditions — strictly historical.

But these historical evaluations are, likewise, conditioned — historically, culturally, socially, existentially. A medieval historian considered as "essential" the events capable of influencing the march of history towards the realization of the City of God, while a modern historical materialist considers as "essential" the events capable of influencing the evolution of history towards the realization of Socialism. Rickert's postulate "what is historically essential must not only be essential for this or that individual, it must be *important for all*" is, thus, Utopian. For a traditionalist like de Maistre, other events are essential than for a Liberal like Michelet; and a militaristic, dynastic historian like Treitschke will give importance to other events than the Socialistic historian Karl Kautsky. The point of view of the historian implies, thus, a system of values which cannot be reduced to everybody's cultural values in Rickert's sense.

Professor Mandelbaum affirms that the consequences of historical events "are embodied in the historical materials" at the historian's disposal and can be ascertained by statements of reality, without the interference of value judgments.[49] But we must not forget that the men who transmitted to us the historical materials had already sorted them, retaining only those events which, according to their standards of values, appeared "essential".

Evidently, the historian, who is himself a part of the historical evolution he retraces, cannot possibly write a history which could be true for a fictitious observer placed outside and above history in an

[49] M. Mandelbaum, *The Problem of Historical Knowledge* (New York, 1938), p.196.

"absolute" space and in an "absolute" time. Moving with the history he retraces, the historian is, in my opinion, comparable to a passenger in a fast-moving train who sees through the window a landscape passing by. How could he design an objective, stable image of this landscape, exempt from individual, variable perspectives? Looking backward, he constantly moves away from the past and sees it only in perpetually changing perspectives. The fact that he can hardly avoid sometimes throwing a glance ahead accentuates the variability of his perspectives of the past.

Historical realists always refer to the established "facts". Carl L. Becker answered them with the following cogent argument:

> Left to themselves, the facts do not speak; ... there is no fact until someone affirms it. ... To select and affirm even the simplest complex of facts is to give them a certain place in a certain pattern of ideas, and this alone is sufficient to give them a special meaning. ... It is, thus, not the undiscriminated fact but the perceiving mind of the historian that speaks.[50]

As we have shown, the historian synthesizes his material not only by means of the general categories of thought but, also and especially, by virtue of the specific categories of historical thought. Each historian deals with one selected aspect of his subject matter. It may be contended that this feature is not peculiar to the study of history, for the exact sciences, also, are selective. Indeed, in describing its objects, each science selects one of the aspects characterizing these objects, disregarding all the others. The chemist sees in a certain piece of marble nothing but a micro-crystalline form of calcium carbonate, while to the archeologist this same piece of marble may be the Niobe of Praxiteles.

And yet, in my opinion, there still subsists a basic difference between the selective approaches of the sciences, on the one hand, and of history, on the other. The selective process in science is not evaluative but purely methodological, a mere consequence of the division of labour. On the contrary, the selective process of the historian is definitely evaluative. The same historical epoch can be described by a great variety of categories or patterns of interpretation, each of which is expressive of a certain set of values. An epoch can, for example, be described as a struggle between human passions (Vico), or between laziness and greed (Kant), or between belief and unbelief — a point of view dear to Goethe and Carlyle, execpt that the German poet interpreted the term "belief"

---

[50] C. L. Becker, *Everyman His Own Historian* (New York, 1935), p. 251.

in a worldly sense and the English writer in a theological way, as a struggle between good and evil, between the forces of heaven and hell. But the same historical epoch could perhaps also be conceived as a battle between reason and unreason, as in Voltaire's conception; or between reason and liberty (Fichte); or as an antagonism between individual and society, a perspective in which Wilhelm von Humboldt was interested; or as a struggle between might and right, tyranny and freedom, nationalism and internationalism, between spiritual and worldly powers, or between exploiting and exploited classes — a point of view stressed by Dialectical Materialism. According to the categories chosen and the selection of appropriate facts, political history can be one of ideas (Hegel), one of civilizations (Voltaire, Spengler, Toynbee, Huizinga), one of great men or "heroes" (Fichte, Carlyle), one of classes (Marx, Engels, Lenin), one of ways of thinking (*Denkweisen*) and opinions (Jakob Burckhardt), one of nations (Ranke), one of international relations (Renouvin), one of religions, of technological achievements, of economic principles, etc. Which of these schemes of interpretation a historian chooses depends, to a large extent, on the set of values governing his mind.

To be sure, there has been some reaction against this great selective freedom of the historian. The German philosopher Nicolai Hartmann rejected all monistic categorical interpretations of history and suggested their replacement by a pluralistic categorical scheme. Believing in a stratified world, with a corresponding stratified realm of categories, Nicolai Hartmann wrote: "History, like the world, is built of many strata. ... History is just as much an economical as a spiritual process; it is the organic as well as the cultural life of the nations."[51] There are historians who truly try to achieve such a pluralistic approach, but they do it with very limited success. The number of data and the variety of aspects offered by the evolution of mankind are too great, and many of the possible historical categories fit to synthesize the data are mutually exclusive. Thus, the historian must make a selection from among the logically possible and empirically applicable synthetic historical categories, choosing those which, according to his personal conception, allow him to give the most plausible explanation of historical events and enable him to integrate those events which, according to his evaluation, are the most important ones. These selections are determined by the historian's Ego. "To eliminate the Ego, in order to make history itself speak" — as Ranke and other nineteenth century historians wanted to

---

[51] N. Hartmann, *Das Problem des geistigen Seins*, 2. Aufl. (Berlin, 1949), p. 19.

do — is a logical and psychological impossibility. Whereas the scientist's approach to reality has to be free from evaluations, history can be written only by an evaluating being. And, as we have seen, our evaluations involve both our personalities and the societies of which we are products. Some of these evaluations reflect certain objective features of the historical reality studied. Others are purely "ideological", mere rationalizations of our or our group's interests. Speaking in the name of the historians, Jakob Burckhardt wrote, in his *Weltgeschichtliche Betrachtungen:* "We can never disengage ourselves completely from the intentions (*Absichten*) of our own time and our own personality."[52] And, even more explicitly, the Swiss historian expressed himself in the introduction to his *Griechische Kulturgeschichte,* from which I translate the following paragraph:

> It will not be possible to avoid a great subjectieve *arbitrariness* in the *selection* of the objects. We are 'unscientific' and have no method, at least not that of others. Starting from the same studies as those which served us to prepare this course arbitrarily, ... another historian would have made another selection and another arrangement and would often have drawn other conclusions.[53]

As we said, the choice of the diverse unifying categories depends to a large extent on the system of values adopted by the historian, and this system often expresses a whole philosophy present in his mind, either explicitly or implicitly. Rejecting the illusion of an absolute objectivity in history, Professor Marrou devised the following excellent formula: "As a knowledge of man by man, history is a way of grasping the past by and in a human thought which is living and committed (*engagée*); it is a complex, an indissoluble mixture of subject and object."[54]

Nevertheless, it would be an exaggeration to conclude that history is entirely fictitious. No serious historian would go so far. In 1938, Professor Raymond Aron published his *Introduction à la philosophie de l'histoire* with the subtitle *Essai sur les limites de l'objectivité historique* — Essay on the limits of historical objectivity. Today, the awareness of these limits has become so general that one should rather insist on the limits of historical subjectivity. One of these limits is logic. Max Weber thought that the directive values which determine the formation of our auxiliary concepts (*begriffliche Hilfsmittel*) are sub-

[52] J. Burckhardt, *Weltgeschichtliche Betrachtungen* (Bern, 1941), pp. 52-53.
[53] J. Burckhardt, *Griechische Kulturgeschichte* (Berlin, 1898), I, p. 6.
[54] H.-I. Marrou, *De la connaissance historique* (Paris, 1956), p. 232.

jective, but he insisted that in the manner of their application the "investigator is bound by the norms of our thought".[55]

No serious historian can underrate the requirements of logic in historical research. As Collingwood says, "history has this in common with every other science: that the historian is not allowed to claim any single piece of knowledge, except where he can justify his claim by exhibiting ... the *grounds* on which it is based."[56]

The determination of the validity of these grounds is, obviously, the task of logic. Even Charles A. Beard, one of the strongest subjectivists among modern historians, recognizes the necessity of a scientific method in history based on logic. But he also insists on the limits of this method in history. The selection and arrangement of the facts and their interpretation according to certain basic axiological ideas is probably the most powerful of these limits. Far from regarding this interference of axiological selective principles as a weakness, Max Weber sees in it a power of history: the inexhaustible character of its content (*die Unausschöpfbarkeit ihres Inhalts*), always offering new aspects capable of stimulating our interest.[57]

If logic is one of the limits of the historian's subjectivity, the other is the document. The historian's choice must be made between these two limits. It is a choice from among documented facts, a choice from among the logical possibilities of their interpretation, a choice of the categories to be used for their synthesis and a choice from among the possible historiographical projects compatible with all those data. I think that these choices are not entirely free, for they are determined by the system of values which, implicitly or explicitly, are present in the historian's mind. These value systems are not freely chosen, but are, to a large extent, a result of the historian's social habitat, an outcome of the development of his personality in given historical, geographical, national, cultural, social, genealogical and psychological circumstances. The interpretation of the historian's own existence in his world will also be determined by the basic set of values which characterize his personality.

Earlier, we have seen that, considered as "provisional syntheses of the typical phenomena of history", historical laws are related to values, for what a historian considers "typical" depends on his set of values. This does not, however, mean that historical laws are completely

[55] M. Weber, *Gesammelte Aufsätze zur Wissenschaftslehre* (Tübingen, 1922), pp. 183, 184.
[56] R. G. Collingwood, *The Idea of History* (Oxford, 1946), p. 252.
[57] M. Weber, *op. cit.*, p. 253.

divorced from objective, empirical reality; for there are values which reflect certain objective features of this reality, features which must be reflected in the evaluations of certain individuals, certain collective groups or of the whole society, if these entities wish to survive and, thus, to continue history. In our last chapter, we shall study more closely this objective aspect of values and its importance for history.

In his recent book, *The Self and the Dramas of History,* the famous American theologian Reinhold Niebuhr mentions a significant example of the impossibility of avoiding value judgments in historical interpretations. Not long ago, two former ambassadors of the United States to Spain, both of them professional historians, published books on the Spanish civil war (1936 to 1939). The one, Claude Bowers, wrote a book *Mission to Spain;* the other, Carleton Hayes, published *Wartime Mission in Spain.* In spite of the identity of the subject matters, the similarity of their titles and of the authors' official functions, the contents of the two books are absolutely antagonistic. While Bowers considers the Spanish civil war as a prelude to World War II, Hayes regards it as a prelude to the cold war between the United States and Russia. "Both are honest historians," writes Professor Niebuhr, "and neither falsified the facts; but they chose very different facts and subjected all relevant facts to contrasting interpretations. Mr. Hayes is a liberal Catholic while Mr. Bowers stands in the Jeffersonian tradition."[58]

Niebuhr recalls that none of the many histories of the French Revolution — written from Jacobin, royalist or Bonapartist points of view — won a definite victory over the others, simply because the French Revolution as such never found a final solution in France's political life. The recent crisis in which the supporters of the traditional republic were ranged against the Algerian right-wing factions was another proof for this contention. Niebuhr thinks that even the decline of the Roman empire ceases to be a *res judicata* as soon as someone tries to prove that there exists an analogy between that period of Roman history and the American New Deal.

All this confirms the thesis affirmed by many philosophers and historians — from Bergson and Croce to Troeltsch and Sartre — that the interpretation of the social past is always in suspense; the importance of historical events is a function of our present and even of our hopes and apprehensions concerning the future. Or, as Carl L. Becker expresses it: "Every generation, our own included, will, must inevitably,

---

[58] R. Niebuhr, *The Self and The Dramas of History* (New York, 1955), p. 54.

understand the past and anticipate the future in the light of its own restricted experience."[59]

These considerations, however, do not contradict our former affirmation that the ideal historian does not evaluate morally or metaphysically and not even politically, but rather historically. For he chooses his historical categories according to his historiographical project, and this project is the expression of his value system. But this project and the values it embodies are historically, socially and existentially conditioned; they express certain tendencies of a definite stratum of present-day society and its orientation toward the future. The two American historians — the one a Liberal, the other a Catholic — who gave such different accounts of the Spanish Civil War had, evidently, different value systems and, consequently, two different historiographic projects: the one based on the assumption that the Spanish Civil War had been the prelude to World War II, the other founded on the theory that it had been the prelude to the Cold War. The difference between their historiographic projects explains the fact that the two historians selected very different events and different historical categories to synthesize and interpret these events. It was in the light of their different historiographic projects that they evaluated the events in different ways. But their historiographic projects themselves express two basic antagonistic orientations in contemporary American society and its attitude to the future: Liberalism and Conservatism. Thus, the two projects mentioned were socially and historically conditioned and, probably, also existentially. Hence, their different axiological orientations.

Were those two historians "partial" in their choice of the facts they interpreted? Certainly, they were "partial" in the sense of showing favoritism, because they had to be "partial" in the sense of being incomplete. Unable to take into account all known facts, even the ideal historian is partial in the second sense and, consequently, also in the first.

When I tried to interpret a fact reported by Rickert, I realized that the multiplicity of historiographical projects brings about a multiplicity of hierarchies and codes of values. Rickert once wrote that the refusal of the German imperial crown by Frederick William IV of Prussia was an "essential" historical fact, while the work of the tailor who made this king's uniforms was historically "unessential".[60] The well known historian, Eduard Meyer, retorted that the tailor was cer-

[59] C. L. Becker, *Everyman His Own Historian* (New York, 1935), p. 253.
[60] H. Rickert, *Grenzen der naturwissenschaftlichen Begriffsbildung* (Tübingen, 1913), p. 290.

tainly not essential to political history but perhaps would be essential to a history of fashions or of the craft of tailoring.

From this contention I am inferring that, for a history of fashions or the craft of tailoring, the refusal of the imperial crown by Frederick William IV would be unessential, since this event did not contribute to the evolution of fashions. On the contrary, the acceptance of the imperial crown by this king could have constituted an essential event in the history of fashions or in that of the craft of tailoring, for this event could have caused the creation of a unique coronation robe.

My conclusion is that what is essential or unessential in history does not depend on Rickert's cultural values but on the directive value of the historiographical project under consideration. This principle entails a plurality of codes of values for the different historians, corresponding to their different projects. As the example just mentioned showed us, the political historian has a different code of values from the historian of fashions. And, obviously, the historians of arts, of ideas, of literature, of philosophy, of the sciences, of technology or political economy, use very different codes of values, each determined by the specific project of their choice. For each of these historians, other events are essential and others are considered as unessential. And within each of these branches — like political history or the history of ideas — there exist, likewise, a plurality of projects characterized by other categories and other directive values, as we have seen in the case of the two American historiographers of the Spanish Civil War. Whoever tries to reduce these different codes of values to a common axiological denominator is wasting his time. He would do better to look for other ways to overcome his intellectual insecurity.

Let us, for the moment, sum up the four essential facts on the axiological implications of history which, up to now, have emerged from our inquiry about the relations between history and values:

1st. History as reality arises from a perpetual will to get out of a present considered as imperfect and to move towards a future dreamed of as more perfect. This opposition of real negative values and positive values, imagined and affirmed by groups, constitutes the life blood of history as reality.

2nd. Values enter the very definition of historical objects; only by its relation to the directive value of a definite historiographical project is an historical object distinguished from any other real, but historically indifferent, object.

3rd. There is a multiplicity of codes of values which determine the essential or unessential character of historical events. Each of these codes of values owes its specific character to a definite historiographical project; the latter is also manifested in the choice of specific historical categories and in the selection of appropriate events.

4th. The choice of an historiographical project and of the corresponding categories is the expression of an original choice of certain basic values, a choice which, in its turn, is historically, socially, culturally and existentially conditioned.

These axiological implications of historiography are not necessarily tantamount to its total axiological subjectivity. To be sure, as relations between objects and appreciating subjects, all values are relative to a subject and, in this sense, all are "subjective". Nevertheless, there are values which one could designate as "supra-individual", namely those which, although being relations between objects and appreciating subjects, are, nevertheless, independent of the individual peculiarities of these subjects. In my book, *Philosophie du rire et des pleurs*, I distinguished, for this reason, the following three classes of values:

1st. *Individual values*, which depend only on the individual peculiarities of the appreciating subjects.

2nd. *Collective values*, which, in spite of likewise being relations of objects to appreciating subjects, are independent of the individual peculiarities of the appreciating subjects; they depend, however, on the collective peculiarities of the groups that affirm them, for example on the collective peculiarities of a certain nation, class, caste, political party or religious denomination.

3rd. *Universal values* which, in spite of likewise being relations between objects and appreciating subjects, are independent of both the individual and the collective peculiarities of those who affirm them.[61]

I shall give some examples. When I say: "The taste of apricots is better than that of peaches" I emit a value judgment, the validity of which is purely individual. The superior hedonic value I affirm is nothing but an individual value, since it depends entirely on the individual peculiarities of me, the appreciating subject.

But let us take the following value judgment: "France, when she let loose the reins of regal authority, doubled the license of a ferocious dissoluteness in manners and of an insolent irreligion in opinions and practices."[62] This is a sentence from Edmund Burke's *Reflections on the Revolution in France*. This judgment, condemning the French Revolution politically and morally, even at its beginnings — Burke's book was

---

[61] A. Stern, *Philosophie du rire et des pleurs* (Paris, 1949), pp. 207-218.
[62] *The Works of the R. H. Edmund Burke*, vol. II (London, 1855), p. 311.

written as early as 1790 — expresses a collective value reflecting the collective peculiarities of the group of which Burke was the ideological spokesman: England's ruling class. Therefore, the author of this sentence and of many others of the same kind was enthusiastically congratulated by the Tories. His king, George III, praised his book on the French Revolution and recommended it to be read by everybody.

In order to give an example of a judgment expressing a universal value, I would say: "Health is better than sickness." The superior value of health with regard to sickness is affirmed by all human beings, independently of the individual peculiarities of the appreciating subjects and of the collective peculiarities of the appreciating groups. Here, we must, of course, set aside certain religious or philosophical schools whose evaluations are not spontaneous but are dictated by definite "systems".

The evaluations of the historians belong to all three classes of the values we have just distinguished. They are, in part, individual; in part, collective; in part, universal. If, in a historian's work, the individual evaluations outweight the two other classes, his work will be more personal. If the collective values predominate, his work will be politically more debatable. If, however, the prevalent evaluations in an historical work are universal, it will be more scientific.

As for Mannheim's ideologies and Utopias resulting from the collective unconscious of the group to which the historian belongs, they obviously constitute collective values. As far as possible, the historian should try to get rid of them. But this possibility is rather limited.

So far as Rickert's "cultural values" are concerned, their author wanted them to be considered as universal, since he insisted that they should be valid "for all". In my opinion, they have, however, all the characteristics of collective values, since they depend on the collective peculiarities of the group which affirms them, and their validity is restricted to this group. For the cultural values of modern Germans, which Rickert wanted to universalize, have certainly very little in common with the cultural values affirmed by the pilgrims to Mecca or by the Parsees on the Ganges. Their collective character places Rickert's cultural values in the neighborhood of Durkheim's social values, which the great French sociologist characterized by writing:

> The social judgment is objective with regard to individual judgments; thus, the scale of values is removed from the subjective and variable appreciations of the individuals. The latter find outside themselves a completely established classification which is not their work and which expresses something quite different from their personal feelings. And they

HISTORICAL KNOWLEDGE AND VALUES

are compelled to conform to this classification outside themselves, for, due to its origin, public opinion has a moral
authority, by virtue of which it imposes itself upon the particular individuals. ... It blames those who judge moral
matters by other principles than those which it prescribes.[63]

Almost the same thing happens in the case of Rickert's cultural values
which the individual feels compelled to recognize out of regard for the
community to which he belongs.

In spite of his postulate that historiography should relate its objects
to values whose validity is recognized by all, Rickert finally realizes
that his cultural values hardly meet this requirement. He admits that
they are only empirical values which result from historical evolution.
Rickert also admits that, in order to evaluate these cultural values and
to be able to ascertain an historical progress, he would need "a standard
of values of suprahistorical validity."[64] "Only after the establishment
of formal values of timeless validity, is it possible to relate to them the
abundance of empirically verifiable cultural values developed in the
course of history."[65]

Rickert admits that the attempt to find a system of timeless supra-
historical values with definite content is "a task just as necessary as
insoluble" (eine ebenso notwendige wie unlösbare Aufgabe)[66]; the reason
is that history develops and always produces new cultural values with
definite content which should find their places in the system. Thus,
Rickert must be satisfied with purely formal values which are, however,
supposed to be transcendent and of unconditional suprahistorical validity. "A value's transcendency" — he writes — "implies timeless validity,
and, therefore, only a timeless reality could be a metaphysical bearer of
timeless values."[67] But what do we know about a metaphysical reality
which could be the presupposition of transcendent values, serving as
standards for judging the cultural values of history? Rickert himself
admits that he knows nothing about them. All he ventures to affirm is
"a necessary indication (eine notwendige Hindeutung) of a metaphysical
relation of the values to empirical reality", but with this vague sugges-
tion "everything that science can say in that respect is exhausted".[68]
Rickert thinks, however, that this vague possibility of an existence of
transcendent, timeless values anchored in a metaphysical world suffices

[63] E. Durkheim, Sociologie et philosophie (Paris, 1924), pp. 122-123.
[64] H. Rickert, Die Probleme der Geschichtsphilosophie (Heidelberg, 1924), p. 119.
[65] Ibid., p. 118.
[66] Ibid., p. 119.
[67] Ibid., p. 153.
[68] Ibid., p. 151.

for philosophy of history and gives it the means to judge the empirical, cultural values, emerging in the course of history.

I think that these transcendent suprahistorical values are only a postulate of Rickert, but a postulate guarantees neither the reality nor the validity of the thing or the idea postulated. In postulating those suprahistorical values, the origin of which is rather mysterious, Rickert believed that he had found an absolute standard by which to judge the empirical values of history and their possible progress. This standard is extra-historical, transcendent and rationalistic. But — as Ernst Troeltsch says — "as soon as one starts from Ideas and standards, one falls into an unhistorical rationalism and loses contact with empirical history and its practice."[69] And Raymond Aron declares that Rickert "eludes the problem of history by the mere fact of assuming a transcendental subject and universal values".[70]

Moreover, I think that, with purely formal values, one cannot avoid axiological relativism, since the true problem of civilization is the perpetual change of the qualitative content of our evaluations, in spite of certain unchangeable forms. Twenty six years ago, I wrote:

> What change constantly in the course of history are the *contents* towards which we direct our will to surmount the subject-object opposition or to erect higher barriers between them. But the fact that a will aiming at surmounting the subject-object opposition confers on its contents a positive value, while the will to elevate barriers between subject and object confers on its contents a negative value — this fact remains immutable and is not affected by the change of the appreciated contents.[71]

In spite of the permanence of this formal principle of my philosophy of values, I ascertained, at that period, what I called and still call *"l'instabilité axiologique de notre monde"*[72] — the axiological instability of our world. It results from the perpetual change of the qualitative contents of our values, dependent on history, geography and social surrounding.

Later, I stated that "what is universally valid is valid for all beings — not only for real beings (*êtres réels*) but also for all possible beings"[73] and I insisted that this was a universality by right and not only in fact.

[69] E. Troeltsch, *Der Historismus und seine Probleme* (Tübingen, 1922), I, p. 162.
[70] R. Aron, *La philosophie critique de l'histoire* (Paris, 1950), p. 293.
[71] A. Stern, *La philosophie des valeurs* (Paris, 1936), II, p. 58.
[72] *Ibid.*, II, p. 58. See also A. Stern, *Die philosophischen Grundlagen von Wahrheit, Wirklichkeit, Wert* (München, 1932), pp. 424-429.
[73] A. Stern, *Philosophie du rire et des pleurs* (Paris, 1949), p. 212.

Today, however, I feel it necessary to add that this universal validity by right must explicitly be restricted to the purely formal relations between ideal objects, such as those of mathematics and logic. As far as values are concerned, they are, however, always linked to definite contents, subject to historical change. It follows that the universality of certain values is only *de facto* and is not independent of the march of history and the different cultural, social and ideological surroundings it creates. Although my formal division of values into individual, collective and universal is applicable to all historical epochs, the concrete contents of the values which are independent of the individual and collective peculiarities of the appreciating individuals and groups change with the historical epochs. This means that, in every historical epoch, *other* values are universally accepted and, therefore, independent of the individual and collective peculiarities of those who affirm them. For example, in the Middle-Ages, the religious values of the Catholic Church were universal in the sense that, according to our definition, they were affirmed independently of the individual peculiarities of the appreciating subjects and of the collective peculiarities of the appreciating groups. Everybody affirmed them: virtuous people and sinners, clergy and nobility, peasants and townspeople, artisans and mercenaries. It is well known that today this is no longer the case and that, even in the Middle-Ages, the universality of the values mentioned above was confined to the Christian community of Europe and did not include such cultural groups as the Arabs, the Chinese and the Hindoos. Consequently, the universality of the Catholic religious values was only a universality relative to a certain period and to a definite geographical and cultural area.

Today, religious values have been replaced by another group of values which, likewise, claim universal validity: the values of modern civilization. They are, indeed, universal in the sense that they are more or less independent of the individual peculiarities of the appreciating subjects and of the collective peculiarities of the appreciating groups. But, also, their universality is only, in fact, limited to the members of Western civilization and is unable to claim timeless, spaceless and supra-historical validity.

We must, however, recall the sentence we used earlier as an example to illustrate universal validity: "Health is better than sickness." This value judgment truly seems to express a timeless, spaceless, supra-historical, supra-social and supra-cultural evaluation; for, in all periods, in all civilizations, in all the regions of this earth, and in all social habitats, men did and still do evaluate health in a positive manner and sickness in a negative way. Linked to the invariable human condition, this evaluation will, probably, be maintained in the future and, possibly, resist all assaults of history. Are we not here confronted with a value of genuine universality?

I think that such a conclusion would not be too daring. The suprahistorical universality of the vital value of health is, however, not due to an unchangeable human "nature" but to the human "condition", which remains identical with regard to life and death. We may here be faced with a possible limit to historical relativism in the realm of values. In a later chapter, we shall take up this problem.

The possibility of establishing a limit to historical relativism in the realm of vital values should not conceal the fact that non-vital values which appear to be universal in a certain epoch and in a certain cultural and social environment are no longer regarded as universal in another epoch and in another civilization. We also saw that with timeless but merely formal criteria we do not escape the historical, geographical, cultural and social relativity of the contents of the evaluations. Troeltsch says: "The man who acts and the history which gives an account of him cannot be understood without the relativity of values."[74]

Why did Rickert try so hard to establish the absolute validity of certain transcendent, timeless, supra-historical values? He tried it, in order to escape the "relativism" and "nihilism" of Historicism. "As a philosophical conception (*Weltanschauung*) Historicism is a monstrosity," he wrote. ". . . It makes a principle of the lack of principles. Therefore, it should be fought most vigorously by the philosophy of history and by philosophy in general."[75]

Considering the importance of Historicism for the final establishment of the relations between history and values, we must now study this movement more closely.

---

[74] E. Troeltsch, *Der Historismus und seine Probleme*, I, p. 214.
[75] H. Rickert, *Die Probleme der Geschichtsphilosophie*, pp. 129-130.

Historicism may be defined by the formula *veritas et virtus filiae
temporis* — truth and value are daughters of time, daughters of
history. Historicism, which rose in Germany towards the end of the
eighteenth century and was developed there in the nineteenth, is an
historical relativism which considers truth, right, customs, ethics and,
in general, all ideas and all values as products of a given historical
epoch, of a specific civilization, or even of a definite national or
regional collectivity. Consequently, these ideas and values are valid
only for the epochs, the civilizations and, in extreme cases, only for the
nations or provinces which produced them.[1]

Since no idea and no value appear to be free from these historical
conditions it seems that there are no transhistorical truths and values
which would allow us to judge of the truths and values created by
different historical epochs. Consequently, *all* ideas and *all* values
created in the course of history would be justified, even the ideas and
values of those epochs which, today, appear to us to be most barbarian.
According to Historicism, we have no right to regard *our* truths and
our values as more advanced than those of the times of the autos-da-fé;
for, in order to be able to measure the superiority or inferiority of
certain truths and values, it would be necessary to possess suprahistorical
epistemological and axiological standards. But, if all truths and all
values are daughters of history, there cannot be any suprahistorical
truths and values able to serve as standards by which to judge the

---

[1] Professor K. R. Popper makes a terminological distinction between *Historicism* and
Historism. With the word *Historicism* he designates the various philosophies claiming
to "have discovered laws of history which enable them to prophesy the course of
historical events." (K. R. Popper, *The Open Society and Its Enemies*, London, 1947,
I, p. 3, and *The Poverty of Historicism*, London, 1957, pp. 105-106). By *Historism*
he means "historical relativism" or "the historical determination of all thought" (*op.
cit.*, II, p. 242). Following the general habit in Anglo-Saxon countries, I shall use the
term *Historicism* to designate the phenomena Popper grouped under the name
Historism.

relative merits of the truths and values created in the course of history. Consequently, it becomes impossible to ascertain any progress in history.

Professor Lalande called Historicism "an equivocal term ..., to be avoided like the majority of terms of this kind which easily engender verbal discussions".[2] Richard von Mises was of the same opinion and designated Historicism as a "catchword".[3] However, these criticisms cannot hide the authentic problem represented by Historicism. It seems to me that Karl Mannheim expressed a very wise opinion when he wrote:

> Historicism is ... neither a mere fad nor a fashion; it is not even an intellectual current, but the very basis on which we construct our observations of the socio-cultural reality. It is not something artificially contrived ..., but an organically developed basic pattern, the *Weltanschauung* itself, which came into being after the religiously determined medieval picture of the world had disintegrated and when the subsequent Enlightenment, with its dominant idea of a supratemporal Reason, had destroyed itself.[4]

I do not think, therefore, that, simply by avoiding the word "Historicism", one can get rid of the anguishing problems raised by the intellectual phenomenon which carries this name.

Historicism is an antithesis; in order to understand it, one has to know the thesis which it denies; namely, natural right, and its presupposition, the concept of a human nature or a human reason considered as unchangeable, eternal, identical throughout the ages, the nations, the civilizations, the social classes.

The concept of a universal human nature and of a natural right inherent in it was one of the great creations of the classical mind of antiquity. Pioneered by Socrates, Plato, and Aristotle, natural right was, in antiquity, especially developed by the Stoics. For the pre-Socratics, right was still something purely conventional. "In God's mind" — said Heraclitus — "all things are noble, good, and just; but men have created the supposition that certain things are just and certain other things are unjust."[5]

With Socrates, Plato, and Aristotle, the notion of nature (φύσις) becomes more and more opposed to that of convention (νόμος). In his *Ethica Nicomachea*, Aristotle wrote: "Fine and just actions, which

---

[2] A. Lalande, *Vocabulaire technique et critique de la philosophie* (Paris, 1928), I, p. 304.
[3] R. von Mises, *Positivism* (Cambridge, 1951), pp. 223-225.
[4] K. Mannheim, *Essays on the Sociology of Knowledge* (London, 1952), pp. 84-85.
[5] *Frag,* 102.

political science investigates, admit of much variety and fluctuation of opinion, so that they may be thought to exist only by convention, and not by nature."[6]

Conventions are known by tradition. But nature is older than tradition. By uprooting the authority of tradition, Socrates and Plato established the authority of nature. It was the Old Stoa which gave wings to the idea of human nature. Its fundamental principle was to live according to nature — ὁμολογουμένως τῇ φύσει ζῆν. Cleanthes teaches that this nature according to which we have to live is κοινὴ φύσις, common nature, which, for Chrysippos, is human nature in particular. Moreover, the law of nature claimed by the Stoics is not a physical law but a moral law.

For the Stoic, there is only one universal reason common to all men. All are members of one body, citizens of one State. Κοινὴ πατρὶς ἀνθρώπων ἁπάντων ὁ κόσμος ἐστίν, said Musonius Rufus[7] — the common fatherland of all men is the cosmos. As citizens of the same universal State — that of mankind — subject to the same law — the law of nature or reason — all men are equal; all have the same rights: natural and rational rights.

This cosmopolitan and humanitarian ideal was especially developed by the Roman Stoics, since they were citizens of a multinational Empire. It was Seneca who proclaimed the principle *homo homini res sacra —* man is to man a sacred thing. The word *humanitas,* absent from the Greek language and literature, is a Latin word and a Roman ideal first cultivated in the circle of Scipio the younger and later propagated by Cicero, Seneca, and Marcus Aurelius.

Thanks to this human fellowship based on one and the same universal reason, all men have, according to the Stoics, the same right to be respected; and all human beings have a duty toward all to be kind and merciful — even toward their enemies. This universal reason, this eternal human nature, carrier of inalienable rights, is certainly one of the noblest heritages which the Christian and the modern worlds received from the Graeco-Roman civilization.

Since Stoicism became the dominant political philosophy of the Roman Empire, its concept of natural right also influenced Roman Law. The latter calls it *jus gentium* and characterizes it as "that which natural reason constitutes in all men" (*quod naturalis ratio apud omnes homines constituit*).[8] Later, a commentator declared that *lex est notitia naturalis*

---

[6] Aristotle, *Ethica Nicomachea,* I, 1094 b.
[7] Stobaeus, *Florilegium,* 40, 9.
[8] *Inst.* I, 2, 2.

a deo nobis insita, ad discernendum aequum ab iniquo[9] — natural law
is the knowledge implanted in us by God in order to distinguish the
just from the unjust. With this principle, the basic moral values seemed
to be removed from the arbitrariness of subjective judgments and placed
on a natural and rational foundation; for *jus naturale est illud quod ex
rerum ipsa natura adaequatum est . . .*[10] — natural right is that which
is adequate from the very nature of things. For the Stoics, nature
mingles with reason; it is rational nature or natural reason. As the
product of universal reason, natural right appears to be valid for all
men, independently of place and time. Thus, the axiological situation,
as seen from the viewpoint of natural right, is much more satisfactory
than that created by Historicism. Unfortunately, the doctrine of natural
right is open to many objections, as we shall very soon see.

In the Middle-Ages, Saint Thomas took up the ideas of the Stoics,
Saint Paul, Saint Augustine, Saint Isidore, etc., and built up the
Christian doctrine of natural right. In his *Summa Theologica*, Saint
Thomas wrote: "There is in man an inclination to things that pertain
to him more especially, according to that nature which he has in
common with other animals; and in virtue of this inclination, those
things are said to belong to the natural law which nature has taught to
all animals" (*quae natura omnia animalia docuit*).[11] The precepts of
natural law are self-evident.

Besides natural law (*lex naturalis*) which is the first rule of reason,
St. Thomas admitted human law (*lex humana*). It is only the natural
law applied to particular matters, depending on circumstances, adapted
to places, times and the customs of the different countries. "Every
human law," wrote the *Doctor angelicus*, "partakes of the nature of
law to the extent to which it is derived from the law of nature. But, if
in any point it departs from the law of nature, it will no longer be a
law but a perversion of law" (*si vero in aliquo a lege naturali discordet,
jam non erit lex, sed legis corruptio*).[12]

During the Middle-Ages, natural right was in no way problematic,
for, metaphysically, it was solidly rooted in the divine law (*lex divina*)
— the old one given to the Jews, the new one given to the Christians —
and, above all, in the eternal law. *Lex aeterna nihil aliud est, quam
ratio divinae sapientiae, secundum quod est directiva omnium actuum,*

[9] Oldendorf, *Jur. natur. gent. et civil.* (1539), II.
[10] Dom. Scoto, *De Jure et Justitia* (1594), III, 1, 2.
[11] *Divi Thomae Aquinatis. . . . Summa Theologica*, Prima Secundae Partis, Quaestio
XCIV, De Lege Naturali, Articulus II.
[12] *Ibid.,* Quaestio XCV, De Lege Humana, Articulus II.

et motionum[13] — the eternal law is nothing else but the principle of divine wisdom directing all actions and movements. In following the inclinations implanted in him by natural law, the medieval Christian was sure that he was on the right way, because, according to St. Thomas' teachings, natural law was regarded as the rational creature's participation in the eternal law.[14]

The situation changed radically when the medieval theocratic order disintegrated under the blows of the scientific discoveries of the Renaissance and under the impact of the Reformation. At that moment, the hierarchy of moral values was in danger of losing its foundation. The revival of Stoic philosophy in the seventeenth century can be explained by the fact that it offered a universal moral system, a "natural right", that all denominations and all occidental nations could accept. In this renewal of Stoicism, the ideas of human dignity and man's natural and rational rights replaced religious dogmas.

From that moment on, the doctrines of natural right developed in a world more and more freed from Christian theocracy. It was the philosophy of Englightenment which now became the great promoter of natural right. Its dominant juridical idea was the dualism of the positive law promulgated by man and the natural law which served as its standard. Thanks to the latter, the legislator could have the good conscience that he had not made unjust laws. In 1748, Montesquieu formulated these ideas in a classical manner, when writing the following in his *Esprit des Lois:*

> Laws, in the widest sense, are the necessary relations which derive from the nature of things. ... The individual intelligent beings may have laws they have made, but they have also laws they have not made. Before intelligent beings existed, they were possible. Hence, they had possible relations and, consequently, possible laws. Before there were established laws, there existed possible relations of justice. To say that nothing is just or unjust except that which is ordered or forbidden by positive laws is tantamount to saying that, before someone drew a circle, all the radii were not equal.[15]

Rarely has the cause of natural right been argued with more penetration than it was in these words of the great French thinker. What enabled Historicism to refute such theses which seem to be the very expression of reason? We shall see soon.

[13] *Ibid.*, Quaestio XCIII, De Lege Aeterna, Articulus I.
[14] *Ibid.*, Quaestio XCI, De Legum Diversitate, Articulus II.
[15] *Oeuvres de Montesquieu*, "Esprit des Lois", Tome 1, Livre 1, Chap. 1 (Paris, 1819), pp. 1 and 3.

It must be emphasized that natural right is far from representing a purely juridical problem. It is rather a problem the solution of which concerns moral philosophy, philosophy of history and of values, just as much as it does the philosophy of law. For "just" and "unjust" are values; they are moral values in the sense that right constitutes the ethical minimum. If this minimum is guaranteed by natural right, then ethics and the philosophy of values have found an absolute starting point from which they can set out in confidence. If, however, this ethical minimum cannot be guaranteed by natural right, then ethics, law and philosophy of values seem to be at the mercy of history, forced to recognize and to sanction all the values and laws history has produced, including those of the concentration camps and of Hitler's gas chambers. This would mean the total victory of Historicism.

The fact that natural right had strongest moral implications was clearly stated by Saint Thomas Aquinas who wrote: *Hoc est ergo primum praeceptum legis, quod bonum est faciendum et prosequendum, et malum vitandum; et super hoc fundantur omnia alia praecepta legis naturae*[16] — hence, this is the first precept of the law, that good is to be done and promoted, and evil is to be avoided; all other precepts of natural law are based upon this.

The French encyclopedists, likewise, recognized the moral character of natural right, and Diderot expressly identified it with ethics. In his classical article on natural right published in the *Encyclopédie*, Diderot wrote:

> Right of nature or natural right, in the widest sense, is used for certain principles that nature alone inspires and which are common to all animals as well as to men. ... More often, one understands by natural right certain rules of *justice* and *equity* which *natural reason* alone has established in all men or ... which God impressed on our hearts (*que Dieu a gravées dans nos coeurs*). ... This natural right is *perpetual* and *invariable;* it cannot be repealed by any convention, not even by any law, nor can anyone be exempted from the obligations it imposes. In this, it differs from positive right, that is, from rules which only exist because they have been established by definite laws. ... Natural right admits nothing but that which agrees with pure reason and equity. ... Consequently, this right is, properly speaking, nothing but the science of customs (*la science des moeurs*) which one calls *ethics.* ... The best treatise of ethics we have is Cicero's book *De Officiis* which contains a summary of the principles of

[16] *Divi Thomae Aquinatis ... Summa Theologica*, Quaestio XCIV, De Lege Naturali, Articulus II.

natural right. ... It tries to demonstrate that there is a natural right independent of human institution and which originates in God's will (*la volonté de Dieu*). He shows that this is the foundation of all just and sensible laws.[17]

As can be seen, the thinkers of the Enlightenment also refer to God as the source of natural right, although their God is no longer that of Aquina's theology but only a supreme law-giver stripped of all supra-rational attributes. I do not deny that this claimed divine origin of natural right was able to produce a psychological effect on certain minds; but I do not believe that it could contribute anything to its logical validity. If natural right is valid, it is so by virtue of its agreement with the principles of nature and reason. If it is revealed as invalid, then its claimed divine origin cannot save it from disappearance. Rationality is in itself a source of validity. Two mathematicians, one of whom believes in the divine origin of reason which the other denies will, nevertheless, arrive at the same conclusions, as soon as they begin to calculate and, thus, put their reason to the test. If natural right is rational, the same will happen with two jurists — whether or not they believe in the divine origin of that right. Moreover, Hugo Grotius, one of the greatest masters of natural law, declared in 1646: *Est autem jus naturale adeo immutabile, ut ne a Deo quidem mutari queat*[18] — natural right is so unalterable that it cannot be changed even by God himself.

Later on, we shall see, however, that the most authentic representatives of the school of natural right come to conclusions absolutely incompatible with one another, in spite of their common claim of the divine origin of their science.

Natural right reached its climax in the American and French revolutions. In 1776, the "thirteen United States of America" adopted the "Declaration of Independence", in which the right of the American people to an existence independent of its former political bonds with the British crown was explicitly derived from "the Laws of Nature". From these laws all the "self-evident" truths are derived which form the basis of the American constitution. Natural right is, thus, the foundation of the political existence of the American nation.

The same can be said of the human rights proclaimed by the French Revolution. They are, also, based on natural law. Article II of the French Declaration of Human Rights reads: *"Le but de toute association*

---

[17] *Encyclopédie ou Dictionnaire raisonné des Sciences, des Arts et des Métiers,* Mise en ordre et publiée par M. Diderot ... et, quant à la partie mathématique, par M. d'Alembert (Paris, 1750), pp. 131, 132.
[18] Hugonis Grotii *De Jure Belli ac Pacis* (Amsterdam, 1646), Lib. I, X, p. 4.

politique est la conservation des droits naturels et imprescriptibles de l'homme. Ces droits sont: la liberté, la propriété, la sûreté et la résistance à l'oppression ..." — the aim of all political association is the conservation of the natural and imprescriptible rights of man. These rights are: liberty, property, security and resistance to oppression.

In Germany, Kant applied the doctrine of natural right in his philosophy of law, and his two critiques are based on the supra-temporal and unchangeable character of reason. In his book, *Der Streit der Fakultäten,* Kant declared that the enthusiasm with which the Europeans had welcomed the French revolution proved "a moral disposition of mankind".[19] It was not without good reason that Marx considered Kant's practical philosophy as "the German theory of the French Revolution".[20] Young Fichte also defended the French Revolution in the name of natural right in his *Beitrag zur Berichtigung der Urteile des Publikums über die französische Revolution* and, also, in his *Zurückforderung der Denkfreiheit von den Fürsten Europas,* etc.[21]

However, after the climax of the French Revolution came the anticlimax of the Prussian reaction and of German Romanticism. These two movements gave the doctrine of natural rights a deadly blow and prepared the way for Historicism. In this struggle, the so-called "historical school of right" was the phalanx of the attacking army. The enemy was the philosophy of Enlightenment, the patron of natural right and mother of the French revolution.

During the Napoleonic wars and after the defeat of the great conqueror, Europe, and especially Germany, wanted to free themselves from the last vestiges of the French revolution by attacking Rationalism. The latter had proclaimed the identity of man throughout the ages and the nations and his rational unchangeable rights, identifying the rational with the natural. But man, the citizen, the people, the eternal rights were all abstractions detached from concrete reality. Opposed to the worship of reason, Johann Gottfried Herder, one of the first Historicists, glorified rather the popular instinct, the unconscious activity of the national spirit of the different nations, especially manifested in primitive poetry (*Urpoesie*).

According to this new romantic philosophy, the instinctive wisdom of the national collectivities was regarded as a safer guide than reason. In contrast to the rationalistic principle *homo intelligendo fit omnia*

---

[19] I. Kant, *Der Streit der Fakultäten* (1798), 2. Abschnitt, par. 6.
[20] K. Vorländer, *Kant und Marx* (Tübingen, 1911), p. 41.
[21] See A. Stern, "Fichte y la revolución francesa", *Cuadernos Americanos,* Mexico, 2, Marzo-Abril 1944, pp. 109-133.

— by understanding man becomes everything — the new romantic irrationalism advocated the principle *homo non intelligendo fit omnia* — by not understanding man becomes everything. The modern historian, Friedrich Meinecke, a great champion of Historicism, speaks with enthusiasm of what he calls man's "creative unreason" (*schöpferische Unvernunft*).[22]

It should, however, be emphasized that, in spite of his worship of the irrational, Herder did not abandon the humanistic ideals of the Stoics and of the philosophy of Enlightenment. For he still regarded mankind as an immense organism and rejected the term "human races" as "ignoble".[23] Many of the later Historicists abandoned this humanistic heritage.

Historicism reproached the Rationalism of the French revolution and the whole Enlightenment mainly with being indifferent to history. In insisting on that which is common to all men — reason — Rationalism had neglected that in which men differ from each other — namely, all those occult and irrational forces which determine the specific personality of each nation and which are manifested in its history. In Historicism, the common rational features of mankind, supposed to be eternal, were superseded by those irrational vital forces which are characteristic of each nation and are the product of a slow historical evolution, of an organic growth in the soil of tradition.

In taking up the ideas of Stoicism, the philosophy of the Enlightenment had believed in an unchangeable rational human nature. Thinking and evaluating rationally, the man of the philosophy of Enlightenment is a man of no particular time and place. Historical rights and religions were considered by the philosophy of the Enlightenment as historical deformations of a natural right and natural religion, veiled by time and place. But this is tantamount to saying that true human nature is not historical and that historical human phenomena are only deformations of man. The new historical consciousness of the late eighteenth and early nineteenth century reacted vigorously against that idea.

Some time before that period, Montesquieu had remarked that he had seen Italians, Frenchmen, Spaniards, etc., but that he had never met the extra-temporal man himself. It was, however, on the claimed existence of the latter that Montesquieu himself built the thesis of natural right. As the jurist Adam Jellinek remarked, the primitive man of natural right had already a completely developed reason. But some time

---

[22] F. Meinecke, *Die Entstehung des Historismus* (München, 1936), I, p. 65.
[23] J. G. Herder, *Ideen zur Philosophie der Geschichte der Menschheit*, 4. B., V, p. 164.

before the downfall of the idols of the Enlightenment, Vico had already suspected that primitive man had been quite different from the rational man of the Renaissance, a conjecture which was confirmed by Father Lafiteau's book *Moeurs des sauvages américains, comparées aux moeurs des premiers temps,* published in 1724. However, for a long time nobody drew the logical inferences from these new anthropological and ethnological data. David Hume recognized in his *Natural History of Religions* that religion was not the child of a *lumen naturale,* the natural light of reason, but rather the expression of the irrational anxiety of primitive man, and that ignorance was the mother of devotion. Nevertheless, Hume maintained the thesis of an invarible human nature. In his *Inquiry concerning the Human Understanding* he wrote for example:

> It is universally acknowledged that there is a great uniformity among the actions of men, in all nations and ages, and that human nature remains still the same in its principles and operations. . . . Would you know the sentiments, inclinations and course of life of the Greeks and Romans? Study well the temper and actions of the French and English: you cannot be much mistaken in transferring to the former most of the observations which you have made with regard to the latter.[24]

Historicism does not conceive of historiography in that way. Instead of insisting on superficial analogies between nations, it tries to capture what is specific in each nation, in each civilization, in each epoch, what distinguishes each of these entities from all the others. Only the nineteenth century was to draw all the conclusions from the new ethnological and anthropological acquisitions by freeing itself from the concept of "human nature". Hegel declared straight out: *"Das Individuum ist ein solches, das da ist, nicht ein Mensch überhaupt, denn der existiert nicht, sondern ein bestimmter"*[25] — the individual is someone that *is* (in a particular time and place), not a man in general, for such a one does not exist, but a particular man. The historical school of Niebuhr, Savigny, Bopp, Böckh, Grimm and Ranke completely eliminated the concept of human nature. What now appears to be man's "substance" is the variable, that which changes in the course of history. Here, we are confronted with a new kind of Heraclitean revolution against the Eleaticism of the Rationalists with their stable eternal concepts.

[24] D. Hume, *An Inquiry concerning the Human Understanding,* Section III, Part I, pp. 94-95.
[25] G. W. F. Hegel, *Vorlesungen über die Philosophie der Geschichte,* ed. Glockner (Stuttgart, 1928), p. 52.

Interpreting the ideas of the historical school which, in part, were his own, Ortega y Gasset wrote: *"El hombre, según esto, no tiene una 'naturaleza', sino una historia. Su ser es innumerable y multiforme: en cada tiempo, en cada lugar, es otro"*[26] — man has no "nature", but he has a history. His being is unnumerable and multiform: at every epoch, in each place he is different. With these basic ideas, the task of the historical school becomes clear: to describe the rich variety of historical appearances, each in terms of that which is individual and incomparable in it.

But, if there is no human nature invariable throughout ages and nations, then natural right has lost its ontological foundation. This fact became evident when in 1814 Friedrich Carl von Savigny, a German jurist of French origin, published his book *Vom Berufe unserer Zeit für Gesetzgebung und Rechtswissenschaft* — on the mission of our time (i.e., his time) for legislation and jurisprudence. Savigny was opposed to the establishment of juridical codes which, "neglecting all historical peculiarities, were supposed to be valid, in pure abstraction, for all nations and all times".[27] Savigny concluded by saying:

> The historical sense is the only protection against a kind of self-deception which is repeated again and again in single individuals as well as in whole nations and ages and which consists in regarding as generally human all which is particular to us. Formerly, by omitting certain conspicuous peculiarities in institutions, one had established a *natural right* which was considered to be an immediate expression of reason. Today there is nobody who would not commiserate with such a procedure. Yet, every day, we see people who regard their juridical concepts and opinions as purely rational, because they do not know their origin. Once we are unaware of our individual connection with the totality of the world and its history, we must necessarily see our ideas in the false light of generality and originality (*Ursprünglichkeit*). We are only protected against this by the historical sense, whose most difficult application is the one which is directed towards ourselves.[28]

Here is a conclusion whose cogency can hardly be denied. A similar inference was used a century later by Lucien Lévy-Bruhl, when he showed, in his *La morale et la science des moeurs*, that the collective

---

[26] J. Ortega y Gasset, *Obras completas* (Madrid, 1952), tomo VI, p. 181.
[27] F. C. von Savigny, *Vom Berufe unserer Zeit für Gesetzgebung und Rechtswissenschaft* (Heidelberg, 1814), p. 5.
[28] *Ibid.*, p. 115.

moral feelings which impose themselves simply in the name of "conscience" are those whose origins we do not know.

Having eliminated natural right as a juridical source, Savigny thought that right had developed organically, like languages and customs, and that it was basically unwritten law, sanctioned by usage, which did not need to be codified. Like language, this right grows with a specific nation and dies when this nation loses its peculiar character. Right is "the common consciousness (*Bewusstsein*) of the people".[29] When nations are young, their right lives and develops in their bosom without being codified, because, under these conditions, language and logic are not yet refined enough. According to Savigny, Roman right has developed as unwritten law sanctioned by usage. When, in the sixth century, Roman intellectual life had ceased to exist, Roman right was codified to save "the debris of better times".[30]

Savigny pleads the cause of a juridical pluralism and sets against natural right not only a multiplicity of national rights but even of regional rights. "It is an error to believe that the general cause will gain more life by the annihiliation of all individual conditions. If one could create . . . a specific self-reliance in each profession, in each town, the whole would gain new strength, thanks to that increased and multiplied individual life."[31]

It is interesting to note that this juridical regionalism was not at all limited to Germany. The contemporary Spanish philosopher of law, José Corts Grau, reveals the parallelism between German and Spanish juridical Historicism. In his interesting *Filosofía del Derecho*, Professor Corts-Grau, who teaches at the University of Valencia, writes:

> That juridical regionalism reminds us in Spain of the figures of the great Aragonese and Catalan jurisconsults, their enthusiasm for customs and municipal laws (*los fueros*), their resistance to legislative unity, on a par with their aversion to political centralism, besides other characteristics peculiar to Spanish juridical Historicism.[32]

In the lives of all great nations, says Savigny, we find an evolution from fresh lively individualities toward vague generalities. Also, civil law follows this path and, finally, loses its specific national character. As time goes on, all peculiarities of national rights are worn away, and, finally, the old nations arrive at the false conclusion that the exhausted

[29] *Ibid.*, p. 11.
[30] *Ibid.*, p. 34.
[31] *Ibid.*, p. 42.
[32] J. Corts-Grau, *Filosofía del Derecho* (Madrid, 1948), I, p. 110.

residue of their right is the *jus quod naturalis ratio apud omnes homines constituit*. Thus natural right would appear to be an error in the perspective of old nations.

To be sure, Savigny was a reactionary, full of hatred for the French revolution which he designated a curse (*Fluch*). Moreover, he was strongly influenced by Romantic irrationalism. But all that did not prevent him from revealing certain weaknesses in the doctrine of natural right.

In our day, those who reject the doctrine of natural right are no longer the reactionaries but, rather, the liberals, while certain reactionary groups make an effort to revive it. With this development, the struggle against the doctrine of natural right and its ontological presupposition, namely unchangeable reason, loses the irrational character it had with the Romantics, with the historical school and, especially, with Savigny. Modern liberal Historicism no longer rejects reason but only unchangeable reason. In fact, Historicism is compatible with the concept of a variable reason in full historical development, always producing new categories.

Of the contemporary thinkers it was Hans Kelsen, the brilliant representative of the Viennese school, a Liberal and a Positivist, who laid bare the chimerical character of natural right with the greatest penetration. He did it by insisting on the impossibility of inferring that which ought to be from that which is. He also showed that, while referring to natural law, each of the great jurists of the past "demonstrated" as "natural" and "rational" whatever he wished — either the ideals of reaction or those of progress.

What characterizes the doctrine of natural right logically is its perpetual confusion between natural laws, on the one hand, and moral and juridical laws, on the other hand. A natural law states that if there is A there is B, while a moral or a juridical law states that if there is A there ought to be B. This means that natural laws are descriptive, while moral and juridical laws are normative. But a normative proposition can never be deduced from a descriptive one.

In order to be able to designate conduct as "good" or "of positive value" or as "bad" or "of negative value", we must presuppose a norm with which this conduct is in agreement or in disagreement. If conduct is in agreement with the norm, it will be said to be "good" or "of positive value"; if it is in disagreement with the norm, the conduct will be "bad" or "of negative value". Since the norm presupposed does not describe what is but decrees what ought to be, its grammatical mood is the imperative, while the statements describing nature are all in the indicative mood. Now, Henri Poincaré showed us the logical impossibility of arriving at an imperative when starting with an indicative. In his essay, "La morale et la science", he wrote:

> If the premises of a syllogism are both in the indicative, the conclusion will also be in the indicative mood. In order to have a conclusion in the imperative, it would be necessary that at least one of the premises itself be in the imperative. Now, the principles of science and the postulates of geometry are and can only be in the indicative, and this is true also of all experimental propositions; on the basis of science, there is and there cannot be anything else. Thus, the most subtle dialectician may juggle with his principles as much as he wants . . . ; all the conclusions he will draw from them will be in the indicative mood. He will never obtain a proposition which says: Do this, do not do that; that is to say, a proposition which would confirm or contradict ethics.[33]

I believe that this demonstration of the great French mathematician not only condemns in advance any attempt to draw a system of ethics from science but, also, reveals the impossibility of a natural right; for what the latter tries to do is to draw imperatives or norms from natural facts which are all conceived in the indicative.

We have seen that the positive or negative value of any form of conduct or of any principle can be defined as their agreement or disagreement with a postulated norm. Now, according to the doctrine of natural right, this norm is presupposed to be inherent either in nature or in reason. Only upon this condition can the thesis be upheld that moral and juridical laws derive from nature or from reason and that they express absolute justice.

In a book published a few years ago in Vienna, *Was ist Gerechtigkeit?*, Professor Kelsen rejects these two presuppositions of the doctrine of natural right in such a conclusive way that it is worthwhile to translating a few sentences of his final judgment, for the latter is tantamount to a death-warrant for natural right:

> As a system of facts, nature has no will, and, therefore, it cannot prescribe a definite kind of human conduct. Starting from facts, that is from that which actually is or happens, one cannot infer what ought to be or to happen. To the extent that the rational theory of natural right tries to derive norms for human conduct from nature, it is based on a fallacy. The same holds for the attempt to deduce such norms from human reason. Norms which prescribe human conduct

---

[33] H. Poincaré, *Dernières Pensées* (Paris, 1913), p. 225.

can only originate in the *will*. And this will can only be a human will, if we exclude metaphysical speculations. ... Human reason can understand and describe; it cannot prescribe. The belief that one can find norms for human conduct in reason is the same illusion as the belief that one can draw such norms from nature.[34]

Perhaps one could assert by way of argument against Professor Kelsen that there are logical norms, the importance of which has been emphasized by Professor Lalande's lucid book, *La raison et les normes*. It seems obvious to me, however, that even the logical norms imply an act of will — that of attaining truth. Only if I want to attain truth, do I have to follow the rules of the syllogism. But, even if we assume that everybody wants to attain truth — although Nietzsche asked "why not rather lies, incertitude and even ignorance?"[35] — that does not lead us far: for logical truth is purely formal, and the conclusions of syllogisms depend on the choice of the premises. And this choice is made by an act of will. All of this brings us back again to Kelsen's thesis that reason cannot prescribe and that will alone can do so.

But, if this is the case, we must ask ourselves how the greatest jurists of all times could, apparently, draw norms from reason. The answer is that the norms ostensibly deduced from reason or nature were, in reality, tacitly presupposed by those jurists, in the form of the chosen premises. *Post festum,* they projected them into reason or nature. All the norms men like Hobbes, Rousseau, Locke, Grotius or Pufendorf pretended to have found in nature or reason sprang from their own will or from that of their employers. The principles of natural reason they declared to have discovered were only their own subjective evaluations presented as intentions of legislative nature or as dictated by timeless reason. If, in spite of the logical rigor of their inferences, these thinkers arrived at such different conclusions so utterly incompatible with one another, it was because, in spite of themselves, they had chosen different premises. As Professor Lalande says, *"le discours ne crée rien par lui-même; il n'est qu'un moyen de transport, un canal conduisant ailleurs l'eau d'une source"*[36] — discourse does not create anything by itself; it is only a means of transportation, a canal which carries the water of a source to another place. This source, we may add, is either will or intuition.

Those among us who cherish the ideals of the American and French revolutions may perhaps regret the dissolution of natural law in a fog

---

[34] H. Kelsen, *Was ist Gerechtigkeit?* (Wien, 1953), p. 38.
[35] Nietzsche, *Gesammelte Werke* (München, 1925), Band XV, I, p. 7.
[36] A. Lalande, *La raison et les normes* (Paris, 1948), p. 123.

of error; for we remember that the principles of these great liberating movements were derived from the "natural and imprescriptible rights" of nations. However, Professor Kelsen showed that, in the course of history, natural right served much more often as a theoretical basis for the strengthening of authoritarian governments against the people than for protecting the people against tyrannical governments. To the question "whose reason it is that shall be accepted as law" Thomas Hobbes answered that it is only the reason of the authoritarian state represented by the prince.[37] For Pufendorf, it was a "seditious opinion" to believe that individual reason could decide what is good or evil, advantageous or disadvantageous for the state.[38] In discussing the question as to whether a tyrant may be brought to order by the people, Pufendorf declared bluntly: "The presumption of justice stands always on the side of the prince."[39]

Although, in Hobbes' interpretation of natural law, the authoritarian state can never be wrong with respect to the citizen, Grotius admits this possibility, but he recommends, by virtue of natural reason, that the citizen ought to endure unjust treatment inflicted upon him by the sovereign state rather than to resist by force. Also Kant declares, by virtue of natural right, that "resistance on the part of the people to the supreme legislative power of the state is in no case legitimate" and that such a resistance is especially reprehensible when "the supreme legislative power is embodied in an individual monarch".[40]

Interpreted in this manner, the so-called "natural" law offers, of course, not the slightest protection to the citizen against the tyranny of the state or the prince. But this was the ordinary interpretation, since the majority of the great jurists of the seventeenth and eighteenth centuries were, in one way or another, in the service of the princes and their authoritarian states.

As for Kant, he was divided between his official duty as a Royal Prussian Government official and his private friendly feelings towards the American and French revolutions. As an official, "natural reason" dictated to him the duty to condemn as illegal any attempt of the people to resist royal tyranny. As a citizen of his age of Enlightenment, "natural reason", however, impelled him to admit the legitimacy of a government which resulted from revolutionary action. Thus, Kant wrote in 1795:

---

[37] Hobbes, *Leviathan*, Pars II, Cap. XXVI.
[38] Pufendorf, *De Jure Naturae et Gentium*, Lib. VIII, Cap. I, Sec. 5.
[39] Pufendorf, *Elementa Jurisprudentiae Universalis*, V, par. 21.
[40] I. Kant, *Gesammelte Schriften*, Band VI, "Die Metaphysik der Sitten", p. 320.

> If, by the violence of a revolution provoked by a bad Constitution, a new juster Constitution were established by illegal means, it must no longer be considered permissible to lead the people back to the previous form of government, although everybody who participated in the revolution by acts of violence or perfidy would, legitimately, be liable to punishment for rebellion.[41]

The examples given make it obvious that the right called "natural" or "rational" only reflects the subjective evaluations of its servants or those of their employers. The consequence is, as Professor Kelsen says, that "there is not one natural-law doctrine but many, advocating quite contradictory principles".[42] According to Hobbes, natural reason teaches that governmental power established in conformity with natural reason is unlimited, "absolute" and "indivisible". According to the "natural" right filtered through the brain of a partisan of absolute monarchy, the sovereignty of the state implies "the absolute use of the sword in peace and war" and "the making and abrogating of laws".[43]

But from the same "natural reason", the Liberal John Locke infers that "the supreme power in every commonwealth ... is not, nor can possibly be, absolutely arbitrary over the lives and fortunes of the people ... for nobody can transfer to another more power than he has in himself, and nobody has an absolute arbitrary power over himself, or over any other, to destroy his own life, or to take away the life or property of another."[44] While natural reason taught Grotius that a nation can renounce its liberty in favour of a king, this same natural reason taught Rousseau that "to renounce liberty is to renounce being a man, to surrender the rights of humanity and even its duties".[45] And, insisting on man's natural imprescriptible rights, young Fichte asked the princes: "Do you believe that men can be inherited like herds of cattle?"[46]

To the Liberal Locke, natural right gives evidence that absolute monarchy is inconsistent with civil society[47] and that only democracy is natural. But to the Conservative Sir Robert Filmer, this same natural

[41] *Immanuel Kant's Sämmtliche Werke* (Leipzig, 1870), "Zum ewigen Frieden", Anhang I, 2. Abschnitt, p. 188.

[42] H. Kelsen, *What Is Justice?* (Berkeley and Los Angeles, 1957), "The Natural-Law Doctrine Before The Tribunal Of Science", p. 151.

[43] Th. Hobbes, *The Elements Of Law*, pp. 87ff.

[44] J. Locke, *Second Treatise Of Civil Government*, Chap. XI, par. 135.

[45] *Oeuvres complètes de Rousseau* (Paris, 1828), "Du contrat social", tome 2, Livre I, chap. IV, p. 122.

[46] J. G. Fichte, *Zurückforderung der Denkfreiheit von den Fürsten* (1793), p. 27.

[47] J. Locke, *op. cit.*, chap. VII, par. 90.

right reveals that it is unnatural for the people to govern or to choose governors. Natural law teaches him, on the contrary, that "God did always govern his own people by monarchy only".[48]

If, more recently, a certain revival of natural right is to be noticed in the conservative circles of some countries, it is because these groups have rediscovered in natural right a means to defend the right of property against Communist threats. Indeed, the majority of the theorists in the seventeenth and eighteenth centuries — from Grotius to Kant — considered private property a natural right. However, Professor Kelsen calls our attention to the *Code de la Nature ou Le véritable Esprit de ses Lois,* published in Paris in 1755, which tries to demonstrate that private property is "against the reason of nature". The world is a table sufficiently provided for all those who are hungry. They are the rightful owners of the dishes. In the name of nature and reason, we must abolish "that monster, the spirit of property",[49] said the *Code.*

This *Code of Nature* ..., originally attributed to Diderot and published by Morelly, was the great book of socialism in the eighteenth century, and Babeuf, the Communist die-hard of the French Revolution, often referred to it. No wonder that in 1940 it appeared in a Russian translation.

All these facts show clearly that natural right is a rather plastic thing, taking all the forms its users want to give it. Having served the cause of reaction much more often than that of progress, the abandonment of the doctrine of natural right does not constitute too harsh a loss for the liberal cause.

Furthermore, if the rights of man cannot be derived from nature or from reason, nothing prevents us from considering them as positive intrinsic values, as ideals, and from proclaiming them as moral and juridical norms. It is in this spirit that the Fifth French Republic maintains the *Droits de l'homme et du citoyen,* as the Fourth one had maintained them. More than that: By virtue of an act of reasoned collective will, these human rights can be promulgated as a positive international law. Without referring to a special source, be it God, nature or reason, the *Charter of the United Nations* reaffirmed, in 1946, its "faith in fundamental human rights, in the dignity and worth of the human person, in the equal rights of men and women and of nations large and small".[50]

Two years later, the General Assembly of the United Nations pro-

---

[48] Sir Robert Filmer, *Patriarcha,* chap. II, par. 10.
[49] *Code de la Nature ou Le véritable Esprit de ses Lois* (Paris, 1910), p. 84.
[50] *Charter of The United Nations* (New York, 1946), p. 2.

mulgated, in a more formal way, the principle of human rights "as a common standard of achievement for all peoples and all nations . . ."[51] In its thirty articles, this *Universal Declaration of Human Rights* became a positive international law, binding for all subscribing nations. It only constitutes, however, a juridical norm established by an act of collective will at a given moment in history, like any other positive law, and does not constitute an eternal law inferred from nature or reason; for such a law does not exist. But this does not prevent all civilized beings from cherishing this law as one of the highest achievements of human society. "Rights are cultural, not natural", as Professor Herbert W. Schneider says.

The doctrine of natural law having been eliminated, the way is open to an unrestrained Historicism. This is not a pleasant situation, but we must face it. Whoever engages in a search for truth has to accept the results of his investigations, wherever they may lead. This is a principle which Professor Leo Strauss, author of the book *Natural Right and History*, apparently does not want to accept. In this book, published some years ago in England and in the United States, Dr. Strauss made a vain attempt to save the doctrine of natural right, by insisting on its absolute necessity for society. "The problem posed by the conflicting needs of society cannot be solved, if we do not possess knowledge of natural right"[52] — he says. However, as we have tried to show, we never possessed such a knowledge but only the illusion of a knowledge of natural right. It was on this illusion that the solution of certain problems of society was based. Should one prefer a useful error to detrimental truth? "The rejection of natural right is bound to lead to disastrous consequences,"[53] declares Professor Strauss. But this is, again, a pragmatic argument which can hardly prevail against a theoretically irremediable situation. The same holds for Strauss' cry of despair, "the contemporary rejection of natural right leads to nihilism — nay, it is identical with nihilism."[54]

In order to rescue natural right, Dr. Strauss refuses no alliance not even one with theology. Max Weber, one of the many opponents of the theory of natural right, had said that only a divine revelation could confer an objective and absolute validity on human norms. But he did not believe in such a revelation. Strauss picked up this piece of straw

---

[51] "The Universal Declaration of Human Rights", adopted in 1948, *Documents on International Affairs*, pp. 855-861 (Oxford, 1952).
[52] L. Strauss, *Natural Right and History* (Chicago, 1953), p. 3.
[53] *Ibid.*, p. 3.
[54] *Ibid.*, p. 5.

which had fallen from Weber's hands and declared: "Philosophy has to grant that revelation is possible."[55] Having chosen the domain of pure theory, we cannot follow Professor Strauss into that of faith.

Since we have no longer the illusion of being able to use the natural-law doctrine as a shield against Historicism, we have now to examine all the implications of the latter. For this purpose an analysis of Hegel's position will prove revealing. We have already quoted the sentence from his *Lessons on Philosophy of History* where he says: "The individual is someone that is (in a particular time and place) not a man in general, for that one does not exist, but a particular man."[56] If man in general, the universal man of the Stoics and of the philosophy of Enlightenment, does not exist, then there is no man able to embody universal reason, no man whose ideas are of timeless supra-historical validity. All that exists is historical man, a child of his epoch who thinks the ideas of his epoch, even when philosophizing. Hegel drew this logical consequence by declaring in a famous passage of his *Philosophy of Law:*

> As for the individual, each is inevitably a *son of his time.* Consequently, philosophy is, likewise, its time apprehended in thoughts. It is just as foolish (*töricht*) to imagine that any philosophy transcends its present world, as it is to believe that an individual jumps out of his time. . . .[57]

If each individual is a son of his time, if all philosophy is only its time expressed in thoughts, it becomes obvious that no philosopher can ever attain or lay claim to absolute truth. Philosophy's absolute truth would then encompass the whole evolution of the spirit in time; that is, its whole history. If a philosopher were to claim to have reached absolute truth, he would, implicitly, be claiming to have accomplished, as a single individual, what only the whole human species can achieve in its progressive evolution from its beginnings to the end of its history.

But, after having recognized these implications, Hegel, nevertheless, laid claim to the absolute truth of his own philosophy, by ascribing an absolute character to his time. He regarded his time as the end of history and, therefore, as an absolute moment. In this way, Hegel tried to escape Historicism — at least with respect to his own philosophy.

Today, we know that Hegel's epoch hardly constituted the end of history. The hundred thirty years which have elapsed since his death have been filled with more history than any other epoch. Moreover,

---

[55] *Ibid.*, p. 75.
[56] G. W. F. Hegel, *Sämtliche Werke, edit. Glockner* (Stuttgart, 1928), Band XI, p. 52.
[57] *Ibid.*, Band VII, p. 35.

who among us would be presumptuous enough to claim that he lives in a privileged epoch, in a supra-temporal time so to speak?

It was not only by affirming the absolute character of his time and his philosophy that Hegel tried to escape the historical relativism resulting from his thesis: all philosophy, i.e. all knowledge, is only its time apprehended in thoughts. He also tried to secure the extra-historical character of moral values. Here is what he said about this subject:

> This inner focus, this simple region of the right to subjective freedom, the seat of will, decision and action, the abstract content of conscience, that wherein guilt and worth of the individual are enclosed — all this remains untouched and . . . completely withdrawn from the noisy din of world history. . . .[58]

But, if, in this way, Hegel withdrew morality from history, he, on the other hand, withdrew history from morality by declaring that world history is above ethics and beyond the reach of moral judgment. The ironical passage is well known in which Hegel castigates the "schoolmasters" who consider themselves morally superior to Alexander the Great, because they did not conquer Asia nor vanquish Darius and Porus. Hegel concluded by saying:

> World history moves on a *higher plane* than that proper to *morality;* the latter includes private convictions, individual conscience, particular will and mode of action. . . . What the final aim of the Spirit in itself demands and achieves, what Providence is doing, all this is *above* the obligations, responsibilities and liabilities which are incumbent on the individuals in regard to their ethics. . . . Thus, the deeds of the great men who are the individuals of world history . . . appear justified. . . .[59]

Carrying out the will of the World Spirit and contributing thus to the necessary progress, to the evolution of the absolute Idea, the great men of history are, according to Hegel, above morality. He even makes fun of those who measure such men by moral standards. Beside Kierkegaard's famous "theological suspension of ethics" Hegel places what may be called *an historical suspension of ethics.*

But, by denying that morality can judge history, Hegel elevated history to the rank of a unique judge of everything which goes on outside the strictly private spheres. With this, he drastically opened all the doors of Historicism.

[58] *Ibid.*, Band XI, p. 68.
[59] *Ibid.*, Band XI, p. 105.

If, in Herder, all cultural and social realities had appeared to be conditioned by their times and their surroundings and, therefore, justified at their historical locus, this idea was to find its metaphysical foundation in Hegel's philosophy. Since, according to the latter, history is the unfolding of universal Reason in time, it follows that "what is reasonable is real; and what is real is reasonable"[60] and that "the real world is as it ought to be."[61] Here lies the justification and even the consecration of all that history has brought forth and a warning to would-be-revolutionaries bold enough to want to change that world which God or History created so "perfectly". What is real is rationally necessary, and, therefore, it does not need any further justification, be it a moral one or any other.

Drawing his inspiration from Hegel, Benedetto Croce thought that medieval tyrants, in crushing basic liberties, were true to their age and in a real sense "liberal". So was the Inquisition, defending a great and necessary institution that was fulfilling the ends of civilization. It is well known that Croce was a modern Liberal and that the judgments just quoted did not express his personal political inclinations. But, representing Hegelian Historicism, he thought that every event was justified by its historical reality which, in its turn, was an expression of logical necessity. For Croce, nothing in history was accidental; to him, as to Hegel, that which had become real was always reasonable. Furthermore, considering historiography as a strictly theoretical activity, Croce wanted to guard it against the value judgments of the historians. "The writing of history", he said, "is simply a logical judgment of the only true kind; it is the bringing of the individual into the universal, the intuition into the category. It, therefore, excludes the intrusion of 'judgments of values' in the proper Herbartian sense, according to which they are extra-logical appendages (*Zusätze*) turning out on analysis to be nothing but expressions of emotion with practical motives."[62]

Interpreting the philosophy of history of his compatriot Croce, Professor Felice Battaglia wrote the following lines, characteristic of Hegelian Historicism:

> The fatal monsters are fatal for the moral reflexion which deplores them ...; for history, which contemplates them, they are only the expression of a logical evolution which, starting from them, moves towards new achievements, profiting even from the slaughters and destructions which cause

[60] *Ibid.*, Band VII, p. 33.
[61] *Ibid.*, Band XI, p. 67.
[62] B. Croce, *My Philosophy* (London, 1949), p. 176.

> the germination of the elements of civilization. ... All this
> brings the true historian, that is to say the pure observer and
> impartial contemplator ... to the conclusion that in history
> there is neither good nor evil. ... In short, Croce says that
> historical thought simply consists in recapturing theoretically
> the necessity of the accomplished fact. ...[63]

In my opinion, Hegel's dictum that "universal history ... is the universal tribunal"[64] is the keystone of Historicism. If there is no extra-
historical authority above history, then history is the supreme judge
of all truths and all values. We see, indeed, with what sovereignty
history condemns to oblivion the truths and values it has produced.
It is Chronos devouring his children. Ernst Troeltsch is quite right when
he declares that neither metaphysics nor the natural sciences are the
true solvent forces of the great religions. These forces are constituted
by history and the relativistic criticism it entails.[65] I think that this
observation of the famous Protestant theologian also illustrates the
drama of conscience of the former Catholic theologian Ernest Renan.

We have seen that, with Hegel and Croce, Historicism results in a
complete amoralism, in the cult of success, in an idolatry of the accomplished fact. According to Hegel, philosophy does not speculate about
anything which is not real. Only that which is real is reasonable.
"Philosophy has nothing to do with an entity so powerless that it had
not the strength to push itself into existence,"[66] he said. In this way,
the Idealist Hegel became the father of that kind of practical Realism
which respects everything that had the strength to become an historical
reality and a success, without any consideration of its moral merits.
This attitude was imitated by the numerous collaborators with the
enemy in all the countries occupied by Hitler during World War II.
Since Nazi Germany had had the strength to impose its domination,
those disciples of Hegel accepted and respected her, without discussing
her right.

Young Nietzsche was one of the first thinkers to oppose vigorously
this idolatry of success and to fight Hegelian Historicism in the name
of morality.

> If every success carries within itself a necessity of reason, if
> every event is a victory of logic or of the idea, let us kneel
> down quickly and hurry kneeling through the whole scale

[63] F. Battaglia, *La valeur dans l'histoire* (Paris, 1955), pp. 76-80.
[64] G. W. F. Hegel, *Sämtliche Werke*, Band VII, p. 446.
[65] E. Troeltsch, *Der Historismus und seine Probleme* (Tübingen, 1922), I, pp. 164-165.
[66] G. W. F. Hegel, *Der Begriff der Religion*, p. 73.

of successes. . . . History always teaches: "it once happened", but ethics says: "you ought not!" or "you should not have". Thus, history becomes an epitome of factual immorality.[67]

Nietzsche was certainly right when he opposed those who consider success as a victory of reason and who regard the accomplished fact as the expression of a logic inherent in history. These are, however, not necessary features of Historicism in general but only of the Historicism of Hegelian metaphysics, which interprets history as a self-revelation of absolute reason, as a kind of logic in action. But the majority of modern Historicists no longer share this metaphysical presupposition of Hegel's and, therefore, no longer regard the accomplished fact as a triumph of reason. They do not extol the rationality of the event. They simply accept it, whether it is reasonable or not.

But Nietzsche's criticism of Hegel's Historicism also has a positive side: it tries to encourage "the great fighters against history", who swim against the latter's current, contrasting their "it should be otherwise!" with the fatalistic "so it is" of history. A similar attitude is adopted by Ernst Cassirer, when he writes: "The great thinkers of the past were not only 'their own times apprehended in thought'. Very often, they had to think beyond and against their times."[68]

This is certainly true, and it is the very condition of any progress of mankind. In his great novel *Clerambault*, Romain Rolland made a moving appeal in favor of the solitary thinkers who are opposed to the currents of their epochs. *"Osez vous détacher du troupeau qui vous entraîne!"* he exclaimed — dare to detach yourselves from the herd which carries you away. And he continued:

> Every man who is a true man should learn how to remain alone in the midst of all and, if necessary, against all. To think sincerely, even if it is *against all,* still means to think *for all.* Mankind demands that those who love it, resist it and revolt against it, when it is necessary.[69]

Nevertheless, in my opinion, it would be erroneous to conclude that those, who, in a given epoch, think against the currents of their time, also think against history and escape its ascendancy. For the solitary thinker who opposes the currents of his time does not rise in an historical vacuum. He rises in an historical world, in a definite civilization and at a certain historical moment, when certain theses have

[67] F. Nietzsche, *Gesammelte Werke* (München, 1922), Band VI, "Vom Nutzen und Nachteil der Historie für das Leben", p. 298-299.
[68] E. Cassirer, *The Myth of the State* (New York, 1955), p. 373.
[69] R. Rolland, *Clerambault* (Paris, 1923), pp. 8-9.

become the credo of the majority. Thus, even the ideas the so-called revolutionary against history proclaims against his time are still thoughts of this time: the antitheses conditioned by the theses of this time. In this way, Nietzsche's and Camus' theses against the Historicism of the nineteenth and twentieth centuries are revealed as the antitheses of the theses of these times and, therefore, as daughters of their times, as children of history who detest their mother.

In the course of history, no antithesis rises *ex nihilo*. All of them grow on historical soil which is impregnated with the ideas of their time and emerge only when the time and the cultural and social surroundings are ripe for them. Rousseau's ideas could not have possibly grown in Egypt at the time of Amenhotep III, and Einstein's could not have bloomed in the Middle Ages. Thus, Nietzsche's revolution against history is revealed as an illusion. Civilized man cannot escape history. Even his ideas against history are ideas of history which will make history. Consequently, Historicism no longer appears to be a choice of modern man but his inescapable destiny. The manifestations of Historicism in contemporary life are, indeed, much more numerous than one imagines — even in the domains of exact sciences and epistemology.

As we said earlier, the central epistemological idea of Stoicism and of the philosophy of Enlightenment was the existence of a universal and unchangeable human reason. A corollary of this idea was the supposition of universal *a priori* categories, such as they appear in Kant's philosophy. The latter considered them as expressions of a supra-temporal understanding (*Verstand*), although he had designed them on the model of Newtonian mechanics, which was a scientific conception linked to its epoch. Since it had, in part, to yield to new scientific conceptions, those of Einstein and quantum mechanics, Newton's mechanics lost part of its validity, and the same holds for Kant's categories, designed on their model. Reason and understanding also develop together with the new empirical data they have to integrate; they do not remain identical throughout the ages, and, therefore, their categories are, likewise, subjected to the law of change which, according to Heraclitus, is the only unalterable thing. Historicism rediscovers Heraclitus' πάντα ῥεῖ, everything flows. By declaring resolutely that "there are no definitive categories in Kant's sense",[70] Einstein expressed a thesis of Historicism, perhaps without noticing it. In fact, many of

---

[70] A. Einstein, "Physik und Realität", *Libres Recherches allemandes*, Paris, juillet 1938, p. 7.

our present-day scientists are Historicists unwittingly, or in spite of themselves.

Professor Nathan Rothenstreich of the Hebrew University in Jerusalem has raised a very significant objection to Historicism in the realm of knowledge. Speaking of the particular historical situation of the Renaissance, which released the various domains of experience from the intermingled relations in which they had been hitherto involved, he wrote: "To be sure, the historical situation of the Renaissance does not create the problem; the problem is based on the very essence of Mind. The historical situation only makes manifest a systematic problem. . . ."[71] This contention is certainly true to a very large extent. We must, for instance, recognize that the theory of relativity and wave mechanics, or Kant's and Bergson's philosophies, are possibilities of thought inherent in the very structure of mind as such, and which, with inner logical necessity, must appear at a certain moment in history, when certain empirical, social and psychological conditions have been fulfilled. This mind, with its timeless inner structure, unfolding in time, would then constitute the most powerful supra-historical entity.

And yet, if we look closer into the problem, we must realize that this "timeless" inner structure of mind is, at every historical period, the *image* of mind, as we *see* it at this given historical period and in this specific cultural surrounding, in conformity with the degree of evolution reached by our theoretical concepts at this historical moment and in this cultural surrounding. The structure of our mind, as we see it today, is no longer the same as it was seen by Aristotle and not even by Kant, who would not have admitted more than his twelve everlasting categories.

In historical retrospective, we can, at every historical moment, give a picture of our mind's structure, taking into account the latest phase of its evolution. At every historical moment, this picture seems to us complete, since it has taken into account all the previous phases of its evolution, including the latest. Often, the latest phase compels us to modify the whole picture, as, for instance, at the moment when Aristotle's qualitative conception was replaced by Galileo's quantitative one; or when the idea of continuity was overthrown by the quantum theory and biological mutation; or when the idea of the absolute was abandoned in favor of relativistic conceptions, etc., etc.

I think that only at the end of history could we possibly have a total

---

[71] N. Rothenstreich, "Historicism and Philosophy, Reflections on R. G. Collingwood", *Revue Internationale de Philosophie*, 42, 4 (Bruxelles, 1957), p. 402.

retrospective of the evolution of mind and, therefore, a view of its supra-historical structure in itself. But we do not know which moment is the last of history. And when the last moment has come, no time is left for the extrapolation of the mind's supra-historical structure. My conclusion is that, at every moment of history, we can only have an historically conditioned view or perspective of the mind's systematic structure and not a supra-historical knowledge of this structure. I believe that this conclusion disposes of Professor Rothenstreich's objection to Historicism.

Although dialectical Materialism rejects the relativism resulting from Historicism, it powerfully contributed to the evolution of the latter. Engels spoke with anger and contempt of the Enlightenment's universal reason and its natural law. Here is what Marx's most intimate collaborator declared:

> We know today that this *kingdom of reason* was nothing more than the idealized kingdom of the bourgeoisie; that this *eternal right* found its realization in bourgeois justice; that *equality* reduced itself to bourgeois equality before the law; that bourgeois *property* was proclaimed as one of the essential *rights of man;* and that the *government of reason,* the *Contrat Social* of Rousseau, came into being, and only could come into being, as a democratic bourgeois republic. . . . This *eternal reason* was in reality nothing but the *idealized* intelligence of the eighteenth century citizen just then evolving into the bourgeois. . . . The state based upon reason completely collapsed. Rousseau's *Contrat Social* had found its realization in the Reign of Terror, from which the bourgeoisie . . . had taken refuge first in the corruption of the *Directoire* and, finally, under the wing of the Napoleonic despotism.[72]

What interests us especially in this philippic is the total rejection by dialectical Materialism of the concepts of universal reason and natural right. Marx and Engels also reproached Feuerbach for speaking always of "man" as such, instead of considering "real historical men" (*die wirklichen, historischen Menschen*). Feuerbach's "man", they said, is, in reality, the German.[73] As we know, the rejection of the concept of man in general and its replacement by the historical men of different epochs and in different countries is also one of the characteristic features of Historicism, and, from this point of view, Marx and Engels would likewise appear as Historicists.

[72] F. Engels, *Socialism Utopian and Scientific* (New York, 1935), pp. 31-34.
[73] K. Marx, F. Engels, *Die deutsche Ideologie* (Berlin, 1953), p. 40.

Marx and Engels also contributed powerfully to the evolution of Historicism by denying the eternal character of the categories and by interpreting them as dependent variables of the social relations of production. In his book, *La misère de la philosophie*, (*Misery of Philosophy*) which Marx wrote in French in response to Proudhon's *Philosophie de la misère* (*Philosophy of Misery*), one can read the following passage, inaugurating a new era not only in political economy but, also, in epistemology:

> The economic categories are only the theoretical expressions of, the abstractions from, the social relations of production. ... The same men who establish social relations according to their material productivity also produce the principles, the ideas, the categories, according to their social relations.
>
> Thus, these ideas, these categories are just as little eternal as the relations they express. They are *historical and transitory products.*[74]

The Marxist idea of the variability of categories, of their "historical" and "transitory" character, is one of the basic ideas of Historicism. Dialectical Materialism is a dynamic philosophy and, therefore, could not possibly admit stable entities such as the eternal human nature of Rationalism and its static categories without evolution. By changing nature, Marx says, man changes his own nature.

In his study, *The Growth of German Historicism,* published in the United States,[75] Professor Engel-Janosi gave a prominent place to Marx, and, in the light of our quotations, this classification would appear to be justified. And yet, it would be erroneous to consider Marx and the Marxists as supporters of Historicism if we define it in terms of our formula, *veritas et virtus filiae temporis* — i.e., as a total historical relativism with respect to truth and values; for this relativism is violently rejected by Marxism.

"*Nicht das Bewusstsein bestimmt das Leben, sondern das Leben bestimmt das Bewusstsein*", Marx and Engels proclaimed — it is not consciousness which determines life, but life determines consciousness. And the life which, according to them, determines consciousness is material life, economic life. "By developing their material production and their material trade, men change their reality and, with it, they also change their thought and the products of their thought."[76]

---

[74] K. Marx, *La misère de la philosophie* (Paris, 1846), p. 88.
[75] Baltimore, 1944.
[76] K. Marx and F. Engels, *Die deutsche Ideologie* (Berlin, 1953), p. 23.

It follows that, according to historical Materialism, the politics, religion, philosophy, right, morality and art of every epoch are only the ideological superstructure of its method of economic production. Consequently, the systems of values embodied in these philosophies, ethics, laws, arts, etc. are reflexions of the conditions of production of their epochs and their corresponding societies and, thus, are relative to them. Is this not tantamount to a total historical relativism? Indeed, Engels wrote that "every class, even every profession, has its own morality..."[77] and that laws only codify juridically the economic relationships which exist in a given society.

But, in spite of this apparent historical relativism, the well-known Hungarian Communist philosopher, George Lukács, declares that "the social determination of the contents and forms of reason does *not entail historical relativism*. In spite of the social and historical conditioning of these contents and forms, the progressive character of every situation and every evolutionary tendency is something *objective,* effective independently of human consciousness."[78]

I translated this passage from the book Professor Lukács published in 1954 under the title, *Die Zerstörung der Vernunft* — the Destruction of Reason. At that time, this thinker was still *persona grata* in Moscow, and, although his book already contains some political anachronisms, it reflects faithfully the philosophical ideas of dialectical Materialism. In effect, Engels had declared that "every new negation increases the tendency towards perfection",[79] and so progress truly appears to be "something *objective,* effective independently of human consciousness".

I must confess that I am unable to imagine an objective progress, independent of human consciousness; for, in order to be able to ascertain and to measure progress, one must have set up a standard of values, a norm, which always results from an act of will and, therefore, presupposes a human consciousness. Otherwise, it would be necessary to admit that, independently of human will and consciousness, nature and society develop toward superior values which are immanent in nature and society. It is, indeed, this idea which Marxism tacitly admits. But such a supposition is possible only by virtue of a teleological metaphysics incompatible with the purely scientific conception which dialectical Materialism affirms so strongly. I believe that we are here confronted with one of the inherent contradictions of Marxist philosophy.

---

[77] F. Engels, *Ludwig Feuerbach and the End of Classical German Philosophy* (Moscow, 1950), p. 59.
[78] G. Lukács, *Die Zerstörung der Vernunft* (Berlin, 1954), p. 7.
[79] F. Engels, *Landmarks of Scientific Socialism,* Chapter 7 (Chicago, 1907).

As for the Marxist affirmation that the social and historical determination of the contents and forms of reason does not entail historical relativism, it is, probably, based on the doctrines of self-alienation and ideology. In Hegel's philosophy, the finite sphere which comprehends nature and mind appears as a self-alienation of God. Dialectics result in the self-reconciliation of the divine spirit. In the philosophy of the Neo-Hegelian Marx, God's self-alienation reappears in the form of man's self-alienation, his transformation into a commodity under the Capitalistic rule. But, after the victory of the proletariate, the totality of man is supposed to be restored in a classless society. Then, he will no longer be the dupe of the ideologies of the bourgeois class, which passes off its own interests as the "general interest". According to dialectical Materialism, the objective standards of values will appear in the classless society, freed from the ideological distortions they underwent during the reign of the bourgeois class.

Thus, the values which form the foundation of the Soviet Union's "Socialist Humanism" are supposed no longer to express the social and historical conditions of a limited society. They are considered the universal standards of mankind.

We quoted Engel's dictum that "every class, even every profession has its own morality". Obviously, this does not mean that for dialectical Materialism all these moralities are of the same value. For Marx and Engels wrote: "The revolutionary class appears, from the beginning, ... not as a class but as the representative of the whole society; it appears as the whole mass of society in opposition to the unique ruling class."[80]

Representing, thus, the whole of human society, the revolutionary class no longer professes, according to Marxism, a class morality but human morality — especially in the society called "classless", in which ideas are supposed to be freed from the ideological distortions of the former ruling class.[81] It is in this way that the moral values of dialectical Materialism seem to escape historical and social relativism, and the same holds for its aesthetic and cognitive values. This does not mean, however, their independence from history and its social conditions. In the course of history, one or the other class can become the vehicle of general moral progress. According to dialectical Materialism, modern

---

[80] K. Marx, F. Engels, *Die deutsche Ideologie* (Berlin, 1953), pp. 45-46.
[81] Engels declared: "Real human morality, superior to class morality and its traditions, will not be possible until a stage of human history has been reached in which class antagonisms have not only been overcome but have been forgotten as regards the conduct of life." (*Anti-Duehring*, p. 129).

history shows that by its material interests the proletariate is pushed towards the realization of a superior morality. The latter is supposed to be a social ethics which secures for the greatest number of members of society the possibility of enjoying the material and cultural values of life. Some of the principles of this social ethics, considered to be objective standards of general validity, have been formulated by dialectical Materialism. The principle expressed in Article twelve of the Constitution of the USSR, "he who does not work, neither shall he eat", represents such a norm of social ethics. In the hierarchy of values of this ethics, the Socialistic imperative "from each according to his ability, to each according to his work performed" is considered to be a value inferior to the Communistic imperative formulated by Marx: "From each according to his ability, to each according to his needs."[82] Dialectical Materialism considers these principles as universal moral norms, historically developed.

The value theory of dialectical Materialism is, thus, neither a pure historical relativism nor a pure absolutism but rather a dialectical synthesis of the two. This also becomes obvious from an analysis of the Marxist concept of truth. "Dialectical philosophy dissolves all conceptions of final absolute truth and of a final absolute state of humanity corresponding to it",[83] wrote Engels. What he denied here were, however, only the so-called "eternal" truths, which could be acquired once and forever, in which his adversary Eugen Dühring believed.[84] But he did not deny absolute truth in the sense of objective standards for our relative historically and economically conditioned knowledge of reality. Lenin interpreted this point of view by saying: "For Engels, absolute truth is made up of relative truths."[85] And elucidating further the dialectical synthesis of absolutism and relativism in Marxist-Leninist Materialism, the Russian theorist and revolutionary writes the following in his book, *Materialism and Empirio-Criticism:* "From the standpoint of modern materialism, or Marxism, the relative limits of our approximation to the cognition of the objective, absolute truth, are historically conditioned; but the existence of this truth is unconditioned as well as the fact that we are continually approaching it."[86]

---

[82] K. Marx, *Critique of the Gotha Programme* (New York, 1938), p. 10.
[83] F. Engels, *Ludwig Feuerbach and the End of Classical German Philosophy* (Moscow, 1950), pp. 17-18.
[84] F. Engels, *Anti-Dühring* (Chicago, 1907), Chap. VI.
[85] V. I. Lenin, *Materialism and Empirio-Criticism* (New York, 1927), pp. 105-106.
[86] *Ibid.,* p. 107.

As our analysis has shown, dialectical Materialism recognizes an absolute trans-historical standard of moral goodness, of which the social ethics of the "classless" society is the closest historical approximation, comparatively speaking. It also recognizes an absolute standard of truth, while admitting the relativity of our factual scientific knowledge, subject to certain historical and economic conditions which determine the degrees of our knowledge, as it approaches absolute truth.

Now the basis of this absolute truth is absolute reality. Since dialectical Materialists consider our sensations as "copies" of the external world, their recognition of absolute truth implies that of absolute reality. Of course, this absolute reality is not regarded as a static immutable entity but, in Lenin's words, as "an eternally moving and developing material mass ... which reflects a progressive human consciousness".[87]

Besides these absolute standards of goodness and truth, dialectical Materialism also recognizes an absolute standard of beauty. The foundation of the latter is likewise constituted by the objective, dynamic reality of nature and society. For beauty is achieved in an art which gives a faithful picture of objective reality. According to the Soviet aesthetician, Mikhail Lifshitz, "art and literature are a *reflection of external reality* or a mirror of objective all-round human practice".[88] Beauty is achieved by an art which gives a faithful image of that reality.

As for natural beauty, the *Bolshaja Sovietskaja Entsiklopedia* declares (in Professor John Sommerville's translation) that it "is not a purely subjective condition of consciousness but ... rests upon definite objective properties and phenomena in nature itself and in the social life of man".[89]

Besides this absolute element in reality, Soviet aesthetics recognizes an element of historical and economical relativity, by declaring that "the feeling of beauty develops in the human being under the influence of historical conditions, in the process of the evolution of his productive activity and of the art and culture rooted therein".

Thus, it is not appropriate to designate Marxism without qualification as an Historicism, as did Professor Engel-Janosi, who used this term in a rather vague sense. Our analysis has shown that dialectical Materialism is an Historicism only insofar as it denies that man in general possesses a timeless unchangeable human nature; Marxism only recognizes concrete historical men, the products of a definite civilization, nation, class

---

[87] *Ibid.*, p. 108.
[88] M. Lifshitz, "Leninist Criticism", in *Literature and Marxism* (New York, 1938), p. 9.
[89] Quoted from J. Sommerville, *Soviet Philosophy* (New York, 1946), p. 134.

and historical epoch. Dialectical Materialism is also an Historicism in the sense that it denies a timeless supra-historical human reason with an eternal, changeless system of categories; it rather affirms that categories are "historical transitory products". Furthermore, Marxism is an Historicism in that it rejects the doctrine of natural right.

On the contrary, Marxism is diametrically opposed to Historicism when the latter denies the existence of absolute standards of goodness, truth and beauty and proclaims the total historical relativity of these values. Dialectical Materialism recognizes the historical relativity of these values only against the background of absolute, transhistorical standards of goodness, truth and beauty. As Professor Sommerville says, "belief in an absolute right is evidently not the same thing as a belief that our knowledge of it is absolutely correct."[90]

Thus, dialectical Materialism realizes that the extent and depth of our knowledge of nature is at any moment conditioned by the phase of the historical evolution of society and of its productive forces and, therefore, is relative to these conditions. But this historical relativism is limited; it is not, so to speak, absolute. Professor Lukács reproaches Spengler for changing "the historical relativity of our knowledge of nature into an absolute principle, by eliminating the fact of a progressive approximation (*Annäherung*) of our knowledge of nature to the objective reality of nature. . . ."[91]

This sentence shows well the objective limits of historical relativism in dialectical Materialism. These limits are constituted by the objective natural and social reality which, although in dynamic evolution, serves as a standard for goodness, truth and beauty.

If this total reality can serve as an absolute axiological and epistemological standard, it is because dialectical Materialists regard it as knowable as it is in itself. But, what proof do we have that we can know objective reality as it is? Dialectical Materialism recognizes that it does not have any theoretical proof and is satisfied with a purely pragmatic one. Pragmatism is, indeed, not an invention of the American philosophers Charles Peirce and William James but was established half a century before them by Marx. In his *Thesen über Feuerbach* Marx enunciated the basic principle of Pragmatism, by writing in 1845: "The question whether human thought has objective truth is not a question of theory but a practical question (*eine praktische Frage*). It is in practice that man must prove the truth, i.e., the reality and power, . . . of

---

[90] J. Sommerville, *Soviet Philosophy* (New York, 1946), p. 92.
[91] G. Lukács, *Die Zerstörung der Vernunft* (Berlin, 1954), p. 370.

his thought. The dispute as to the reality or non-reality of thought which is isolated from practice is a purely scholastic question."[92]

In his Introduction to the English translation of his book, *Socialism, Utopian and Scientific,* Engels dealt with the epistemological problem, applying the principles of Marx's pragmatism. When the Idealist speaks of the objects and their qualities, Engels says,

> he does not actually mean these objects and qualities, of which he cannot know anything for certain, but merely the impressions which they have produced in his senses. Now, this line of reasoning seems undoubtedly *hard to overcome by mere argumentation.* But, *before there was argumentation, there was action. Im Anfang war die Tat* (in the beginning was action). And human action had solved the difficulty long before human ingenuity invented it. The proof of the pudding is in the eating. From the moment we put these objects to our own use according to the qualities we perceive in them, we subject to an infallible test the correctness ... of our sense perceptions. If these perceptions have been wrong, then our estimate of the use to which an object can be put must also be wrong, and our attempt must fail. But, *if we succeed* in accomplishing our aim, if we find that the object does agree with our idea of it and does answer the purpose we intended it for, then that is a *positive proof* that our perception of it and of its qualities, *so far, agree* with reality outside ourselves.[93]

Theoretically, this pragmatic argument does not convince me. In my opinion, practical success in handling things according to the idea we have of them only proves that, to a certain extent, there exists a correspondence of some kind between the sense data and the symbols by which we represent them in our theories. This correspondence is, however, never one between an original and its copy. The incessant abrogation of older symbols which have rendered good services and their replacement by new ones, because the old symbols no longer serve to explain and control newly discovered sense data, is a proof that none of them ever "copied" "absolute" reality and that probably none of them ever will copy it. For a whole century, Augustin Fresnel's wave concept of light and its mathematical theory allowed us to explain theoretically and to control practically all know optical phenomena. But, after the discovery of the photoelectric effect, a new theory was needed and a new picture

---

[92] K. Marx, "Thesen über Feuerbach", 2, in *Die deutsche Ideologie* (Berlin, 1953), pp. 593-594.
[93] F. Engels, *Socialism, Utopian and Scientific* (New York, 1935), Introduction to the English edition, 1892, pp. 13-14.

of the structure of light. They were afforded by Einstein's theory of photons or light quanta, a dialectical synthesis of Newton's corpuscular and Fresnel-Huygen's wave conception of light. The correspondence between Einstein's symbols and the known optical phenomena goes farther than that between these phenomena and Fresnel's symbols. But in no case has this correspondence been revealed to be one between an original and its copy. In view of new empirical findings, the theory of photons may some day need a modification or a replacement by another theory, and so on *ad infinitum*. None of them will ever have been a *speculum naturae*, a mirror of nature. And, even if it had been such a mirror of reality, we would not know it; for, besides our knowledge, we have nothing with which we would be able to compare this knowledge. Kant showed this clearly. Thought does not copy reality; it changes the empirical data into formal symbols, in order to understand and control the phenomena.

Engel's proof that we can know reality in itself is, thus, only a pragmatic proof and in no way a theoretical one. If we cling to pure theory, as it suits theoretical philosophy to do, the thing in itself remains unknowable. And with the disappearance of a knowable absolute reality disappear also the absolute standards of our evaluations, so that our problem of historical relativism remains unsolved.

In contemporary philosophy, Historicism reappears in *Existentialism*. The Historicist implications of the latter become obvious as soon as we examine some of Heidegger's, Ortega's and Sartre's ideas. Existentialism, especially as represented by Sartre, has been reproached for its disdain of history and its anti-historical orientation. I think, however, that by starting with existing man, Existentialism has been forced into Historicism. For while being is timeless and unlimited by space, existence is always here and now — *hic et nunc*.[94] Man always exists at a certain place at a certain moment; he is a "man-in-the-world", a concrete man, "situated" historically, geographically, culturally and socially. To emphasize the essential necessity and indissoluble character of this association between man and his world, Heidegger hyphenated the words designating man's existence and his world. Sartre followed his example. "The compound expression 'being-in-the-world'," Heidegger writes, "already shows in its coinage that a unitary phenomenon is meant thereby."[95] Elsewhere, Heidegger declares: *"Zum Dasein gehört*

---

[94] Cf. A. Stern, *Sartre — His Philosophy and Psychoanalysis* (New York, 1953), p. 6.
[95] H. Heidegger, *Sein und Zeit* (Tübingen, 1949), p. 53.

wesenhaft: Sein in einer Welt"[96] — being in a world is an essential part of existence. Finally, he affirms that being-in-the-world always means being-with-others (*Mitsein* or *Mitsein-mit-Anderen*).

At first glance, these affirmations seem to be truisms; and yet, philosophically, they have important implications. By insisting that concrete man is a man in the world, that he always exists at a certain place and at a definite epoch — that he is always "situated" historically, geographically, culturally, socially — Existentialism involves a defiance of the classical concept of man in general who, identical throughout the ages and nations, is a timeless, spaceless, extra-historical man, a man without a world: in short, an abstraction. On the contrary, Existentialism's "situated" man is an historical man. Abandoning the rationalist concept of man in general — timeless, extra-spatial and supra-historical — Existentialism enters the broad current of contemporary Historicism.

In Heidegger, this fact is more obvious than in Sartre. According to the German Existentialist, "the being of existence is, in principle, historical",[97] because it is temporal. Existence is a concretion of time. Summing up these ideas, Heidegger declares: "The thesis of the historicity of existence does not state that the worldless subject (*das weltlose Subjekt*) is historical but ... the one which exists as being-in-the-world. ... The historicity of existence is, essentially, the historicity of the world."[98]

Not being determined by any essence, Heidegger's man is "free", but his freedom is limited by the fact of being "cast" into a destiny. This *"Geworfenheit"*, this fact of being cast into the current of historical time, is one of the fundamental unalterable features of the human condition. We cannot change this current. We have to accept the historical conditions of our existence. We may try to understand them, to interpret them, but that is all.

This interpretation, however, is historically conditioned, since every truth is relative to existence. Thus, no thinker can give more than the truth of his own existence, which is historical. With this, we have come to the core of Historicism and its thesis, *veritas filia temporis*. The former is not only manifested in the evaluation of theoretical truth but, also, in the practical imperatives of Heidegger's Existentialism. We have already seen that, for Heidegger, man as such does not exist. What exists is the man of a given historical epoch with his historical and national environment. As a pure existence, the individual is cast into

[96] *Ibid.*, p. 13.
[97] *Ibid.*, p. 392.
[98] *Ibid.*, p. 388.

a certain situation. Thus, "to act" can only mean that man has to start from this historical situation into which he finds himself cast, to accept it voluntarily, instead of allowing himself to be impelled by it. This is a Stoic and Nietzschean idea which consists in willing one's own destiny and which, basically, changes an unavoidable necessity into a virtue. This doctrine also constitutes a link between Heidegger and Hegel. The latter distinguished two kinds of men: the uprooted man who lives outside his time, and the man who inserts himself into his historical time and through whom time acts. The life of the uprooted is senseless; it is a *"faule Existenz"*,[99] an idle existence, because it does not insert itself into the round of duties which its epoch imposes upon it. In Hegel's conception, such an uprooted existence is not in agreement with the rational divine plan, the fulfilment of which is world history. Therefore, Hegel does not recognize any duty of timeless validity, and Heidegger adopts this view. For the German Existentialist, the moral duty is always the duty of a definite period, the duty to do what the historical moment requires. Having no essence and being a pure existence in the state of becoming, the man of Existentialism has no character. Being an empty envelope, the individual can, according to Heidegger's postulate, insert himself voluntarily into any historical situation in which he finds himself cast, by acting in the way required by that historical situation and according to its meaning. That is what Heidegger himself did, when Nazism took over Germany. To be sure, Heidegger's phenomenological philosophy of historical man is supposed to elevate us above the relativism of man in history, but I am not convinced that it does so.

The Spanish philosopher José Ortega y Gasset anticipated some of the positions of Heidegger's Existential Historicism and, also, many of Sartre's theses. Ortega established his important principle, *"Yo soy yo y mi curcunstancia"*[100] — I am I and my circumstance — thirteen years before Heidegger; and, seventeen years before the German philosopher, he insisted on the fact that human existence is a coexistence with other people. Ortega showed the organic unity between man and his specific surroundings, his *circum-stantia,* the things which stand around him and determine his outlook. This section of reality into which a person is cast and which may be the Sierra of Guadarrama, a Parisian boulevard or the Broadway of New York, is considered as the natural entrance which leads Gonzalez, Durand or Smith into the world. These circumstances form the other halves of their persons.

[99] G. W. F. Hegel, *Sämtliche Werke,* Band XI (1928), p. 68.
[100] J. Ortega y Gasset, *Obras completas* (Madrid, 1950-52), t. I, p. 322.

Thus, Ortega's man is a man of a certain place. He is, also, a man of a certain time. *"El hombre es lo que le ha pasado, lo que ha hecho"*,[101] says Ortega — man is what has happened to him, what he has done. Our past has become a part of our present, which means that each of us is a product of his history and of his group's history.

Ortega's man is, thus, not the rationalistic abstraction of a man without a world, outside space and time. He is an historical, geographical, regional man. "Man has no nature, but he has a history."[102] He *is* his history, his own and that of his ancestors, the latter being transmitted to him by the society in which he lives. Man is not a thing, he is drama, in the original sense of the Greek word δρᾶν, to act. According to Ortega, "to exist" means to invent projects of doing and being which correspond to a man's specific circumstances. His history, his previous experiences, together with his circumstances, constitute the basic limitations of his future possibilities. In order to be able to choose and to decide, man has to know his vital circumstances and both his and his group's past, which, in fact, has become a part of his circumstances. In so doing, man is guided by a concrete reason, vital or historical reason. It is a narrative reason, for in order to understand life — individual as well as collective life — one must tell a story. If this man or this nation are doing this, it is because they have done that. This historical narrative reason alone can elucidate life. It tries to "liquify" (*fluidificar*) every fact by revealing its origin and evolution.

As a dynamic Heraclitean thinker opposed to Eleaticism, Ortega declares that whoever tries to understand man, this reality *in via*, this eternal pilgrim, must get rid of all stable concepts and learn how to think by virtue of dynamic concepts. *"Toda noción referente a la vida específicamente humana es función del tiempo histórico"*[103] he says — every concept which refers to a specifically human life is a function of historical time.

Now, this is pure Historicism; for, if our concepts are functions of historical time, then there are no supra-historical stable concepts capable of serving as permanent standards for judging the concepts created in the course of history. Ortega adopts Historicism freely and consciously. Here is what he writes about this question: "It is extremely comic to condemn Historicism, because it produces and corroborates in us the consciousness that man is changeable in all directions and that nothing

[101] *Ibid.*, t. VI, p. 41.
[102] *Ibid.*, p. 41.
[103] *Ibid.*, t. V, p. 540.

concrete is stable in him. As if a stable being — for example a stone — were preferable to that which moves!"[104]

To give even more emphasis to his judgment in favor of Historicism, Ortega quotes Galileo's word: *"I detrattori della corruptibilità meriterebbero d'esser cangiati in statue"* — the detractors of corruptibility would deserve to be changed into statues.

Far from seeing a blemish in perpetual historical change, Ortega considers it an ontological privilege of man and the very condition of his progress. Only the man who is not enchained by the past is able to progress. He alone can always migrate towards the possibilities of his future. It is in this new sense that Ortega uses the word "progress". It does not imply the idea of an evolution towards higher values, since historical reason can only judge this question *a posteriori*. To Ortega, "progressing" simply means to exhaust, by experience, all the possibilities of existence, to profit from earlier experiences, to conserve them, to surmount their shortcomings. *"Progresar es acumular ser, tesaurizar realidad"*[105] he says — to progress means to accumulate being, to treasure up reality.

Having no "human nature", man is, to Ortega, the sum of his acts — just as to Hegel, Malraux and Sartre. Declaring that man has no other nature than the one he has made,[106] Ortega admits that man builds up his own essence, which is preceded by his existence. Therefore, I have classified this Spanish philosopher as an Existentialist. I have tried to show, however, in an essay published in Spanish,[107] in what respects his thought has to be considered as Essentialism. Values, for instance, are in Ortega's eyes absolute, timeless, supra-historical essences. This view is incompatible not only with Existentialism but, also, with Historicism. We may say that Ortega and any other philosopher is an Historicist to the extent to which he is an Existentialist.

Although much more radical than Ortega's Historicism, the Historicism of Sartre is much less obvious, for it is only implicit. It needs a little analysis to bring it to light.

Like Ortega, Sartre too rejects the concept of human nature and, with this, he makes the first step towards Historicism. As an Existentialist, he denies that man's essence precedes his historical existence. "If God does not exist," he writes, "there is at least one being in which existence

---

[104] *Ibid.*, t. VI, p. 41.
[105] *Ibid.*, t. VI, p. 43.
[106] *Ibid.*, t. VI, p. 41.
[107] A. Stern, "¿Ortega - existencialista o esencialista?", *La Torre*, Revista general de la Universidad de Puerto Rico, Num. 15-16, Julio-Diciembre, 1956, pp. 385-399.

precedes essence, one being which exists before it can be defined by any concept, and ... this being is man. ..."[108]

It is well known that Sartre's Existentialism is a consequence of his atheism. According to him, there is no "human nature", for there is no God to conceive it. Thus, man is nothing but what he makes of himself in the course of history. If there is no human nature hovering above history as a supra-temporal essence, then there is no universal man, no archetype-man who could serve as a standard by which to judge the different types of men emerging in the course of history. Consequently, the historical men become the only men, and each of them is justified in relation to his epoch, without any of them occupying a privileged position.

This is pure Historicism. It becomes imperative as soon as one abandons the Platonism of Ideas, wich are absolute essences; and by its very definition, Existentialism is an anti-Platonism. For while Platonism proclaims the primacy of universal essences over individual existences, Existentialism consists in proclaiming the primacy of individual existences over universal essences. Consequently, Existentialism must also deny that the individual values which we posit by our evaluations are determined by essences or general norms existing before those values. According to Existentialism, the essences do not arise before the existences but after them. This means that, in evaluating, the authentic Existentialist is not determined by any previously given essence or norm, by anything outside himself. He judges subjectively without any objective support and is responsible for his judgment or evaluation. Or, as Sartre expresses it: *"Ma liberté est l'unique fondement des valeurs* — my freedom is the only foundation of values, and nothing, absolutely nothing justifies me in adopting this value rather than that, this hierarchy of values rather than another."[109]

Since, according to Existentialism, there are no timeless value-essences, the values emerging in the course of history, thanks to the evaluations of existing men, are the only values in the world. Consequently, there is no supra-historical value allowing us to judge the historical values. If Sartre does not believe in progress, it is probably also because the Historicism implicit in his Existentialism does not offer him any supra-historical values and hierarchies of values which would allow him to verify and to measure any such progress in history. Thus, Historicism appears to be an unavoidable consequence of radical Existentialism.

[108] J.-P. Sartre, *L'existentialisme est un humanisme* (Paris, 1946), p. 21.
[109] J.-P. Sartre, *L'être et le néant* (Paris, 1949), p. 76.

And yet, even the Historicism of Sartre's Existentialism has its limits. On the one hand, the author of *Being and Nothingness* admits that there is no human nature, that "every epoch develops according to dialectical laws" and that "men depend on the epoch and not upon a human nature".[110] On the other hand he admits, however, a kind of human universality under the name of *condition*. By human condition he understands, with other thinkers, the totality of *a priori* limits which circumscribe the fundamental situation of man in the universe. The historical situations vary. What never varies is the necessity for man to be in a world, to live, to act in order to maintain himself in existence. What likewise never varies is the fact that man loves and hates, that he procreates, that he falls ill, that he suffers, that he knows he must die, that he fears death and that he dies. This is a kind of human universality which we may, indeed, regard as trans-historic, and, in a sense, as absolute. Sartre is thus right in declaring that, in spite of the non-existence of a human nature and in the midst of a constantly changing history, the "human condition" allows us to preserve enough universal principles to understand any human project; it may be that of a modern American or European, that of a medieval Chinese, of a Greek of the Periclean age or a Sumerian's. Of course, inside this very general framework of the human condition, the projects of men exhibit the impress of their epochs, of their societies, and of the value systems by which the latter are governed. Sometimes, when the subject is a primitive man, a civilized person has difficulties in understanding his projects, unless he has a knowledge of primitive psychology and of the collective ideas by which it is governed. Nevertheless, there remains a common ground: that of the human condition. "Although human projects may be different," writes Sartre, "at least none of them remains completely strange to me, because they all present themselves as attempts to overstep these limits (of the human condition) or to push them back or to deny them or to adapt oneself to them."[111]

With the undeniable universality of the human condition, a breach becomes visible in the solid masonry of *Historicism*. Sartre did not draw this conclusion, for he did not study the Historicist implications of his Existentialism. In my opinion, the fact that men do and always did accept the human condition is the expression of certain fundamental evaluations, common to all men, in all civilizations and all historical

---

[110] J.-P. Sartre, *L'existentialisme est un humanisme* (Paris, 1946), p. 136.
[111] *Ibid.*, p. 69.

epochs. Since these inferences go far beyond Sartre's philosophy, we shall discuss them in a separate chapter.

Another limit of Historicism in Sartre's Existentialism seems to be the idea of liberty as a means of escaping from the "facticity" of nature and history. Mme Simone de Beauvoir even defined morality as "the triumph of liberty over facticity".[112] Ortega y Gasset had already pointed out that our reaction to the circumstances is not imposed upon us in the same way as a certain orbit is prescribed to a planet. The circumstances (in Sartre's terminology, the "facticity") always offer us several possibilities from which we may choose according to our "project".

Sartre insists that this project is "free". Nevertheless, I think that the possibilities from which we can choose our projects are historically, culturally, economically and socially determined: historically and economically by the institutions created by the society in which we live and by its past and present situations: socially and culturally by the value systems and ideologies by which this society is ruled and by the collective unconscious which motivates its members. All these determinations are limitations of our freedom of choice, according to the logical principle *omnis determinatio est negatio*. Let us examine a characteristic example given by Sartre:

> The motives for Clovis' conversion were the political and religious conditions of Gaul, the relative strengths of the episcopate, the great landowners and the common people. . . . Nevertheless, this objective appreciation can be made only in the light of a presupposed goal and within the limits of a project of the Ego towards this goal. In order that the power of the episcopate could be revealed to Clovis as a motive for his conversion . . . , he must first have posited the conquest of Gaul as his aim.[113]

With this example, Sartre tried to show that, in spite of all motives, man's project is free. More than that: Facts and events become motives only in the light of a free project. Without challenging this very interesting conclusion, I think that the choice of a free project is always historically, economically, culturally and socially conditioned and, by the same token, limited. In the case of Clovis, it was conditioned by the historical constellation which showed Gaul to be an object of possible conquest and by the axiological conceptions of the epoch which saw in

---

[112] S. de Beauvoir, *Pour une morale de l'ambiguité* (Paris, 1947), p. 64.
[113] J.-P. Sartre, *L'être et le néant* (Paris, 1943), p. 522.

absolute royal power the highest social value. Thus, it becomes obvious
that we can choose our projects only within the limits of the possibilities
offered by the natural, economic, and historical situation, so that, even
by our free choice, we cannot escape from the prison of history. In the
Middle Ages, for example, a young European, gifted in philosophy or
letters, could only choose an ecclesiastical career, since this was the only
one which, at that historical epoch of Western civilization, offered the
possibility of intellectual activity. A man with scientific interests could,
at that time, only become a mechanic. In a similar way a young Hindoo
was, for centuries, limited in his "free" choice of a life project not only
by his natural gifts but, also, by the caste into which he was born — by
luck or by misfortune.

Even in our modern society, historical constellations greatly influence
the free choice of our projects. Today, thousands of American boys and
girls are choosing a scientific career, because public opinion as well as
private and governmental scholarships encourage such a choice. The
reason is the current historical constellation with its strong scientific,
technological, industrial, and military competition between the United
States and Russia. This historical constellation has even slightly modified
the American hierarchy of values, in giving the scientist a social prestige
he never before enjoyed in this country. Nobody could deny that social
values greatly influence man's choice of his life project. These social
values are, as we just saw, variables of historical constellations.

By these examples, I have wanted to show that our freedom in
choosing our projects, on which Existentialism insists so strongly, can
be carried out only within the framework of the naturally, economically, and historically given possibilities and of the evaluations historically developed in a given society. The freedom mentioned does not,
therefore, afford any possibility of escaping from the prison of history,
just as it does not allow us to escape from nature.

Sartre does not believe in a prescribed march of history, since men
are free and will decide tomorrow what history will be the day after
tomorrow. "By the past, I belong to universal temporality, by the
present and future, I escape from it,"[114] he says. Freedom means to him
commitment to action in order to change the present and to construct
a future. But do we, by this present and future action, escape from
history? I do not think so: for we cannot commit ourselves to collective
action to change the present and build a new future without creating

---

[114] *Ibid.*, p. 259.

history, a new history, which will envelop us and "situate" us — ourselves and our descendants. Essence is a timeless supra-historical abstraction, but existence is basically historical; it is always "situated" historically. Whatever the existing man may do, he is entangled in history. History is his destiny, from which he cannot escape.

VII. THE LIMITS OF HISTORICISM

Historicism is the *enfant terrible* of contemporary philosophy. Denying the eternal and suprahistorical validity of philosophical and scientific truths as well as that of moral and aesthetic values, Historicism expresses theoretically what the histories of philosophy, of the sciences, of ethics and of the arts show us empirically. If philosophy cannot refute this testimony of history, it at least does not want the vanity of its aspirations to eternity to be exposed on its own ground by a philosophical doctrine; for Historicism is a philosophical doctrine and not an historical one. Therefore, we are confronted with an abundance of philosophical attempts to refute Historicism. Of these attempts we have already mentioned Professor Leo Strauss' arguments. Applying an inference often used in order to refute relativism, Professor Strauss reproaches Historicism with refuting its own thesis. Here is what he writes:

> Historicism asserts that all human thought or beliefs are historical and, hence, deservedly destined to perish; but Historicism itself is a human thought; hence, Historicism can be of only temporary validity, or it simply cannot be true. To assert the Historicist thesis means to doubt it and, thus, to transcend it. ... Historicism thrives on the fact that it inconsistently exempts itself from its own verdict on all human thought.[1]

To invalidate this argument, one could have recourse to the theory of types, according to which no property can be ascribed to itself. But, instead of hiding ourselves behind a question of form, let us rather admit that Historicism cannot claim timeless validity without violating its very principle; for, if it affirms that all human thought is historical, at whatever epoch of history, and that there will never be any trans-historical truth or value, Historicism claims trans-historical validity for its own thesis, thus refuting it. But, if Historicism limits itself to affirm-

[1] L. Strauss, *Natural Right and History* (Chicago, 1953), p. 25.

ing that, by virtue of the categories at our disposal at this moment of history, human thoughts, beliefs and values appear to be historically conditioned and limited, it is free from contradiction. Since, besides the categories of our epoch, we have no others at our disposal — those of the past being, in part, regarded as no longer valid, and those of the future being unknown — we must say that, in our epoch, Historicism appears to be a well established theory. The fact that we cannot affirm the eternal, timeless, trans-historical validity of Historicism does not exclude the possibility of its being valid for the present historical epoch which gave birth to it.

In spite of being a Phenomenologist who believes in an "ideal in itself" of such eternal "essences" as values or logical and mathematical entities,[2] Nicolai Hartmann admits that Historicism, as "the historicity of the historical consciousness" (die Geschichtlichkeit des Geschichtsbewusstseins), is a condition which cannot be abrogated. All attempts to surmount Historicism run up against a "solid wall".[3]

Ernst Troeltsch established what he himself called a theory of historical relativity by writing: "Just as, in the physical sciences, every computation of a movement depends on the position (Standort) of the observer, so, in history, every standard is irremediably determined by the spot where one is located and from which it originates."[4]

Now, we know that, temporally, the place where one is located cannot be any other than that of present time. As Hegel reminded us in his Philosophy of Right, it would be foolish to imagine that anyone could "jump out of his time", for everybody, including the philosopher, is "a son of his time".[5] Even our anticipation of the future, which influences, counter-currentwise, our interpretation of the past, is a present act. One must, therefore, give up any attempt to find absolute timeless standards of eternal and universal validity. Nevertheless, Troeltsch urges us not to renounce the search for standards. But what kind of standards can we apply, since absolute, timeless, universal standards do not exist?

As far as present history is concerned, we shall, naturally, apply present standards. The categories and values, which, in this case, serve as standards, have developed organically with the historical process they are supposed to interpret and to evaluate. Therefore, they will be adequate for the latter.

---

[2] N. Hartmann, Ethik (Berlin, 1926), p. 136, etc.
[3] N. Hartmann, Das Problem des geistigen Seins (Berlin, 1949), pp. 32-34.
[4] E. Troeltsch, Der Historismus und seine Probleme (Tübingen, 1922), I, p. 169.
[5] G. W. F. Hegel, Grundlinien der Philosophie des Rechts (Stuttgart, 1928), p. 35.

As for past history, the problem is more delicate. Here, Troeltsch recommends what he calls *"immanente Kritik"*. "To understand an epoch means to measure it according to its own nature and ideal, however complicated they may be."[6] This is, certainly, a very difficult task; for it would not suffice for the historian to rediscover the value system of the past epoch he is studying. It would be necessary for him to restore these dead values to life, so that he feels them in his own heart, for, otherwise, he would not be able to understand and judge the epoch studied according to its own ideals and standards. Without referring to Troeltsch, Professor Raymond Aron asks: "Is it even possible to recover a value system which is no longer ours, without disfiguring and transfiguring it?"[7] He seems to doubt it, and I am not convinced either. In this respect, Goethe's dictum has kept all its validity:

> *"Mein Freund, die Zeiten der Vergangenheit*
> *Sind uns ein Buch mit sieben Siegeln.*
> *Was ihr den Geist der Zeiten heisst,*
> *Das ist im Grund der Herren eigner Geist,*
> *In dem die Zeiten sich bespiegeln."*[8]

(My friend, times past are to us a book with seven seals. What you call the spirit of the times is basically those gentlemen's (the historians') own mind in which the times are reflected.)

If the historian truly succeeds in reviving the dead values of certain past epochs by trying to forget their significance for our present-day feelings and if he judges according to these revived standards, the artificial character of his judgment will be obvious and he will shock the sensibility of his modern readers. We had an example in Croce's statement that, in crushing basic liberties, medieval tyrants were only faithful to their age and, in a sense, liberal and that the Inquisition defended a great institution which was necessary for civilization.

Troeltsch did not go to these extremes. He believed rather that, in the first place, the historian should measure a past epoch or a foreign civilization according to its own standards but that, afterwards, he should compare them with those of his own epoch or civilization. "In this case, we judge ... the foreign world not only according to its own but, also, according to our own standards. From these two different directions a new specific movement will ultimately result.[9]

[6] E. Troeltsch, *Der Historismus und seine Probleme* (Tübingen, 1922), I, p. 172.
[7] R. Aron, *La philosophie critique de l'histoire* (Paris, 1950), p. 155.
[8] *Goethes Faust*, I, p. 30.
[9] E. Troeltsch, *op. cit.,* I, p. 172.

I believe that it should be possible to delimit more precisely the use of these two standards of values. It seems obvious to me that the historian who studies a foreign or past civilization must try, within the limits of possibility, to rediscover its value systems and to "understand" it through empathy. Only in this way would he be able to reconstruct the motivations of the historical agents and to explain their reactions. In my opinion, he should, however, renounce any attempt to impose these standards upon his own judgment or upon his reader's minds. For we can judge only by virtue of our own standards — those of our epoch and our civilization. A judgment based upon a standard of dead values — dead in themselves or dead to our feelings — would not be a true judgment but an erudite caricature, an artificial purely intellectual construction, devoid of the emotional roots of a true value judgment.

But, if we judge past or foreign civilizations according to our own present standards, do we then not fall into the error of a new absolutism? Do we not, in this case, follow the road of Voltaire, who regarded the spiritual values of the century of Louis XIV as absolute standards, as norms for measuring the values of past civilizations and as "the example for posterity"?[10] Evidently, we cannot decree the absolute supra-historical character of our values by a *sic volo, sic jubeo,* for our values are only historical products relative to our historical, geographical, cultural, social and economic situation.

I think, however, that it is not necessary to commit all these errors and that there exists a middle of the road between the extremes of absolutism and the total relativism of an unbridled Historicism. It is evidently insincere to say, like the pure Historicists, that the Middle Ages had a "right" to burn the so-called witches, since this usage corresponded to its standards of values. I call such an affirmation insincere, because it does not correspond to our present emotional reactions and only constitutes a kind of intellectual snobbery. We cannot jump out of our time, out of our skin.

Nevertheless, we do not need trans-historical values or a "privileged" moment of history to refute the affirmation of an uncompromising Historicism that every historical epoch and every foreign civilization has a "right" to barbarity, if the latter corresponds to their historically developed standards of values. In my opinion, we may declare today that the stake was a barbarian institution, although it corresponded to the religious and moral evaluations of the Middle Ages, without proclaiming implicitly the absolute trans-historical validity of our present

[10] *Oeuvres complètes de Voltaire* (Paris, 1878), tome XIV, p. 155.

evaluations. We may judge other epochs and other civilizations by virtue of our own standards of values as long as we recognize the relativity of our standards to our epoch and our civilization and that we recognize the right of future and foreign civilizations to judge of our standards by virtue of theirs.

Rickert and other thinkers expressed the fear that the non-recognition of absolute transhistorical values would open the road to nihilism. In a similar way, Professor Leo Strauss identifies the rejection of natural right with nihilism, since natural right represents absolute trans-historical values in a concrete form. While trying to avoid the fallacy he calls *reductio ad Hitlerum*[11] — a cheap substitute for the *reductio ad absurdum* — Professor Strauss insinuates that without natural right we cannot condemn Hitler's barbarities. I do not believe, however, that in order to escape nihilism we need absolute values. We are citizens of our modern civilization, a civilization with humanitarian ideals. Ideals are directive values. We believe in these values and in these ideals of our epoch and of our civilization, we feel them vibrating in our hearts, we affirm their validity in our judgments. This is not nihilism! Nihilism is the lack of belief in values. Since we live in the present epoch and not in eternity, we may be satisfied with values valid for the present epoch. A trans-historical eternal validity would not contribute anything to our belief in values which developed with us and which we consider, therefore, as ours.

Thus, we may condemn Hitler's barbarity, without resorting to an eternal natural right, simply by virtue of the fact that this barbarity is in flagrant contradiction to the moral conscience of our epoch and of any other epoch which shares our humanitarian ideals.

Here, another limit of Historicism is revealed. For the humanitarian ideal which our epoch has elevated to a high degree by translating it into social institutions is an heritage from antiquity, especially from the Greek and Roman Stoics. Seneca's principle, *homo homini res sacra* — man is to man a holy thing — is still our ideal, although we no longer share the Stoic conception of a universal unchangeable human nature. In order to affirm the ideal mentioned, it is enough to recognize the human condition with its greatness and miseries. While admitting today — thanks to history and ethnology — the diversity of men, we have a deeper consciousness of what unites us, and this implies certain values.

[11] L. Strauss, *Natural Right and History* (Chicago, 1953), p. 42.

If our humanitarianism is revealed as an heritage from antiquity, then it becomes obvious that we evaluate not only according to the standards developed by our epoch but, also, by virtue of certain values created by previous epochs and civilizations which we have incorporated into our civilization.

The same holds for our truths. Einstein's theory of Relativity and quantum mechanics could not have been discovered by Thales, Pythagoras, Archimedes, or Euclid. Not because these thinkers lacked the necessary genius. What was missing in them were all the empirical and theoretical findings accumulated and selected from the Renaissance up to now. Without Galileo there could have been no Newton; without Newton no Einstein. Thus, instead of saying *veritas et virtus filiae temporis* — truth and value are daughters of time — we should rather affirm the principle, *veritas et virtus filiae temporum* — truth and value are daughters of the times, of all times, of the present as well as of the past. For without the past there would not be any present.[12]

With this, we have not refuted Historicism and it was not our intention to do so, but we have pushed back its limits. Every epoch has its truths and its values, but they rest on certain truths and values of previous epochs; not on *all* truths and all values of previous periods, but on *selected* truths and values of these epochs. Our present epistemological, moral and aesthetic conceptions have little in common with the corresponding conceptions of the Middle Ages and very much in common with those of the Greeks. Nevertheless, we no longer consider slavery compatible with a humanitarian morality and we no longer are satisfied with contemplating nature in a general way, but we force nature to answer concrete questions by submitting it, by means of appropriate experiments, to extraordinary conditions. Without what we regard today as our ancestors errors, we would not have arrived at what we call today our truths.

When Spengler urges us to abandon all standards, he asks of us something superhuman, inhuman, and he contradicts himself. On the one hand, he represents the most radical historical relativism; on the other hand, he cherishes the illusion of surmounting it with his "Copernican" conception of history, without realizing that the latter conception is, likewise, conditioned by his epoch and his civilization. Thus, he proposes the most contradictory theses. He reproaches our historians for

[12] Professor Risieri Frondizi was right in saying: "Change supposes elements which are conserved, and the permanence of these elements is what secures historical continuity." (R. Frondizi, "El historicismo y el problema de la verdad", *Dianoia*, 1957, p. 344).

considering Western Europe as a steady pole, while great histories of millennial duration are made to revolve around it. "We select one landscape as the natural center of the historical system. Here is the central sun. From it all the events of history receive their true light."[13] When Spengler criticizes this "Ptolemaic" system and when he tries to replace it by a "Copernican" system, in which foreign and past civilizations weigh as much as, and sometimes even more, than ours, Spengler only continues Voltaire's work. It was this French thinker who undertook and carried out such a project for the first time, completely conscious of what he was doing, in his *Essai sur les moeurs et l'esprit des nations*. In imitating Voltaire, Spengler is followed by Toynbee, as he is in many other respects.

Neither the historian nor the philosopher will deny the merits of such efforts to mitigate our cultural provincialism. But Spengler went much too far, when he imagined that, with his approach, he could overcome historical relativism. He seemed indeed to believe this, when he wrote: "Now, at last, it is possible to take the decisive step of sketching an image of history which no longer depends on the accident of the observer's standpoint in this or that period — in his period. . . ."[14] This certainly is not possible, and Spengler's own historical relativism, manifested in the rest of his work, as well as his nationalistic provincialism, refute his illusion of a history independent from the observer's historical, geographical and cultural standpoint. Here are some of the statements of Spengler which contradict his claim to an historiography independent from the observer's "standpoint": "We men of occidental culture are, with our historical sense, an exception and not a rule. World-history is *our* world picture and not that of 'mankind'."[15]

When Spengler wrote "there are no eternal truths; each philosophy is an expression of its own time and only of its own time",[16] he just repeated Hegel's thesis that "philosophy is its time apprehended in thought".[17]

Finally, Spengler draws the logical conclusion from his historical relativism by writing: "With this, the claim of higher thought to possess general and eternal truths is abolished. Truths exist only in relation to a certain type of mankind. My own philosophy would, then, only be

---

[13] O. Spengler, *Der Untergang des Abendlandes* (München, 1923), I, p. 22.
[14] *Ibid.*, I, p. 127.
[15] *Ibid.*, I, p. 20.
[16] *Ibid.*, I, p. 56.
[17] G. W. F. Hegel, *Grundlinien der Philosophie des Rechts* (Stuttgart, 1928), p. 35.

the expression and reflection of the occidental soul, ... and only in its present, civilized phase. ...."[18]

The best proof of the failure of Spengler's attempt to write a history which is "independent" from the observer's historical, geographical, and cultural standpoint is the provincial narrowness of his own view of German history. "There is no nation which has stood on the same pedestal for centuries", he wrote. "The Prussian-German nation has had the mighty moments of 1813, 1870 and 1914, and that is more than others have had."[19]

But one could ask Spengler: What do these ephemeral successes mean for the history of India, China, and Mexico, or the Arabic world? Obviously nothing. With the narrow perspective of a German jingoist, Spengler showed the vanity of his aspiration to historical universalism, just as did his compatriot Hegel, who saw in the German nation the final one chosen of the World Spirit. As prisoners of their nationalistic German provincialism, these two thinkers considered the moon much bigger than Jupiter and Saturn. It is not in this way that one overcomes the Ptolemaic conception of history.

Oscillating between the illusion of an historiography which is "independent" from the standpoint of the historian and an extreme historical relativism, Spengler urges us to eliminate from history all our own standards of value and to consider as equal all the truths which have emerged in the course of history in all civilizations. "For different men there are different truths. The thinker must admit the validity of *all* or of *none*",[20] he wrote.

I believe that this Spenglerian "thinker's" point of view is quite artificial. One cannot remain *au dessus de la mêlée* — above the conflicts of the millennia. Woe to the nation which does not believe in its truths and values! It will never create anything and will fall into a paralyzing scepticism. But there is no necessity for us to live without such a belief in our truths and values! While realizing that they are relative to our historical epoch and to our civilization, we believe in our values and truths for the simple reason that they are daughters of our time and that they, therefore, represent the axiological and epistemological consciousness and conscience of our epoch. It is in the very name of Historicism that we can insist on the validity of our standards for our epoch and for our civilization.

[18] O. Spengler, *op. cit.*, I, p. 63.
[19] *Ibid.*, I, pp. 49-50.
[20] *Ibid.*, I, p. 33.

Since our values are the only ones we are able to feel and our truths the only ones which can convince us, our prejudice in their favor is almost inevitable. But, as I said before: We may judge other epochs and other civilizations in the light of our own standards of value as long as we recognize our own standards as being relative to our own epoch and our own civilization and as long as we recognize the right of future and foreign civilizations to judge our standards in the light of theirs.

The recognition of the historical relativity of our truths and values is, as we saw, not necessarily tantamount to scepticism and to the abandonment of our ideals. In a moving passage from his novel *Jean Barois,* the great French writer Roger Martin du Gard expresses an idea and a sentiment to which we subscribe entirely:

> Our manner of conceiving justice and truth is infallibly condemned to be surpassed by the coming ages. We know it. But far from discouraging us, this certitude, this hope, are the most efficient stimulants for our present impetus. The strict duty of every generation is, thus, to go as far as it can in the direction of truth, to the extreme limit of what it can see vaguely — and to stick to it desperately, *as if* it could claim to reach absolute truth.[21]

I call this a courageous and noble Historicism. Spengler's is defeatist. If we consider our truths and our values as just as valid or as little valid as those of the Inquisition or those of the Chinese under the Chow dynasty, then nothing is left in history which would be worth defending. The "decline of the West" would then become an inescapable necessity.

In order to know to what extent our truths are historically variable, we must first clarify what we mean by "truth". There are thinkers who consider truths as values. According to Rickert, for example, "truth can only be defined as the particular value which belongs to judgments. ... What I affirm must please me, what I deny must displease me."[22] I do not believe, however, that truth *is* a value. I affirm that truth *has* value. To me, truth is only a carrier of values, not a value-quality like goodness and beauty. Doubtless, truth is useful; it pleases and it is accompanied by feelings of enjoyment. But these feelings could be absent; yet truth would still subsist. I do not deny feelings of cognitive pleasure and displeasure, but they do not found truth, they only accompany it.

In my opinion, truth is a certain epistemological relation which I shall determine in a moment. As such, it can be a carrier of all kinds of

[21] R. Martin du Gard, *Jean Barois* (Paris, 1923), pp. 275-276.
[22] H. Rickert, *Der Gegenstand der Erkenntnis* (Tübingen, 1892), pp. 61, 66.

values: moral, aesthetic, instrumental values, etc. Besides, truth is the carrier of one specific value: cognitive value. Unlike truth, the cognitive value is endowed with the essential character of all values, that is to say, with the property of being graduated and of establishing hierarchies. The fact that truth itself is lacking in this typical property of all values shows that it is not a value. An action is good, better or best; a symphony is beautiful, more beautiful, or most beautiful. But a proposition cannot be "truer" than another one, nor can it be "the truest".

In his *Traité des valeurs*, Louis Lavelle declares that he does not agree with me on this point, since the probabilism of modern science establishes degrees of truth.[23] My answer is that there are no degrees of truth but only degrees of probability. Doubtless, we can ascribe to one truth a higher cognitive value than to another truth. But then, the cognitive value is the value and not the truth. The latter is only the carrier of a value.

But what is truth itself? Formal or logical truth can be defined as a certain relationship between a proposition and other propositions which are called its premises. This relationship is defined by the rules of syllogism. As for material truth — scientific and philosophical — it is the applicability of certain propositions to our observations.

The truth of scientific and philosophical propositions does not consist in the fact that the symbols employed are copies of a reality existing outside theoretical thought. In my opinion, the truth of scientific and philosophical propositions consists in the fact that they are valid for a reality outside theoretical thought: namely, our empirical reality. To be valid means to be applicable to empirical reality in such a way that the factual relations among the parts of empirical reality appear as logically and mathematically necessary relations and can be derived from those propositions. For the sciences, this empirical reality is that of the objective world, including man. For philosophy, this empirical reality is the objective world in its relation to man as a subject.

Truth as the applicability of certain propositions to our experience is, thus, reduced to the fact that our observations are derivable from those propositions. In examining the work of this century's great scientists, we find that their concepts of truth correspond more or less to our definition. Some of them add, however, some specific requirements. To Mach and Duhem, the principles of science are abbreviated economical descriptions of observed facts. To Henri Poincaré, the affirmations and definitions of science are simple "conventions" which are theoretically

[23] L. Lavelle, *Traité des valeurs* (Paris, 1951), Tome I, p. 562.

free. But, in practice the scientist chooses the most convenient ones (*les plus commodes*), those which allow him to order the phenomena with the simplest constructs according to Mach's principle of economy of thought rather than according to Kepler's principle, *natura simplicitatem amat* — nature likes simplicity. For we really know nothing about what nature likes or dislikes. Finally, these constructs are tested by experience and prediction.

In Einstein's epistemological conception, these elements are united. For the creator of the Theory of Relativity, science works with what he called *"freigebildete Begriffe"*[24] — freely-formed concepts. They correspond to Poincaré's "conventions". To Einstein, the physical theories and their laws are free creations of the imagination. This freedom, however, is restricted by the following requirements: The physical laws must be logically compatible among each other, their number should be as small as possible and conclusions logically derived from them must be testable by observation.

Since the symbols and categories which compose our scientific theories are conventions chosen because of their simplicity, our scientific theories never stop changing in the course of history. Every convention exhibits the impress of its time and is, therefore, basically historical. Scientific theories, thus, appear as alternative and historically conditioned modes of representing observed facts, and they are "true" to the extent to which they represent these empirical facts. But the sphere of observable facts also varies in the course of history. It grows without respite. Thus, in the course of history, every scientific theory is superseded by another, applicable to the facts observed with greater simplicity and allowing us to derive newly discovered empirical facts without too many auxiliary hypotheses.

As can be seen, there is not and there cannot be any "eternal", "transhistoric" truth in science. If there were any, this would mean a progressive petrification of science and, finally, its death. *Mors immortalis:* death alone is immortal. As far as I am concerned, I prefer variable and living truths to eternal dead truths.

Since, in each epoch, philosophy posits and solves its problems at a different level of general knowledge, using, as tools of thought, the categories and symbols which correspond to these different levels, it cannot escape the law of history, which is that of change.

We have been told again and again that Historicism does not allow

---

[24] A. Einstein, "Physik und Realität", in *Libres Recherches Allemandes* (Paris, 1938), I, p. 9.

us to conceive of the idea of progress, for, in order to ascertain and to measure progress in history, it would be necessary to have trans-historical standards. I do not believe that this is necessary. For three centuries, our civilization has believed in progress and has measured this progress by establishing standards or norms of values with which it has compared its achievements. To be sure, these standards are themselves historically conditioned; they are children of our modern times, of our western civilization, as is the very idea of progress. This fact only precludes the trans-historical validity of the idea of progress and of its standards, but it does not prevent this idea and its standards from being valid for our civilization and our modern times which created them.

Since the days of Condorcet and Turgot, the standards of values by which progress is measured have not stopped changing. They take the form of ideals, of directive values or norms, which we carry in front of us while marching through history. Mobile as ourselves, these standards always precede us.

As far as science is concerned, the standard by which it measures its progress is, at present, constituted by the idea of a discipline which unites the greatest simplicity of its laws with the greatest number of observable facts derivable from these laws. The standard by which our civilization measures political progress is now represented by the idea of a State in which the freedom of each individual can coexist with the freedom of all — an ideal formulated by Kant. And the standard by which we measure our technological progress is now represented in our civilization by the ideal of a society in which human physical work is reduced to a minimum by a total mechanization of industrial production.

These ideals are strictly those of our epoch and of our Western civilization. In the Renaissance, for example, "natural magic" (*magia naturalis*) as opposed to "diabolical magic" (*magia diabolica*) was considered a legitimate part of science, and its ideal was, in Pico della Mirandola's terms, "to marry the earth with heaven". This famous Italian Neo-Platonist wrote, in 1486, in his *Conclusiones: "Magia naturalis licita est et non prohibita. Magia est pars practica scientiae naturalis. ... Nulla est scientia, quae nos magis certificet de divinitate Christi quam magia,"* etc., — natural magic is legitimate and not prohibited. Magic is a practical part of natural science. There is no science which proves more the divinity of Christ than magic, etc., etc.

When Pico della Mirandola says that *"magiam operare non est aliud quam maritare mundum"* — to practice magic is nothing else than to marry with the world — he illustrates this process by referring to what the Greeks called συμπάθεια, a kind of penetration of the secrets of nature by empathy. Goethe's Faust wished to know "what holds the world together in its innermost" (*"was die Welt im Innersten zusammenhält"*),[25] and with these words he expressed the scientific ideal of his time. Meanwhile, critical philosophy has discarded that ideal and standard, realizing that they are beyond our means.

Just as the ideals of science have changed in the course of history and, with them, the standards by which to measure its progress, so the political ideals and standards have been transformed. During the first decades of the nineteenth century, the political ideal and the standard by which to measure political progress was, for the majority of European countries, the constitutional monarchy. This ideal has now been dead for a long time.

I have not only wanted to show by these examples the extreme historical variability of ideals or directive values and standards. I have also wanted to make it clear that, in spite of this historical variability of ideals and standards, we may ascertain a progress in history. For each civilization and each epoch creates its own ideals and standards and, thus, opens up a road for new possibilities not yet realized in history. Representing the axiological consciousness and conscience of its epoch, each of these ideals and standards is valid for its epoch. If all values, all norms and standards were transhistorical and eternal, this would be tantamount to a total inertia of mankind's axiological consciousness. Measured by our standards of values, this would be hardly an ideal condition. If we are faithful to our ideals of progress, we should not condemn Historicism.

It would be a great mistake to believe that progress is a law inherent in the evolution of mankind, for this belief would presuppose a teleological metaphysics, the validity of which could not be demonstrated. On the contrary, we see that, in the course of history, certain societies have not progressed at all and are remaining stable. But our society progresses, and we can ascertain this when we measure its achievements against the norms we have given ourselves and which serve us as standards. Since we are creating the historical social reality by virtue of our activities, the norms which we give ourselves as standards necessarily influence this historical and social reality. Far from being a gift of history, progress reveals itself as a result of the work of the human collectivities, guided by the norms which they give themselves and which serve as their standards.

Will this progress continue and will it spread over other civilizations?

---

[25] Goethes *Faust,* I, p. 22.

These are questions which can only be answered by the philosophy of history, with the cooperation of sociology of knowledge. Professor Pitirim Sorokin studied these questions in his monumental work *Social and Cultural Dynamics*. The second volume of this book is devoted to the "Fluctuations of Systems of Truth, Ethics, and Law".

Sorokin studies these fluctuations in the influence of the main epistemological currents especially in the Graeco-Roman and Western cultures. He reduces these currents to the three great systems which he calls "Ideational", "Idealistic", and "Sensate". Each of these systems has a concept of truth of its own characterized by a specific criterion.

The Ideational system represents the truth of faith which is superrational and supersensory. In this system, theology is the greatest of sciences and divine inspiration is regarded as the main source of truth. In the ideational system, the method of verification consists of comparing every proposition with a corresponding passage of the Holy Scriptures. Any proposition which agrees with the Holy Scriptures is considered true. Basically, this system, which Sorokin calls "Ideational", corresponds to Comte's theological stage.

As for the system which, in Professor Sorokin's terminology, is called Idealistic, it is a mixture of Rationalism, Empiricism and revealed faith. The main source of what this system considers "truth" is human reason, with subsidiary admission of sensory and revealed truths. Referring to these three sources of truth, the Idealist, in Sorokin's sense, tries to show their perfect harmony. Basically, this system, called "Idealistic" by Professor Sorokin, corresponds to Comte's metaphysical stage.

Finally, the Sensate system is based on the testimony of our senses reinforced by their extensions, such as microscopes, telescopes and all scientific apparatus. This testimony is completed by logical and mathematical reasoning. In this system, science is regarded as the highest authority in all matters of truth and references to religious faith are mostly rejected as superstitions. This system is called „Sensate", because it considers theoretical constructions as pure hypotheses, as long as they have not been verified by the testimony of the senses. Even such a highly abstract theory as Relativity was recognized as true only after having been verified by certain astronomical observations. As it has not yet been tested by observations, the Unified Field Theory is still considered to be an hypothesis. Obviously, Sorokin's "Sensate" system corresponds to Comte's positive stage.

Since we live in a civilization and an age of scientism, we are prone to believe that scientific truth is the only system of truth and that everything outside it is fallacious and superstitious. But an impartial investigator of socio-cultural phenomena, like Professor Sorokin, calls our attention to the fact that the supporters of metaphysical and religious truth, likewise, consider their concepts of truth as the only valid ones. And this is an undeniable fact, even today. Scholars like Jacques Maritain or Arnold Toynbee regard scientific truth as an inferior degree of truth revealing only the most superficial aspect of reality. According to these thinkers, reality reveals itself only in metaphysical and religious truth.

Of course, we may object that only the scientific interpretation of reality is empirically verifiable, both by the testimony of our senses and by the realization of our theoretical predictions, while metaphysical and religious systems cannot be verified empirically. But then, the representatives of metaphysical and religious systems may reply that empirical verification is only a requirement of our scientific way of looking at the world and that, if we consider empirical verification as necessary, it is only because we have adopted scientism. For those who do not adopt it, empirical verification is in no way a necessary requirement of truth. Thanks to their metaphysical reasonings or to their religious intuitions, they are so strongly convinced of their theses' truth that they can dispense with empirical verification.

What Professor Sorokin's sociology of knowledge tries to prove is summed up in the following paragraph:

> When a culture passes from, say, the Ideational to the Sensate type, or vice versa, all its art, philosophy, religion, science, ethics, and law undergo the same profound transformation. From this standpoint, the volume attempts to demonstrate that what a given society regards as true or false, scientific or unscientific, right or wrong, lawful or unlawful, beautiful or ugly, is conditioned fundamentally by the nature of the dominant culture.[26]

In other words: what appears to be beautiful or ugly, moral or immoral, true or false, what is considered to be a valid criterion of truth and what is not — all this is a function of the socio-cultural variable. Since the latter changes in the course of history, Sorokin's Sociologism is tantamount to Historicism.

In order to determine the fluctuations of the different systems of truth mentioned, Professor Sorokin and his collaborators, Professors Lossky and Lapshin, made the following investigation: They estimated the comparative rise and fall in the influence of each system of truth

---

[26] P. A. Sorokin, *Social and Cultural Dynamics* (New York, 1937), vol. II, p. VII.

by the number of its supporters from among the majority of prominent thinkers in the field in each twenty-year period and in each one-hundred-year period from 580 B.C. to A.D. 1920. The objective criteria of the comparative influence of each thinker included the number of monographs devoted to each of them, the approximate frequency with which their names were mentioned by their contemporaries, their successors, etc.

What resulted is a very interesting piece of statistics. In Professor Sorokin's interpretation, it refutes the popular opinion that there exists a linear trend consisting of a progressive increase of empirical, scientific truth at the expense of metaphysical and religious truth. He believes that the generality of this opinion is only due to the fact that we live in a scientific civilization which considers empirical verification as the only valid one. According to Sorokin, our contemporaries repeat the formulae of Turgot, Condorcet, Saint-Simon and, especially, the following of Comte: that, in the course of its evolution, mankind passes from the theological through the methaphysical to the positive stages of its mind. "It is apparent that the formula is wrong," says Professor Sorokin. "The data presented support the theories of G. B. Vico and others on trendless fluctuation rather than the theories of other scholars on the linear trend of growth. ... However improbable it may seem, it is possible that, in some future time, the present empirical system of truth will also decline. It is at least as probable as the belief that, in the future, the empirical system of truth will grow perpetually."[27]

I cannot accept this opinion of Professor Sorokin's, for I do not believe that the chances of a growth and decline of scientism in the future are the same. Professor Sorokin's statistics show clearly that, in the last five centuries, the empiristic system of truth has been continually rising. The detractors of this system may speak of science as a "false god" or a "sacred cow";[28] they may condemn what they call "the counterrevolution of science".[29] They can, nevertheless, no longer live without the benefits of science and no longer think without the methods of empirical verification. Although science is a *succès de scandale*, it is a success. It gives man such great power that one can hardly imagine that he would some day voluntarily renounce it. To be sure, the light of Graeco-Roman antiquity was followed by the darkness of the Middle Ages. But Greek science was theoretical and the privilege of a small

---

[27] *Ibid.*, II, p. 33.
[28] A. Standen, *Science Is a Sacred Cow* (New York, 1950).
[29] F. A. Hayek, *The Counterrevolution of Science* (Glencoe, 1952).

caste. In contrast to modern science, it never changed the way of life of the great masses of men.

Professor Sorokin tries to justify his thesis by pointing out that there has never been a Spencerian evolution from the less differentiated to the more differentiated status. But it was by refuting these same "evolutionary illusions" of Spencer that Professor André Lalande arrived at a conclusion opposed to Professor Sorokin's: i.e., that science not only assimilates things among themselves, in the sense of Émile Meyerson, and the things to the minds, but that it also assimilates the minds to each other. The more civilization advances, the more one can see how the diversity of customs, of moral, intellectual and juridical conceptions disappear in the world.

To be sure, with its belief in progress, our scientific and technological civilization is only one of many produced in the course of history. It is not only temporally but also spatially limited. For, on this same planet on which we live, hundreds of millions of men — for example the Hindoos — do not believe in progress and do not consider empirical verification as the only valid criterion of truth. Nevertheless, by its very nature, our scientific civilization is spreading over the earth by way of a progressive assimilation of minds to each another. In my opinion, capitalism and communism, this time on the same side of the fence, have powerfully contributed to this progressive assimilation of the oriental civilizations to the scientific technological civilization of the West. The following well known passage from the *Communist Manifesto* illustrates this point very well:

> The bourgeoisie, by the rapid improvement of all instruments of production, by the immensely facilitated means of communication, draws all, even the most barbarian nations, into civilization. The cheap prices of its commodities are the heavy artillery with which it batters down all Chinese walls, with which it forces the barbarians' intensely obstinate hatred of foreigners to capitulate. It compels all nations, on pain of extinction, to adopt the bourgeois mode of production; it compels them to introduce what it calls civilization into their midst, i.e., to become bourgeois themselves. In a word, it creates a world after its own image.[30]

One century after these lines were written, Marxism succeeded capitalism in propagating among six hundred million Chinese the ideal of Western science, technology and progress. Today, the oriental civiliza-

---

[30] K. Marx, F. Engels, *Manifesto of the Communist Party* (New York, 1932), p. 325.

tion of China hardly knows any other criterion of truth than that of Western science and is devoting itself to technological projects of amazing dimensions. Japan, too, entirely adopted modern technological scientism, and India is increasingly penetrated by it. For the first time in history, *one* civilization is tending to become universal on our earth. And this process will continue, for, as Professor J. Robert Oppenheimer says, "the world cannot endure half-darkness and half-light".[31]

One could object that only Oppenheimer's evaluations as those of a modern Western scientist motivate him to regard as "half-dark" the condition of man in certain non-scientific non-technological civilizations. To us intellectuals, knowledge is an intrinsic value and we are prone to suppose that this is everybody's evaluation. "To be learning something is the greatest of pleasures not only to the philosopher but also to the rest of mankind,"[32] says Aristotle. Let us take care not to fall into such generalizations!

But, if one cannot affirm the universal supra-historical character of the intrinsic value of knowledge, its instrumental value is, in my opinion, of suprahistorical validity. The reason is that the instrumental value of knowledge is based on intrinsic evaluations which are bound up with the human condition. While denying a human nature, we admit — like Sartre, Malraux, and other contemporary thinkers — the existence of a human condition, which, common to all men, is manifested in a fundamental attitude to life, suffering and death. The historical situations are changing and so are the intellectual and moral capacities of men. What does not change in the course of history is the fact that man is a being conscious of his existence, that he is in the world, that he has to act in order to maintain himself in existence, that he loves and hates, that he propagates himself, falls ill, suffers, tries to escape from suffering, that he knows he must die, fears death and finally dies. In my opinion, this human condition is a constant in history; it is suprahistorical, independent of civilizations and their degrees of evolution, and also independent of social habitats. Here we see, indeed, a breach being opened in the solid wall of Historicism.

The fact that men do accept and always have accepted their human condition is, in my opinion, the expression of certain fundamental evaluations, common to all men, of all civilizations, of all historical epochs and all social habitats. These evaluations consist in ascribing to

[31] J. R. Oppenheimer, "Science and Our Times", *Bulletin of the Atomic Scientists* (Chicago), vol. VII, Nr. 7 (Sept. 1956), p. 235.
[32] Aristotle, *De Poetica*, 1448 b.

life and health a positive value and to suffering and death a negative one. These values, which I call existential, are intrinsic, for they are affirmed for their own sake. These intrinsic existential values necessarily entail certain instrumental values. For everything which preserves life and alleviates human suffering becomes a positive value, everything which threatens life and increases suffering becomes a negative value. Thus it has been at all times and thus it is in all places. The difference between the civilizations and historical epochs with regard to these existential values consists only in the evaluation of the means by which this common human project of living and fighting the sufferings of life can be achieved. For the Australian primitive, this means is magic, as it was for the medieval European; for modern occidental man, it is science, especially pharmacology, chemistry, medicine, hygiene, technology, the struggle against ignorance and superstition.

I used the term "project of living" common to all men. Obviously, here it is not a question of a consciously devised act of mankind, which, itself, is only an abstraction. However, it is obvious that, in accepting the human condition with all it implies, men of all times and all civilizations resolve to face it, as far as it is possible. It is that which I call the project of living common to all men of all ages, all civilizations, all social habitats.

The evaluation of what constitutes an appropriate means for carrying out the project of living is variable; it is historically and socially conditioned. Conversely, the values which form the basis of this common project to face the human condition — that is the positive value ascribed to life and health and the negative value ascribed to suffering and death — are timeless, invariable, suprahistorical, trans-social, for they originate in the common and invariable human condition, face to face with life and death. These values are truly universal in the sense that they are independent of the individual peculiarities of the evaluatting subjects and independent of the collective peculiarities of the evaluating groups. They are, also, independent of the civilizations and their historical and social variations.

Even Buddhism and Christianity do not deny the positive value of life. The Nirvana means only the dissolution of individual life in the living ocean of the universe. It preserves the essential character of life, which is lacking in a rock. In an analogous way, what the Christian prefers to earthly life is not the inanimate condition of the rock; it is the blessed life in the hereafter which shares with terrestrial life the essential criterion of being life.

In accepting the human condition and in projecting (or resolving) to face it, men of all epochs have established certain fundamental existential values. They constitute an objective transhistorical standard by which to measure the instrumental values able to realize these existential values. Life and health having been established as intrinsic positive values and suffering and death as intrinsic negative values, everything capable of preserving life and of alleviating the sufferings and miseries of human existence becomes a positive instrumental value; everything which threatens life and increases human suffering becomes a negative instrumental value. Now, it is easy to prove objectively by definite experiments that biochemistry, medicine, hygiene and the struggle against ignorance are more effective means of alleviating human misery and of lengthening the human life span than magic.

The fulfilment of the human project of living requires certain objective conditions, the determination of which no longer depends on subjective tastes but on an objective, empirical and rational examination of the most suitable means of reaching the desired ends. The instrumental values borne by these means will, then, only reflect the objective requirements imposed upon us by the execution of the project of living. By comparing the magic means used by primitive civilizations with the scientific means used by our modern civilization, the superiority of the latter can be measured objectively by a comparison of the results obtained in the two cases.

With these assertions, we have established an objective limit to Historicism and its principle, *veritas et virtus filiae temporis*. We have, also, refuted Spengler's "absolute" relativism with its thesis of the equivalence of all the truths and values that have emerged in the course of history in the different civilizations. To be sure, the majority of scientific and philosophical truths vary in the course of history, just as do most of the cognitive, moral and aesthetic values. But the proposition that, for the realization of the intrinsic values expressed in the human project of living, science and technology represent higher instrumental values than magic — this proposition is of suprahistorical validity, for it is based on objective facts demonstrable at any moment of history by definite experiments. Also, the standard of these instrumental values is removed from historical and social variations, because it is constituted by the intrinsic values expressed in the general transhistorical acceptance of the invariable human condition.

If, thus, modern occidental man believes in the superiority of his civilization, his pride is not vain; for it is based on the incomparable power of this civilization to face the human condition, which is the permanent fixed pole amid the perpetual flight of historical events.

VIII. HISTORICAL PROJECTS AND VALUES

We have just shown that there are certain limits to Historicism, the most important of which is the invariable human condition with regard to life and death. This constitutes a transhistorical fact and the fixed pole amid the perpetual flight of historical events. Let us appreciate it at its face-value without overrating it: for it is not an Archimedean point which could enable us to lift up the whole world of Historicism and to overthrow it. The human condition is not a human nature. While the latter was supposed to contain the universal, transhistorical, eternal standards of all truths, all values, and all principles of right and morals, the acceptance of the human condition by all men only throws into relief some isolated transhistorical standards.

In accepting the human condition, we have said, the men of all epochs, all civilizations, and all social habitats adopt the project of facing it. This project of living, common to all men, shows that they ascribe and always have ascribed a positive value to life and health and a negative value to suffering and death. Therefore, we considered these existential values which are bound up with the project of living as transhistorical values, independent of the different epochs, civilizations, and social environments.

Although they are not very numerous, these existential values are of great theoretical importance; for they constitute supra-historical objective standards which enable us to measure the degrees of all instrumental historical values, capable of furthering the realization of the transhistorical project of living. In this way, we have been able to demonstrate the higher instrumental value of our scientific technological civilization as a means, unmatched in history, of alleviating human suffering and of lengthening the human life span — two essential aims of the transhistorical human project of living.

Thus, Historicism can no longer declare that *all* values are daughters of their respective times and that one cannot prove their transhistorical validity. On the one hand, we have discovered some intrinsic existential values, the transhistorical validity of which cannot be denied, since it is expressed in the acceptance of the human condition by the men of all epochs and all civilizations in their common project of living. These existential values are, as we said, the positive value ascribed to life and health and the negative value ascribed to suffering and death.

Besides, the whole domain of instrumental values is not subject to the ascendancy of Historicism. Of course, the means capable of promoting certain intrinsic values are developed in the course of history. But, at any moment in history, the instrumental value of these means with regard to a given intrinsic value can be verified in a way which is objective and of transhistorical validity.

In this way, it can be demonstrated by objective experiments that, for the preservation of the intrinsic values of life and health, asepsis and antibiotics are higher instrumental values than antiseptic methods. Since life and health are transhistoric values, affirmed and reaffirmed in the human project of living, they will always be fit to serve as standards by which to measure the degrees of the instrumental values of different epochs, capable of furthering that transhistoric project. In the next century, there will probably be remedies which surpass penicillin in their power to preserve human lives, and in two centuries' time they will be still more powerful. Thus, the instrumental values capable of promoting such transhistoric intrinsic values as life and health form a hierachy, the recognition of which no longer depends on the subjective "tastes" of the different epochs but on the objective properties of these means. As long as men maintain their common project of living —that is to say, as long as there is history — it will be possible to demonstrate in an objective and transhistorically valid way that the method of throwing silver iodide from an airplane to clouds is a more efficient way of making rain than the magic dances of the primitives in honor of the god of rain. And a more efficient means of reaching a desired end is a higher instrumental value, the degree of which is independent of the tastes and predilections of the different historical periods and civilizations.

Thus, at least, the superiority of the instrumental value of the scientific technological civilization — if not the superiority of its intrinsic value — can be demonstrated objectively and with transhistorical validity; for the result of a comparison between the effects produced by scientific methods and by magical procedures will always be the same, at any historical epoch and in any cultural and social environment.

Here, an objective aspect of values becomes noticeable, an aspect which traditional philosophy for a long time neglected. But, recently, several thinkers have tried to show the insufficiency of the methods which regard the subject as the only source of all values and reject the object as a negligible factor. In the United States, John Dewey insisted on the "transactional" character of values.[1] Values are, indeed, always revealed in transactions between subjects and objects. "Evaluative judgments cannot be arrived at ... without going outside the 'value field' into matters physical, physiological, anthropological, historical, socio-psychological, and so on,"[2] Dewey declares.

Another American philosopher, Professor Iredell Jenkins, threw into relief with admirable clarity the objective requirements which our biological and social environments impose upon us and to which our evaluations must respond. Here is what Professor Jenkins wrote:

> Man then becomes a creature who must satisfy the objective conditions of life, but who encounters real subjective alternatives in the ways he can satisfy them. ... Finally, values become both reports of conditions that life imposes and expressions of the individual's response to these conditions. Values are obligatory because they define the general demands and possibilities with which life confronts the human creature; they are preferential, because they incarnate what each man seeks to realize and create through his life.[3]

To me, it seems to follow from the foregoing that, as soon as man has adopted the project of living, he must fulfil the objective — biological, social, and other conditions necessary for the conservation of life, and his evaluations must reflect these objective requirements which the execution of the project of living imposes on him. A system of values incompatible with these objective requirements of life would, in the long run, make the conservation of life impossible.

If this is so, then the objective side of values has, of necessity, causal implications. Professor Werkmeister insists very strongly that evaluative judgments are partly rooted in our understanding of causal chains. It is possible, he says, that an object — for example a certain dish — which, at present, occasions a pleasure, is causally linked to a state of affairs which, at a later time, occasions an intense disvalue experience, for example an illness. In this case the causal connection "provides a factual framework for a contextual re-evaluation of the present felt value".[4]

---

[1] J. Dewey, "The Field of 'Value'", *Value, A Cooperative Inquiry*, edit. by R. Lepley (New York, 1949), p. 69.
[2] *Ibid.*, p. 77.
[3] I. Jenkins, "The Present Status of the Value Problem", *The Review of Metaphysics* (New Haven, Conn.), Sept. 1950, p. 109.
[4] W. H. Werkmeister, "An Empirical Approach to Value Theory", *The Personalist*, vol. XXXVI, No. 4 (Autumn, 1955), p. 357.

The values based on relations established by natural laws are those which Professor Viktor Kraft calls "natural values".[5]

These objective causal aspects of values confirm the ideas which Johannes Erich Heyde expressed thirty-six years ago. According to this thinker, the evaluation is a progressive knowledge of the object of value and is based on what he called the *"Wertgrund"*[6], the reason for the value. When asking "Why does this object have value?" we must distinguish between the fact on which the value is based and the fact in which it consists. The value of an object may be based on its utility, but it does not consist in this utility. It consists in the relation of this object to a feeling of the subject. But when this feeling of value is linked with the object because of its utility, the latter is the reason for its value. Because I have recognized — let us say, the healing power of a certain remedy, I ascribe to it a positive instrumental value, which is not restricted to the moments when it gives me relief. Because it creates in us a state of serenity and peace of mind to hear a symphony by Mozart, we ascribe to it a high aesthetic value, which is, also, not restricted to the time of our hearing the music, but is permanent. Because the reading of a certain book of Pascal's reveals to us certain truths and frees us from certain doubts, we ascribe to it a high cognitive value, again, not restricted to the moments when we read the book. Although the feelings of relief, beauty, serenity, intellectual satisfaction etc. caused by these objects of value are felt only at certain moments, the relations of these objects to these feelings are permanent. The "permanent" character of these evaluations — although subjected to changes due to new experiences — is manifested by the relative identity of our evaluative judgments on their objects at different times.

Professor Risieri Frondizi, who did very much to clarify the problems of contemporary axiology, showed that values exist and are meaningful only within definite concrete situations and circumstances.[7] In ascribing to certain goods "permanent" values, i.e. values not restricted to the moments when we actually feel them, I do not think that we deny the influence of concrete situations and circumstances. I believe that we imply those situations and conditions in which these values can manifest themselves in full. For example, in affirming the positive aesthetic value of a symphony by Mozart, we imply that it is performed by highly qualified musicians and in external circumstances which do not impair

[5] V. Kraft, *Die Grundlagen einer wissenschaftlichen Wertlehre* (Wien, 1937), p. 192.
[6] J. E. Heyde, *Wert, eine philosophische Grundlegung* (Erfurt, 1926), p. 161.
[7] R. Frondizi, ? *Qué son los valores?* (Mexico, Buenos Aires, 1958), pp. 125-136.

the listener's contemplation. And, in affirming the "permanent" value of a certain remedy, we imply that the patient takes the prescribed amount and does not suffer from other ailments which would cancel its healing power.

These examples show that our value judgments have reasons, that they are, to a certain extent, rational. What, in my opinion, remains irrational in the domain of axiology is the fact that a positive value feeling is linked, for instance, to a psychological state of serenity or to the revelation of certain purely speculative truths.

I think that both of these relations — the rational as well as the irrational — are subject to historical changes. To give an example of an historical change in the rational component of our evaluations, I would say that a remedy highly valued in the Middle Ages may no longer be considered a positive value, *because* modern science has replaced it with more efficient ones. The conjunction "because" shows clearly the rational character of this historical change in our evaluation. But it is also conceivable that in very active, dynamic epochs or in very utilitarian pragmatic types of civilizations, serenity, peace of mind, or the revelation of purely speculative truths may no longer be felt to be positive values. I think that such an historical change in human evaluations would concern the irrational component of axiology. The rightness of the rational type of change mentioned can be proved, the wrongness of the irrational change referred to cannot be proved, although it may be felt by those whose evaluations are not utilitarian.

As we saw earlier, there are, however, evaluations which have hardly changed in the course of history and have also been identical in different civilizations and classes: the attribution of a positive value to life and health and of a negative value to suffering and death. If it were otherwise, there would not be any history. For, in the widest sense, history is the carrying out of the common human project of living. But the realization of this project would be impossible without a positive valuation of life and health. Only because of these valuations do we have a history.

The great importance of the common human project of living lies in the fact that it is the inescapable condition of all history. As long as men maintain this common project, as long as they accept the unchangeable human condition and resolve to face it, there will be history. If, some day, mankind were to refuse to accept this human condition and to give up the project of living, following Schopenhauer's advice, history would stop at the same time.

It is the common human project of living which creates history, and the perpetual execution of this project is the condition of any continuation of history. As an *a priori* condition of all history, the human project of living is, thus, necessarily transhistorical and not merely *de facto*. Thus, the existential values which this project implies are also of necessity, transhistorical.

But, besides these existential values (life and health), there are many others, the affirmation or negation of which are not expressed in the transhistorical human project of living. These values, which we shall call non-existential, remain subject to history and its variations.

The main difference between these two classes of values consists in the fact that the values we call existential are based on transhistorical postulates — those affirmed in the human project of living — while the values called non-existential are based on historical postulates. But this difference does not exclude features which are common to existential transhistorical values and to non-existential historical values. For, as soon as a postulate is adopted and established as a norm — be it a transhistorical or an historical postulate — it serves as a standard by which to determine the positive or negative quality of any given value and to measure its degree. Only the postulate adopted as a norm can bestow validity on a value or on an evaluative judgment. Any value in agreement with the postulate adopted as a norm will be positive; any value in disagreement with this postulate will be negative. A value cannot be verified "in itself", but only relatively to a standard adopted as a norm. Let us give some examples:

In order to be able to qualify conduct as "good" or "bad", an object of art or nature as "beautiful" or "ugly", a proposition as "meaningful" or "meaningless", one must have postulated norms of the "good", the "beautiful" and the "meaningful", against which the conduct, the object of art or nature and the proposition can be tested. According to their agreement or disagreement with these norms, we shall ascribe to them positive or negative moral, aesthetic or cognitive values.

It follows that any concrete value can be defined in terms of agreement or non-agreement of an action, a proposition and an object with a postulated norm. Thus, one of the essential problems of the philosophy of values is to determine the source of these postulated norms which serve as standards for the values of different civilizations and epochs. The question whether these normative postulates are transhistorical or whether they emerge from history is answered by us in the following way: the normative postulates of existential values are transhistorical; the normative postulates of non-existential values are historical. The norms set up in the course of history by the different civilizations and nations determine their value systems and set a special impress upon each of them.

But how do these different normative postulates arise which serve as value-standards for the different civilizations and epochs? This is another essential question concerning the relations between value and history which we shall try to answer.

First, we have to ascertain that every norm results from an act of will — be it an individual or a collective will. In both cases, this will is human. As for the existential values, this will is expressed in the acceptance of the human condition by the men of all epochs and all civilizations and in their project of facing this condition. Representing a transhistorical phenomenon, the project of living is based on a trans-historical postulate: it is the postulate that life and health are positive values, that suffering and death are negative values and that life should be lived with a minimum of suffering. This postulate which serves as a norm for all values related to existence is, obviously, not always formulated, but it constitutes the logical supposition tacitly admitted in the human project of living.

As for the non-existential values, the will which sets up the normative postulates is always an historically conditioned will. What this historical will has in common with the transhistorical will behind the existential values is the fact that it sets up norms, normative postulates which serve as standards for other values. Nothing but the postulate adopted as a norm by an act of will can confer validity upon all the values belonging to the value-system of a certain domain, a certain civilization or epoch.

As soon as the postulate is adopted and recognized as a norm, all acts, objects and propositions agreeing with it acquire a positive value and all those in disagreement acquire a negative value. The diversity of the postulates adopted as norms by the different civilizations, nations and historical epochs explains their diversity.

Obviously, the norms postulated are themselves values. I call them "values of the first degree", while the values for which they serve as standards are "values of the second degree". If, theoretically, all values of the first degree, that is all norms, arise from certain acts of will — individual or collective — practically all these acts of will appear concretely in the form of definite projects. We have seen it in the case of the existential values, the normative postulate of which is embodied in the transhistorical project of living. The same holds for the non-existential values, the normative postulates of which are always embod-ied in definite historical projects.

If, logically, every project presupposes an act of will, we may say that, psychologically, every act of will appears in the concrete form of a project. Only in or through a project do we become conscious of our volitions and evaluations. In the beginning, neither of the two exists in an abstract state. Thus, I should say that the projects are the particularizations of our volitions and evaluations. Only after the genesis of the project and, sometimes, even only in the course of or after its realization, do the evaluations it implies separate from the project and become crystallized as concepts which can be grasped in an abstract way.

As soon as a project is conceived and, with it, a normative postulate is adopted, we always have to do something in order to realize the project and to live according to the postulated norm. The totality of actions necessary for the realization of a given project is what one calls the duty. Since the project and the normative postulate it implies are things willed, it follows that our duties result from our volitions. If our duties seem sometimes opposed to our volitions, it is because the objective of our will — our personal project or the collective project of our group — is general, while the duties it imposes are particular. Only, because we *want* to live in society and enjoy the security this life offers, we ought to submit to the laws of that society and also accept their unwanted consequences, such as the limitations which life in socitey imposes on the free manifestation of our impulses.

One remembers Kant's distinction between hypothetical imperatives and the categorical imperative. He called an imperative "hypothetical" which requires an action only in order that another end which has been willed may be attained. On the contrary, the "categorical" imperative commands an action because it is good in itself and objectively necessary, without any reference to an end outside itself. Kant's categorical imperative thus constitutes an unconditional duty.

In my opinion, there are, however, no unconditional duties, for any duty is conditioned by a volition, by a will expressed in a definite project. But, if all imperatives are hypothetical, because they are conditioned by a project wanted and by a norm postulated, then there is no categorical imperative. Nevertheless, I do not deny the validity of the imperative Kant called categorical. I only deny its categorical character. In my opinion, Kant's imperative "act only on that maxim whereby you can at the same time will that it should become a universal law"[8] is hypothetical because it is conditioned by the human project of

---

[8] I. Kant, *Grundlegung zur Metaphysik der Sitten*, 2. Abschnitt, p. 44.

living in society, peace and security, with a maximum of freedom. Since man is a ζῷον πολιτικόν, a political or social animal, this project enjoys a high degree of generality; hence, the high degree of generality of the imperative which Kant called "categorical". I think that only when this imperative is adopted as a norm, does it constitute a standard by which to judge all moral acts. And it *is* adopted as a norm — at least tacitly — as soon as the human project of living in society is adopted.

At a previous stage in our inquiry, we quoted the example of a certain king's tailor, unessential for political history but possibly essential for the history of fashions. This example led us to the conclusion that the political historian uses a different code of values from the historian of fashions and that, generally, the different historiographical projects imply different codes of values. To every project there corresponds another code of values, and each of these codes is characterized by another normative postulate.

When examining other domains, we find that the validity of this principle is not limited to historiographical projects but extends to all human projects. The physicians, the lawyers, the scientists, the teachers, the journalists, the soldiers, the businessmen, etc., are distinguished from one another by their different collective projects, and each of these projects implies a different code of values dominated by a different normative postulate. Thus, there exists a professional ethics for the physicians, conditioned by their common project of saving human lives and of alleviating the physical and mental sufferings of men. The professional ethics of the lawyers is conditioned by their common project of assisting their fellowmen who are in possible or real conflict with the law or who are deprived of the law's benefits. The professional ethics of the teachers is conditioned by their common project of instructing the youth and requires, for example, the explanation of the subject matter without bias. The professional ethics of the soldiers is conditioned by their common project of defending their country, while the professional ethics of the businessmen is conditioned by their project of providing people with commodities.

As for the professional ethics of the scientists, it is at present experiencing a crisis, owing to certain changes in their projects. The invention of nuclear weapons, for instance, raised the ethical problem of the scientists' responsibility for the use of these discoveries.

According to the differences between the projects, there consequently exists a plurality of moralities, including both individual and collective moralities. Among the latter, we may distinguish the professional ethics, the ethics of political parties, of classes, of nations, and, finally, the ethics of mankind. Let us designate this state of affairs as moral pluralism. Since every individual has personal projects and, besides, participates in diverse collective projects, he has different codes of values, the imperatives of which are sometimes conflicting. A man has, for example, a project as a father, a project as a husband, a project as a member of a professional group, another as a member of an association, of a political party, etc. Besides, he participates in the collective project of his nation, of his church, of his class, the minority group to which he may belong, etc. Finally, each man participates in the collective project of mankind by virtue of being a specimen of *homo sapiens.* Since each of these projects entails another code of values, the conflicts of values are sometimes inevitable for the individual. That which, according to the code of one definite project is a positive value appears as a negative value according to another project which a certain man has adopted.

Sartre tells of one of his students who came to see him during the German occupation under the following circumstances: his elder brother had been killed by the Germans in 1940 and his mother lived alone with him and found consolation only in him. This young man now had the choice between escaping to England in order to enlist in the Free French Forces or staying with his mother and helping her to make a living. In the latter case, he would have had to abandon his country and his idea of avenging his brother's death.

To Sartre, this example demonstrates man's "abandonment" (*délaissement*) in his choice of values.[9] To me, it proves one of those conflicts of values resulting from the diversity of our projects, each of which entails another code of values. In my opinion, one can distinguish three different projects between which the young man mentioned was divided: his project as a son, his project as a brother, his project as a citizen. According to the code of values arising from his project as a citizen, his flight to England and his enlistment in the Free French Forces was a positive value and a moral duty. This code of values coincided with that arising from his project as a brother, but conflicted with the code of values arising from his project as a son. The latter summoned him to help his mother and, consequently, to abandon his country and the idea of avenging his brother's death.

The dilemma of the young man resulted thus from the fact that each project entails a specific ethics with specific imperatives. In view of the diversity of human projects, conflicts between the different codes of

[9] J. P. Sartre, *L'existentialisme est un humanisme* (Paris, 1946), p. 39ff.

values they impose upon us are extremely probable. The way to resolve such a conflict of values in a concrete case is either to abandon one or several of the conflicting projects or to violate certain values implied in their codes. Both alternatives are mostly tragic, according to my definition of the "tragic" as a loss of values which could have been avoided and which, nevertheless, occurs.[10] To be sure, it could have been avoided, but only by sacrificing other positive values arising from other projects. We must accept these tragic losses which reveal the precariousness of human values. It is the price we have to pay for the pluralism of human projects which enrich our lives and are the moving forces of history.

Besides the *different* moralities required by the diversity of human projects, there is, however, *one* morality conditioned by the only project common to all men: that of facing the human condition, the project of living without too much suffering. The code of values derived from the universal human project of living constitutes *basic human ethics*. As we know, this human project of living is due to the positive evaluation of life and health by all men of all times, all civilizations and all social habitats. From these existential values, affirmed in the human project of living, the code of values of basic human ethics is derived. Bound up with this project, the basic code of human ethics must also take into account the objective, biological and social conditions necessary for the conservation of human life in nature and society. Otherwhise, human life could not be preserved on our earth, and history would not be able to continue.

Since the human project of living is supra-historical, the code of values derived from it — that is, basic human ethics — is likewise of supra-historical validity. It is valid for all times, all civilizations and all social habitats, since the human project of facing the unchangeable human condition is, likewise, common to all times, all civilizations, and all social habitats. Since life in society is one of the objective conditions necessary for the conservation of the life of man, that social animal, it seems to me that Kant's categorical imperative constitutes a fundamental principle of human ethics. As we have said, this imperative is not really "categorical", for it is not unconditionally valid. It is valid only on the condition that man has adopted the project of living and of living in society. But this condition has always been fulfilled in history and must always be fulfilled in history, for, otherwise, there would not be any history.

[10] A. Stern, *Philosophie du rire et des pleurs* (Paris, 1949), p. 252.

The code of values derived from man's transhistorical project of living postulates the positive value of man and his life. I think that the best epitome of this basic human ethics is Seneca's sentence: *homo homini res sacra* — man is to man a sacred thing.

With the unchangeable human condition, the transhistorical project of facing it, that is, of living, and the code of values ensuing from this project under the name of basic human ethics, we finally have found a supra-historical standard by which to judge the values of all historical projects. This supra-historical standard allows us to condemn with transhistorical validity all attacks against the only supra-historical values: human life and health, and the objective conditions necessary for their preservation on earth. This means that, in the name of our supra-historical basic human ethics, we are entitled to castigate all violations of the sanctity of human life, all killings, all cruelties, all sufferings willfully imposed on men in any epoch of human history. We are, thus, entitled to condemn the fights with wild animals imposed on the Roman gladiators, the stakes of the Inquisition, Hitler's gas-chambers, and the secret executions ordered by Stalin; for, whatever the "conceptions" of a given historical period or civilization may have been, life and health were always appreciated as positive values, for men always wanted to live without suffering. Thus, no historically conditioned customs, dogmas or traditions had a right over and above the supra-historical values of life and health.

There exists a great human solidarity opposed to death and suffering, a solidarity due to the project of living, common to all men. If, in the street, we witness, by chance, an accident in which a stranger is involved, our only preoccupation is to be assured that the person concerned was not killed and that his or her life can be saved. As soon as we get this certainty, we feel relieved, as if we had won a collective victory over death. This moral solidarity is due to our common human project of living and to the code of values derived from it.

If we call this code of values basic human ethics, it is because it refers only to the basic values of human existence: life and health. Since the latter are existential values, we may designate fundamental human ethics *existential ethics*. Only these basic existential values are affirmed in the transhistorical human project of living and they alone can be objects of a transhistorical existential human ethics. All other human projects are historically conditioned and entail that great variety of specific, historically conditioned moralities which we analyzed earlier under the name of "moral pluralism".

The recognition of human life and health as basic supra-historical existential values, protected by a supra-historical code of existential ethics, does not exclude the possibility that an individual may sacrifice his life and health to his idea. Socrates and other great individuals were examples. The ideal an individual values higher than his life or health is, however, always due to an historically conditioned project. Since he adopted it, he may sacrifice his life and his health in its service; but only his own life and his own health. He has no right to sacrifice to his ideal the lives and health of other people, the value of which they have affirmed by adopting the project of living. As existential supra-historical values, life and health are presuppositions of all non-existential historical values and, therefore, have precedence over them.

When I say that life and health are basic human values, that does not mean that they are the highest values. As basic values, they cannot be the highest ones. Nicolai Hartmann has shown that, if organic life is based on material being, if psychic life is based on organic life and spiritual life on psychic life, then the lower stratum is always stronger, and the higher stratum depends on it. But this does not prevent the higher strata from enjoying a certain degree of liberty and autonomy.[11]

I think that, in an analogous way, life and health are the stronger values, since they constitute the existential foundations and conditions of all superior values, that is, of aesthetic, intellectual and certain moral values developed in the course of history in different civilizations, and these higher values depend on the lower ones. But this does not prevent the higher historical values from enjoying a certain degree of liberty and autonomy with regard to the vital, existential, transhistorical values. The stronger value is the one which imposes itself with greater vigor. It is not necessarily the higher one. Existential human ethics offers only an ethical minimum, but it is the basic one nevertheless.

At the beginning of our inquiry, we insisted that history is the development of the *res publica* and not that of the *res privata*. Consequently, the historical projects are always collective projects. Every time an individual project ends up by influencing the march of history, it is because it has been adopted by a collectivity. This happens, for instance, in the case of scientific discoveries, technological inventions or artistic creations.

What are the collectivities whose projects determine history? For Hegel, they are the States, for Marx, the classes. Probably, both of

---

[11] N. Hartmann, *Das Problem des geistigen Seins* (Berlin, 1949), pp. 16-18; and N. Hartmann, *Aesthetik* (Berlin, 1953), pp. 82-85 etc.

these entities are carriers of historical projects. Nevertheless, the national State appears to be the main promoter of collective historical projects. The collective projects of Catholicism and Protestantism were embodied in powerful States, and, in this form, they confronted each other in the Thirty Years' War. Only after having been adopted by the Arab States and by the Ottoman Empire did the project of Islamism conquer the Orient and push to the gates of Vienna. Even the class project of Communism was realized only after becoming the collective project of a great State: Russia. Thus, is becomes understandable why nations which had lived for a long time without a State — the Poles, the Czechs, the Jews — longed so ardently for a new existence as States. The State is still the most efficient tool for carrying out collective historical projects.

Since the national State is the main author of historical projects and of the values the latter imply, we must ask ourselves: What is a State? This question was asked by Ernest Renan in an epoch-making lecture he gave at the Sorbonne in 1882. Renan's point was that nothing material suffices to make a nation, for a nation is a spiritual principle and not a group determined by blood, language or the configuration of the soil. According to this great French Humanist, two things constitute that spiritual principle, that collective soul called nation:

> The one is in the past; the other in the present. The one is the common possession of a rich legacy of memories; the other is the present consent, the desire to live together, the will to continue the claim of the heritage received undivided. ... In the past, an heritage of glory and of regrets to be shared, in the future, a common program to be achieved. ... Thus, a nation is a great solidarity constituted by the sentiment of the sacrifices made and of those which one is still disposed to make.[12]

Finally, in a formula which has become famous, Renan declared: *"L'existence d'une nation est ... un plébiscite de tous les jours"* — the existence of a nation is a plebiscite repeated every day.

Half a century after its proclamation Renan's thesis was taken up and modified by José Ortega y Gasset. The Spanish philosopher agreed with Renan's view that the principle of the nation is neither blood nor language, since, in France, in England, and in Spain, the community of blood and languages has been an effect of the unification of the State and not its cause. "At its origin, the State consists of the mixture of

---

[12] E. Renan, *Opuscules et discours,* "Qu'est-ce qu'une nation?" (Paris, 1882), pp. 26-27.

bloods and languages, it represents a victory over any natural society,"[13] says Ortega.

It was Renan's thesis of the plebiscitary character of the State which became predominant in Ortega's doctrine, but only after some criticism and modifications. Ortega reproached Renan's thesis with being "archaistic", because it insists that a nation's existence "supposes a past". If a nation only consisted of its past and its present, says Ortega, nobody would be interested in defending it against a possible attack. *"Al defender la nación defendemos nuestro mañana, no nuestro ayer,"*[14] he declares — in defending the nation we defend our "tomorrow" and not our "yesterday". We want a future in which our nation's existence continues.

The basic difference between the two thinkers' doctrines of the nation consists of the fact that Renan insisted on the past and the future as two factors of equal importance, while Ortega insisted on the future alone, excluding the past. After all, Renan was a child of the nineteenth century and a conservative Liberal. *"J'aime le passé, mais je porte envie à l'avenir,"* he said in his autobiography[15] — I like the past but I am longing for the future. Ortega, on the contrary, was a man of the twentieth century and a futurist. *"Nada tiene sentido para el hombre sino en función del porvenir,"*[16] he wrote — nothing has meaning to man except in terms of the future.

Ortega's futurism is intimately linked with his concept of the project. A long time before Sartre, Ortega had insisted on the moral necessity for man to commit himself to a definite project. As if he wanted to establish the anti-thesis to Gide's thesis of *"disponibilité"*, Ortega wrote: *"Una vida en disponibilidad es mayor negación de sí misma que la muerte"*[17] — a disposable life is a greater negation of itself than death. Unlike Sartre, Ortega insisted on the moral necessity of a project not only for individuals but, also and especially, for collectivities. Thus, a nation is for the Spanish thinker basically "the project of an action and a program of collaboration".[18]

It was only in the sense of a collective project of the future that Ortega interpreted Renan's formula of the nation as a plebiscite repeated every day; for a plebiscite decides only about the future. The Spanish philosopher concluded that the essence of a nation is composed of two

[13] J. Ortega y Gasset, *Obras completas* (Madrid, 1951), tomo IV, p. 252.
[14] *Ibid.*, t. IV, p. 266.
[15] E. Renan, *Souvenirs d'enfance et de jeunesse* (Paris, 1883), p. X.
[16] J. Ortega y Gasset, *op. cit.*, t. IV, p. 266.
[17] *Ibid.*, t. IV, p. 239.
[18] *Ibid.*, t. IV, p. 258.

ingredients: first, a project of total community (*convivencia*) in a common enterprise; second, the adherence of people to this project. The adherence of all creates that internal solidity and cohesion which distinguishes the modern national State from the antique States.

To have a common project means to wish to achieve a common future. From this springs Ortega's Futurism. At the end of the eighteenth century and the beginning of the nineteenth, neither the links of blood nor those of language, culture, and a common historical past could prevent the separation of the United Colonies from England and of Latin America from Spain, for neither England nor Spain was any longer able to offer the Americas inspiring projects of a common collective future. The plebiscites of the future decided against England and Spain. And, therefore, the common past, on which Renan had insisted, was useless, for it is the future which models nations, as it were, contrary to the stream. When there is a common future, concludes Ortega, then the ancestors, the remembrances, the heritage of glories and regrets serve as "consolidating forces; but nothing else".[19]

This thesis of Ortega's may be shocking for traditionalists. It is, nevertheless, well supported by undeniable facts. The enormous growth of the United States resulted from the immigration of millions of people who had no American ancestors and, therefore, did not share this nation's past. What these immigrants had in common with the American nation was rather her future, her collective project of prosperity in freedom and the values linked with this ideal.

To be sure, such an integration is easier in the case of new nations such as those of America; it is, however, not impossible in respect of ancient nations. It happens, indeed, that certain rather exceptional individuals become members of an ancient foreign nation by virtue of a profound affinity between their mode of evaluation and that of the nation of their choice. Let us take the example of Napoleon Bonaparte: He was born in Corsica in 1769, one year after this island had become French. He had no French ancestors. What he had in common with France was not the past but the future, a glorious future which he proposed to this nation and of which he became the chief architect. Napoleon and Paoli had the same Corsican and Italian ancestors; Paoli fought against France, Napoleon for France. After a short period of his youth in which he hated the French, Napoleon became a Frenchman by adopting a new manner of evaluating — that of the French.

---

[19] *Ibid.*, t. IV, p. 267.

Jacques Offenbach, Guillaume Apollinaire (whose true name was Wilhelm Apollinaris de Kostrowitzky), Marie Curie-Sklodowska, and many other glories of France had no French ancestors. But thanks to an elective affinity based on a community of values and ideals, they became integrated into the French national community and enriched its cultural patrimony.

In a similar way, the Greek Domenicos Theotocopoulos became a Spaniard under the glorious name of El Greco, the Englishman Lord Byron became a Greek, the Englishman Huston Stewart Chamberlain a German, and Cosima Wagner, the daughter of a French mother and an Hungarian father, changed into a German woman, with all her virtues and vices. All these transformations were based on an elective affinity in the domain of values.

The examples I have just given show clearly that a nation is characterized by a certain way of evaluating, or, in other words: a nation is a community of values and ideals. This is my own doctrine of the nation, a consequence of Renan's and Ortega's but which neither of them has formulated. It appears, especially, to be a logical development of Ortega's thesis, according to which a nation is a collective project. If the Spanish thinker did not recognize that the project is the source of the codes of values, it was because his value theory was only a re-issue of Scheler's and, therefore, basically essentialistic and unhistorical. "Values," says Ortega, "are something objective, not subjective ... To evaluate is not to give value to something which did not have it in itself; it is to recognize a value residing in the object."[20]

If, according to this thesis common to Ortega, Scheler and Nicolai Hartmann, values are universal objective essences, they come before the subjective historical existences. Therefore, they cannot proceed from the historical projects of these existences. Instead of trying to derive the values from the historical projects, Ortega accepted Scheler's non-historical, ontological hierarchy of values.[21]

My own axiological point of view is diametrically opposed to that of Ortega and the German phenomenologists. For, to me, there exists a total solidarity between the project — be it historical or transhistorical

---

[20] *Ibid.*, t. IV, "Introducción a una estimativa", pp. 325-327.
[21] A critique of Scheler's and Hartmann's axiological doctrines is to be found in my book *Filosofía de los valores*, Second revised edition (Buenos Aires, 1960). See also R. Frondizi's penetrating refutation of Scheler's axiological objectivism in *¿Que son los valores?* (Mexico, Buenos Aires, 1958). For a critique of Ortega's axiology see my article "¿Ortega - existencialista o esencialista?", *La Torre*, Universidad de Puerto Rico, num. 15-16, Julio-Diciembre 1956, pp. 385-399.

— and the code of values which corresponds to it. To each project corresponds a different code of values, and each of these codes is characterized by another normative postulate. Only the postulate adopted as a norm by an act of will can confer validity on all values belonging to a certain system. This act of will is bound up with a definite project.

According to my thesis, the different collective projects appearing in the course of history, and especially the collective projects of the groups called nations, give birth to the different codes of values.

If every nation is characterized by a specific collective project, by the will to do something in common, and if this specific collective project gives birth to a specific code of values, it follows that each nation is a community of values of the second degree, that is, of values conditioned by the value of the first degree affirmed in the basic national project. Only a person who has adopted the common code of values of the second degree, which characterizes a given nation at a given moment of history, is ready to make the sacrifices necessary for the realization of this nation's collective project. But the fact that a person has adopted this collective project also shows that he or she has affirmed the value of the first degree, the norm this project implies.

I said that, logically, each project presupposes an act of will and that, psychologically, every act of will is particularized in a definite project. Only in and by a project do we become conscious of our volitions and of our evaluations of the first degree. Thus, the project is the particularization of our volitions and evaluations of the first degree which, to begin with, are not formulated in terms of abstract concepts. Let us remember Spinoza's statement about the relation between will and value which reads: *"Constat itaque ex his omnibus, nihil nos conari, velle, appetere, neque cupere, quia id bonum esse judicamus; sed contra, nos propterea aliquid bonum esse judicare, quia id conamur, volumus, appetimus, atque cupimus."*[22] This means that we do not endeavour, want, desire nor covet anything because we judge it to be good; but on the contrary, we judge that something is good because we endeavour, want, desire and covet it.

In my opinion, the particular way in which this value-creating will manifests itself is the project. Often, the values a project implies crystallize, become conscious and separated from the project only in the course of or after the execution of the project. Only then, can these values be expressed in abstract concepts.

---

[22] Spinoza, *Ethica ordine geometrico demonstrata,* Pars III, Schol. ad Prop. IX.

A code of values is composed of two elements: first, of the norms affirmed in a definite project. We designated these values of the first degree. Second, of the radiated and instrumental values ensuing from the norms postulated. These values of the second degree develop in the course of historical time out of the norms bound up with the project. Together, these two classes of values form the code of values of a given system. Often, the fundamental project to which a nation or a civilization owes its birth has already been forgotten, but the collective evaluations which it expressed have become completely crystallized and now form the code of values by means of which this particular nation or civilization is distinct from all the others.

What is the influence of historical time on the projects and the value systems bound up with the latter? This influence is reciprocal. The collective projects and their codes of values submit to the influence of history and exert their influence on history. On the one hand, persons and groups can only choose their projects from the possibilities offered at a certain moment in history and in a certain cultural and social environment. In this way, the projects are results of history. But, on the other hand, history is also a result of the projects. These statements are not contradictory. For, if the present project results from past history, it is future history which will result from the present projects.

I think that the collective project is the keynote of a nation's or a civilization's value system. For those who adhere to such a collective project, the fundamental and directive value it affirms — that is, the collective ideal — is an intrinsic value. The latter confers an instrumental and a radiated value on all means proper to the furthering of the realization of the collective project and to the accomplishment of the victory of the ideal it incorporates.

The term "radiated" value (*Strahlwert*) was proposed by William Stern.[23] An example will clarify its meaning: aviation is not only appreciated as an instrumental value suitable for the achievement of utilitarian ends. Aviation is also appreciated as a new content of personal life which gives the person a new feeling of power and sovereignty over the forces of nature. Thus, aviation which, as an instrumental value of a fast, time-saving means of transportation, was detached from the person becomes a part of this person, a carrier of a value which the human person "radiates" over its component parts.

When a nation has a collective project, a common ideal and, with it, a collective directive value, it does not necessarily follow that its mem-

---

[23] W. Stern, *Wertphilosophie* (Leipzig, 1924), p. 44.

bers also affirm the same instrumental values. The members of a group may, indeed, have the same project and, nevertheless, have different opinions about the means of realizing it. The majority of disputes in parliaments result from such different instrumental values put at the service of a common project, a common ideal. Nevertheless, the fact of serving the realization of the same collective project orientates the different instrumental values of a nation in the same direction. The radiated values of a nation will, likewise, have more or less the same character, since they reflect the rays emitted by the same intrinsic values: those expressed in the nation's fundamental collective project. These facts explain the unity of style which characterizes the evaluations of a nation's members.

The primary axiological fact is, thus, the collective project which, with its intrinsic directive values, determines a nation's radiated values and orientates its instrumental values in the same direction. We may speak of a value field created by the collective project; for, because of the project's function of orientating instrumental and radiated values in the same direction, its action is comparable to that of a magnetic field. The value field created by the collective project is responsible for the typical manner of evaluating which characterizes the members of a given nation at a certain historical epoch and determines what we call their "style" of evaluating. If, for instance, the basic collective project of a nation is heroic, then its whole system of values will have a heroic style. If the basic collective project of a nation is mercantile, its whole system of values will be permeated with mercantilism. Individual evaluations will then occur within a mercantile value field.

In general, the realization of a national collective project gives birth to a new project, which, in its turn, gives a new justification to a nation's historical existence. If the character of the new collective project differs considerably from that of the previous one, the whole code of values of the nation will be modified. In this respect, German history offers excellent examples. During the second half of the eighteenth and at the beginning of the nineteenth century, the Germany of Classicism, Romanticism and Idealistic philosophy seemed to have no other national project than the one Goethe assigned to it in his dramatic poem, *Pandora:* the project of dominating the ideal world, the world of thought and poetic imagination. It was France, symbolised by Prometheus, which, according to Goethe, was to govern the world of political and military realities. But, in the course of the nineteenth century, the national project of Germany changed radically, and the proverbial "country of the poets and thinkers" (*das Land der Dichter und Denker*) became Bismarck's nation of "blood and iron" (*Blut und Eisen*), whose collective project was military conquest and rule by force.

After Germany's unification in 1871, her political and military projects merged with another one: that of surpassing all other European nations in material production, in industry and commerce. And we saw how rapidly the whole code of values changed in all parts and all social layers of the German people. The cult of ideas was superseded by the cult of material prosperity and military force. The radical change in that nation's code of values could not have occurred, had not the great majority of the Germans accepted the new collective projects. It is well known that the Germans accepted them enthusiastically, with very few exceptions — such as Nietzsche.

This enthusiasm was still stronger, when, after World War I, a new collective project emerged in Germany: that of withdrawing from Western civilization, of putting military force at the service of world conquest in order to "rejuvenate" mankind by the idea of racial purity, by the dethronement of the intellect and by the establishment of a hierarchy of "master"-races and "slave"-races. This new collective project gave birth to a new code of values which the overwhelming majority of Germans accepted with a fearful headlong haste, especially after 1933. This new code, which totally governed the German nation for twelve years, proclaimed the positive value of violence and the negative value of right; the positive value of instinctive impulses and the negative value of intelligence; the positive value of a hierarchy of masters and slaves and the negative value of the equality and dignity of individuals and nations; the positive value of autocracy and blind obedience, the negative value of democracy and self-determination, etc. Transforming the values of all domains — moral, aesthetic, social, religious, juridical, political and cognitive — the new German code, brought about by the collective project called National-Socialism, even changed the criterion of truth. The world was appalled to see that even German university professors and other leading intellectuals accepted Alfred Rosenberg's and Professor Carl Schmitt's formula of "organic" thruth expressed in the words: True is what is useful to the German people.[24]

When, in 1945, the collective project of National-Socialism was drowned in an ocean of blood and flames, the code of values to which

---

[24] A. Rosenberg, *Der Mythus des zwanzigsten Jahrhunderts* (München, 1934), p. 669 etc., and C. Schmitt, *Über die drei Arten des rechtswissenschaftlichen Denkens* (Hamburg, 1934), p. 26.

it had given birth disappeared. It is still too early to tell what will be the new collective project to which the German people will devote its energies and what code of values will ensue from it. At present, the collective project of Western Germany seems to be limited to the realization of the so-called "economic miracle" (*"Wirtschaftswunder"*), the categorical imperative of which is: Get rich!

Other nations have shown more historical continuity in the axiological field, either because they had fewer collective projects — although sometimes of a much wider scope — or because their projects were inspired more or less by the same ideal. Sometimes, the original project to which a nation owes its existence determines its character so decisively that it hardly changes in the course of history. All its collective projects then follow the same pattern, and its code of values is not much modified in the course of history.

In the code of values of contemporary Spain, for example, honor, fidelity to faith and pride still occupy an outstanding position. These are the predominant values which were developed in the course of the realization of the two great collective projects to which the Spanish nation owes its historical existence: the first one, which lasted from the eight to the end of the fifteenth century, consisted in expelling the Moors from the Iberian peninsula and in restoring the unity and purity of the Catholic faith. With the fall of Granada, in 1492, this project was achieved. This date coincided with the discovery of America by Columbus, and with this event emerges the second gigantic project which was to occupy Spain for the following centuries: that of conquering, colonizing and Christianizing the new world. This collective project was also successfully achieved.

These two collective projects of the widest range show a certain continuity and determined the Spaniards' national character and code of values in an ineffaceable manner. The Spaniard of our day is still the *hidalgo,* the knightly personality of the times of Queen Isabel the Catholic, with his virtues and limitations. Vainly did Cervantes, with his *Don Quijote,* warn his compatriots against the danger of running after the phantoms of the past, while around them other nations discovered new realities.

A virile vigorous man procreates children; a nation in full bloom procreates projects. A nation lives as long as it continues to invent new collective projects which captivate the imagination of its citizens, so that they accept the sacrifices necessary for their realization. These collective projects can only succeed, if they respond to the needs of the nation which adopts them and if they are compatible with the vital interests of society as a whole. Anyway, by giving themselves new projects, by imposing new norms upon themselves, the nations create new codes of values. When a nation ceases to procreate new projects capable of gaining the adherence of its citizens, then it *dies,* for it has no longer anything to achieve in history. For a while, the values which crystallized out of its earlier collective projects continue to remain in force, for they do not have to give way to new values. But, slowly, they weaken and, finally, disappear. When the code of values characterizing a nation has disappeared, the nation disappears also. After Rome had ceased to be the power unifying the ancient world by a grandiose juridical administration and by the propagation of Stoic Humanism, her last great project was exhausted. The code of values linked to this project remained in force for a time, then disappeared. Odoaker killed only a corpse. Hegel was quite right when he said that a nation can die a violent death only when it is already naturally dead.[25]

In 1898, after Spain had lost the remaining vestiges of her American colonial empire, the greatest Spanish thinker of that epoch, Miguel de Unamuno, published an essay under the title *La vida es sueño* — life is a dream. This essay expresses the lassitude and renunciation of any historical rôle on the part of a nation which has become incapable of inventing new collective projects. Here is what Unamuno said or, rather, passionately exclaimed:

> *¡Que le dejen vivir en paz y en gracia de Dios, circundado de áurea sencillez, en su camisa de hombre feliz, y, sobre todo, que no se tome en vano el nombre de su fe para hablarle de la España histórica, conquistadora de reinos, en cuyos dominios no se ponían ni el sol ni la injusticia! ¡Que no le viertan veneno pagano de mundanas glorias en su cristiano bálsamo de consuelo! ¡Que le dejen dormir y soñar su sueño lento, oscuro, monótono, el sueño de su buena vida rutinaria! ¡Que no le sacrifiquen al progreso, por Dios, que no le sacrifiquen al progreso![26]*

In this moving page of beautiful Spanish prose, Unamuno implores the world to allow the humble Spaniard a peaceful life, without speaking to him about historical Spain, the conqueror of kingdoms where the sun did not set and injustice did not disappear. The Spaniard should be allowed to sleep and to muse away the slow monotonous dream of a simple, routine life. And with passionate emphasis Unamuno asks that

[25] G. W. F. Hegel, *Sämtliche Werke* (Stuttgart, 1928), Band XI, p. 115.
[26] *Ensayos y sentencias de Unamuno* (New York, 1932), "La vida es sueño", p. 32.

the Spaniard should not be "sacrificed to progress" and that one should "not pour the pagan venom of wordly glories into the Christian balm of his consolation".

Later on, in his famous book, *Del sentimiento trágico de la vida*, Unamuno tried to give a new project to his nation: that of being the tragi-comic Don Quijote among the nations, a living expression of a people's refusal to submit to logic and science, that is, to the modern world and its truth. The ultimate aim of this project, says Unamuno, is "to save the Middle Ages from the Renaissance, in order not to lose the treasure of its infancy".[27]

I doubt very much whether such a project could gain the adherence of a nation. The past cannot be brought to life again. Likewise, I cannot accept Unamuno's thesis that even a restoration of the past would be tantamount to the creation of a future.[28] Historically speaking, such a restoration would be sterile, for a project which does not create new values, values not yet realized in history, has no historical reason for being.

Every true historical project proposes that a nation change its destiny. What Unamuno proposed to his nation was only to want its destiny. Therefore, this project was not able to stop the separatist tendencies which, from the beginning of the twentieth century, had been manifest among the Basques, the Catalans and other peoples forming the Spanish nation. Much more realistic than Unamuno, Ortega y Gasset explained these separatist and particularist tendencies as being the lack of a suggestive collective project justifying the life in common of the different Iberian provinces in the same State. In his book, *España invertebrada*, Ortega wrote: "Spain is disintegrating. Today, it is less a nation than the cloud of dust which remains when a great nation has passed, galloping along the great road of history".[29]

However, Professor Americo Castro, the famous Spanish historian, is less pessimistic. *"Henos, pues, ante una cultura que a la vez se afirma y se destruye en una continuada serie de cantos de cisne,"*[30] he says: we are confronted with a culture which affirms itself and destroys itself at the same time in a continual series of swan-songs. Indeed, at the beginning of the twentieth century, when the world spoke of "moribund Spain", an artistic, literary, philosophical and scientific renaissance went on in Spain and greatly enriched the cultural values

[27] M. de Unamuno, *Del sentimiento trágico de la vida* (Madrid, 1913), p. 314.
[28] *Ibid.*, pp. 312-313.
[29] J. Ortega y Gasset, *Obras completas*, III, p. 71.
[30] A. Castro, *España en su historia* (Buenos Aires, 1948), p. 21.

of our time. The establishment of the Republic and the heroism it showed during the Civil War from 1936 to 1939 also proved that the Spaniards are still capable of a great collective effort in the service of an historical project.

Such a collective effort can hardly be overestimated, even if it fails: for the fact that a group gives birth to some great men still does not change it into a nation, as long as it is not united by a collective project. During the centuries of the dispersion, the Jews produced an amazing number of great men — in the sciences, in philosophy, literature, politics, and the arts — without, however, forming a nation. Only their new collective project of Zionism and its realization in Israel recreated the Jewish nation.

Let us now return to our thesis that it is the intrinsic directive value, that is, the ideal affirmed in a collective project, which determines the whole system of a nation's radiated values, gives a definite orientation to its instrumental values and impresses a certain style on the evaluations of its members. As we said before: if the collective project of a nation is heroic, its whole system of values will have a heroic style. If, on the contrary, a nation's collective project is mercantile, its whole system of values will be permeated with mercantilism. As an example, we could take Spain in the sixteenth and seventeenth centuries. At that time, the whole nation was engaged in the double project of the Counter-Reformation and the Christianization of its American colonial empire recently acquired in great maritime and military adventures.

The religious and heroic fervor of this collective national project was communicated to all the branches of national life. The painting, architecture and literature of this epoch — especially in Toledo, city of El Greco and prime center of Spanish Catholicism — manifested this religious, heroic, visionary character which emanated from the collective political and military project of the nation. The directive value or ideal of the latter determined the whole system of values of the nation, including its artistic values.

The same holds for Dutch painting in the seventeenth century, which reflected the basic values affirmed in the collective project of this nation: the affirmation of a life which cherishes worldly treasures, overseas commerce, the material abundance resulting from it, the markets exhibiting the riches acquired as a result of the people's industry and common sense, the folk dances, good living, the enjoyment of life here below. Life-affirming art, Calvinism (which sees in material prosperity a proof of divine grace), the style of every-day life and the current way of evaluating things and events — all this reflected the directive values of the Dutch nation's collective project orientated towards worldly treasures and the gifts of the oceans.

Another example is afforded by the Soviet Union: There, all evaluations — in the domains of literature, art, music, philosophy, law, politics, technology and, even, of science — are totally determined by the collective project of the nation: that of establishing and consolidating a Communist economy and society. The ideal, the directive value affirmed in this project, is the norm by which all other values achieved by the Soviet peoples are measured. The latter become instrumental and radiated values of the directive intrinsic value of the nation's collective project. All this affirms our thesis that it is the collective project with its norms which changes a nation into a community of values.

"*Schätzen ist Schaffen*" — to evaluate is to create, said Nietzsche.[31] The typical manner of evaluating which characterizes each of the great nations and distinguishes it from all the others is, thus, of necessity, manifested in the domain of creating values. From this springs the specific character of the artistic, moral, intellectual, religious and social values created by the different great nations of history: China, India, Egypt, Israel, Greece, Rome, Italy, Spain, France, England, Germany, Russia, the United States.

This will which creates national values, intimately linked with a nation's collective project, may be considered a kind of general will — even more general than Rousseau's *volonté générale*, since it encompasses the totality of a nation's manifestations — its cultural and personal manifestations as well as its political ones. But, as Rousseau showed us in his *Contrat social*, the general will is not necessarily the will of all (*la volonté de tous*).[32] Indeed, not all members of a nation evaluate in the same way, but the average is characterized by a certain style of evaluation. This style, common to the majority of a nation's members, is neither due to their "blood" nor to their "race" but simply to the acceptance by the individuals of the normative values affirmed in the nation's collective projects. If the latter reveal a certain historical continuity, those normative values determine a nation's pedagogical system, are propagated by education, become traditional and leave their impress on the character of the whole nation. Then, even everyday evaluations of the individuals reflect the code of values which characterizes the whole nation. Being engaged in the same collective project

---

[31] F. Nietzsche, *Also sprach Zarathustra*, I, p. 86.
[32] *Oeuvres complètes* de Rousseau (Paris, 1928), tome II, "Du contrat social", chapitre 3, p. 147.

— consciously or not — most Americans, of whatever descent, judge in more or less the same way all questions concerning the general outlook on life. Perhaps, it is for this reason that two political parties are sufficient to express the political will of a nation of one hundred eighty million people. And even these two parties only symbolize two different ways or means of reaching the same end: the fulfilment of the collective project which characterizes the American nation in modern history. In other words: the two parties and those whom they represent affirm the same intrinsic normative values and only differ as far as instrumental values are concerned.

In one of his books, André Maurois says: "To interest a Frenchman in a boxing match, one must tell him that his national honor is at stake. To interest an Englishman in a war, nothing is better than a hint that it resembles a boxing match."[33] I think that this amusing observation indicates basic differences between the codes used by each of these nations to determine the value of things and actions. Each of these codes results from the norms affirmed in the one collective project of the nation which contributed most to shape its destinies. The collective project uniting the British nation has been, for centuries, that of ruling the oceans, of colonizing remote overseas countries in order to exploit them for the benefit of the national economy. This project has always been permeated by the Greek idea of ἀγών, of "contest", of a struggle against competitors, the aim of which is not purely utilitarian. It should also be a test to demonstrate, *urbi et orbi,* the superiority of the winner. The whole British code of values expresses these sportsman-like standards, as Maurois' witty remark exemplifies.

Here is another humoristic observation by a French writer which deserves the philosopher's attention: In his book, full of gracious irony, *Les carnets du major Thompson,* Pierre Daninos writes:

> The American pedestrian who sees a millionaire passing by in a Cadillac dreams secretly of the day when he will sit in his own. The French pedestrian who sees a millionaire passing by in a Cadillac dreams secretly of the day when he will be able to force the millionaire out of his car, so that he will have to walk like everybody else.[34]

Far from being merely a joke, this penetrating psychological observation throws into relief the different codes of values used by the American, with his *optimism of prosperity,* and by the Frenchman, with his

---

[33] A. Maurois, *Les silences du colonel Bramble* (Paris, 1921), p. 10.
[34] P. Daninos, *Les carnets du major W. Marmaduke Thompson* (Paris, 1954), p. 48.

optimism of equality. Danimo's witty remark explains, better than erudite sociological treatises, why, for example, the United States has no leftist parties and why France has.

But it would be necessary to take the matter further and to seek the reasons for this obvious difference in the codes of values of these two great nations in the difference in the collective projects which presided over their destinies and, thus, formed the styles of their evaluations.

It is well known that the Pilgrim Fathers who arrived in America on the *Mayflower* in 1620 had mainly religious preoccupations. They had left the Church of England because, on its separation from Roman Catholicism, it had retained too many ceremonies of the latter. After twelve years of exile in Holland, these "Separatists" emigrated to America. Their collective project was to bring up their children in their own language and to practise their religion according to their own consciences, without being molested by the orders of the British Government. Therefore, they decided to set up an autonomous government.

The Puritans, who arrived a few years after the Pilgrims, were also motivated by religious considerations. Unlike the Separatists, they had decided to stay within the Church of England but to "purify" it of its Roman Catholic residues in a new community, representing an "aristocracy of righteousness".

But soon, these theological and moral projects were eclipsed by the unlimited economic possibilities offered by the incomparable wealth of that boundless almost untouched continent that was North America at the beginning of the seventeenth century. The project of the American colonists and of the crowds of immigrants who joined them became more and more prosperity in freedom by the exploitation of the American continent's natural resources. In order to be able to carry out this project, the American colonists needed a maximum of freedom of action. While their original project had required the non-intervention of the government in religious matters, their new project emphasized the non-intervention of the government in economic matters. Only this non-intervention was able to guarantee to the American the enjoyment of the fruit of his labour. Thus, to the American, "freedom" became tantamount to "free enterprise". I would say that free enterprise is the highest instrumental value of the American collective project of prosperity by the exploitation of the new continent's wealth; for free enterprise is considered the only efficient means to carry out this project. As it gave a feeling of independence and of power to those engaged in it, free enterprise also became the chief radiated value in the United States. Prosperity in this freedom is the intrinsic value of the American collective project, its ideal and norm. These intrinsic, instrumental and radiated values determined the whole American code of values, molded the national character and are manifested even in the every-day evaluations of the average American.

In 1950, the famous American historian Henry Steele Commager published his remarkable book, *The American Mind*. The passages I am going to quote from it seem to corroborate my thesis that the code of values of the American nation — as that of any other nation — is only a reflexion of its dominant collective project. Referring to the nineteenth-century American, Professor Commager writes:

> Nothing in all history had ever succeeded like America, and every American knew it. Nowhere else on the globe had nature been at once so rich and so generous, and her riches were available to all who had the enterprise to take them and the good fortune to be white. As nature and experience justified optimism, the American was incurably optimistic. . . . The American saw the present with the eyes of the future. . . . In every barefoot boy he saw a future president or millionaire. . . . His culture too was material. . . . As he himself expected economic success next year or the year after, he had little envy of those who achieved it this year. . . .[35]

I think that this latter remark of Professor Commager's confirms Danino's observation. The optimism justified by the past allows little room for envy. In the following, Professor Commager describes what we would call the American "code of values" in the nineteenth century:

> He (the American) was accustomed to prosperity, resented anything that interfered with it, and regarded any prolonged lapse from it as an outrage against nature. . . . The worst that could be said against a law was that it was harmful to business. *Whatever promised to increase wealth was automatically regarded as good,* and the American was tolerant, therefore, of speculation, advertising, deforestation, and the exploitation of natural resources, and bore patiently the worst manifestations of industrialism.
>
> All this tended to give a quantitative cast to his thinking and inclined him to place a *quantitative valuation* upon *almost everything.* When he asked what was a man worth, he meant *material worth* . . . The American was incurably utilitarian, and it was appropriate that the one philosophy which might be called original with him was that of instrumentalism. . . . His religion, too, . . . was practical. . . . Braggartism became a virtue and criticism a vice. . . . Where

[35] H. S. Commager, *The American Mind* (New Haven, 1950), pp. 5, 6, 13.

shrewdness in speculation had been elevated to a public service, he was not inclined to look too critically at the means
whereby success was achieved. He ... resented government
interference with free enterprise far more than private interference with government enterprise. The self-made man, not
the heir, was the hero, and by "made" the American meant
enriched.[36]

I believe that this American code of values, as outlined by Professor
Henry Steele Commager, is a faithful reflection of the basic collective
project to which the nation owes its existence. As I said, this project
was prosperity in freedom by the exploitation of the American continent's material resources. All that could promote and facilitate the
execution of this project became necessarily a positive value; all that
could delay or hinder its execution became a negative value. Only this
genesis explains the American code of values, as we find it in Professor
Commager's outline.

In the passages quoted, the well known American historian talks only
of the nineteenth-century American. However, in the final chapter of
his book devoted to the American of the twentieth century, Professor
Commager shows that the American character basically remained the
same. "The differences are quantitative and material rather than
qualitative and moral," he says.[37] Referring to the twentieth-century
American, Commager writes: "His culture was still predominantly
material, his thinking quantitative, his genius inventive, experimental
and practical. ... He was still suspicious of culture but avid for it. ...[38]

Indeed, in the twentieth century, the American code of values is, in
many respects, still the same as it was a century before. When the
average American of our day is asked what a certain person is worth,
he still answers by indicating a sum in dollars. As for things and
institutions, he appreciates them only when they are "the world's
biggest" — a sentence one can hear and read dozens of times every day
in American advertising. The quantitative type of evaluation is, as these
examples indicate, still predominant in American civilization. In my
opinion, this social phenomenon can be explained by the fact that,
basically, the collective project of the American nation has not changed.
Only the means of achieving it have become more complex.

And yet, during the twentieth century, many important changes have
taken place in American society which studies like Steele Commager's,

[36] *Ibid.*, pp. 7, 8, 9, 12, 13.
[37] *Ibid.*, p. 409.
[38] *Ibid.*, p. 410.

Max Lerner's,[39] William H. Whyte's Jr.[40] etc., have pointed out most competently. To me, the most striking change is America's emergence in the twentieth century as a first-rate power in the fields of science and literature. Today, the American novel is read and admired in all European and Asiatic cultural centres and translated into many languages. American plays are given on the best European stages, and the oldest most revered European universities have created chairs for American literature. It no longer is considered an annex to English literature. In France, a growing number of students major in American literature.

As for science, the United States during the last decades has made substantial contributions in the fields of nuclear physics and chemistry, in biochemistry, astronomy, genetics, medicine and many other fields. Within a few years, American writers have won a considerable number of Nobel Prizes in literature, and American scientists have obtained the lion's share of scientific Nobel Prizes.

And yet, most of these cultural events have passed along the fringe of American national life, almost unnoticed by the great mass of the people. While boasting his nation's material quantitative achievements, the average American is not proud of his writers and — at least, in pre-Sputnik days — never showed any esteem for his scientists. Some prominent American writers are better known in Paris, Vienna, and Tokyo than they are in Washington or Dallas. Many of them are harshly criticized, because they prefer ugly truths to beautiful lies.

As for the scientist, he is still considered a dangerous non-conformist and ridiculed as an "egg-head". Speaking of nineteenth-century American culture, Professor Henry Steele Commager says: "No people was more avid of college degrees, yet nowhere else were intellectuals held in such contempt or relegated to so inferior a position; and in America alone the professor — invariably long haired and absent-minded was — an object of humor."[41]

The fact that this approach had not changed very much during the first half of the twentieth century became obvious after the psychological shock this nation suffered at the launching of the first and second Sputniks. Suddenly, it became obvious that in order to survive, American civilization had to change its evaluation of the scientist and the teacher. But this is a very difficult task, because it means a modification

[39] M. Lerner, *America As A Civilization* (New York, 1957).
[40] W. H. Whyte, Jr., *The Organization Man* (New York, 1956).
[41] H. S. Commager, *op. cit.*, p. 10.

of the American code of values, as it has developed historically out of this nation's basic collective project. To make this change a little more palatable, journalists and radio commentators had first to prove to the average American that "scientists are human". This was, indeed, a phrase used in an article by Mr. Alton L. Blakeslee, Associated Press Science Reporter. "Scientists Not Just Oddballs" was the article's title, and it explained that not all of them are ... "absent-minded, self-centered, godless, or dull". To make scientists and professors in general more acceptable to the American public, Mr. Blakeslee found it necessary to insist that "some are avid football or baseball fans. ... Like other people, they marry, have children, work in parent-teacher associations or the Boy Scouts, vote and argue politics, worry about bills, fix up the house on weekends."[42] On January 27, 1958, the National Association of Broadcasters called on the nation's broadcasters to urge Americans to "respect learning and knowledge and make ignorance unfashionable".[43]

All these efforts, considerably diminished after the launching of the first American satellite, made obvious the low position the intellectual occupies in the American scale of values. I am referring to this situation only as an example to corroborate my thesis that a nation's code of values is the result of the basic postulates affirmed in its fundamental collective project. Almost since the beginning of American history, this collective project has been prosperity in freedom by the exploitation of this continent's rich material resources. The main carrier of this project is the businessman — especially, the great business executive. Hence, the incomparable prestige he enjoys in American society, where he occupies the highest rank of the social pyramid. He supervises higher education, and scientific research depends greatly on his munificence. There is no European counterpart of the "boards of trustees" or of "regents" which characterize American universities.

For all these reasons, American civilization is often called a "business civilization", and the national community a "business community". It was a President of the United States — Calvin Coolidge — who defined the American purpose by saying: "The business of America is — business." As the nation's basic collective project has not essentially changed since the beginning of its history, I am convinced that America's code of values, likewise, cannot undergo much transformation. Referring to America's national purpose, Walter Lippmann wrote, in

---

[42] *Los Angeles Herald and Express,* Nov. 18, 1957, p. A-10.
[43] *Los Angeles Times,* Jan. 28, 1958, Part I.

1960: "The ultimate ends are fixed. They are lasting and they are not disputed. ... The innovation, which is now beginning, will be in the means, in the policies and programs and measures, by which the ultimate ends of our free society can be realized in the world today."[44] Taking these facts into consideration, we understand why the "Sputnik-shock" did not basically transform America's code of values but only slightly modified it. The revelation of Russia's unsuspected achievements in science and technology only made clear to the average American that scientists and teachers represent instrumental values indispensable for the carrying out of this country's collective project in the new international situation. Therefore, some people realized that the scientist's and professor's social prestige and their material reward should be raised. But this modification in the attitude of American public opinion does not imply a recognition of the scientist's or the philosopher's intrinsic values as fountain-heads of intrinsically valuable ideas. Such a recognition would hardly be compatible with the basic postulate of America's collective project and the code of values derived from it.

It would be more difficult to establish the relation between the French code of values and the collective project from which it emanates. The two millenia-old history of France is much more complex than that of the United States, and many collective projects have succeeded each other since the struggle between Julius Caesar and Vercingetorix. The derivation of the different national codes of values from the collective projects to which they owe their validity would be an interesting task, but it would be outside the scope of the present inquiry, which is intended only to show the existence of a relation between a nation's code of values and its collective project. Besides, I wanted to determine the nature of this relation and illustrate it by some examples. I believe that I have carried out this plan. As for France, I shall limit myself to the following remarks:

I believe that the main collective project with which the French nation has identified itself for more than a century and a half has been the worldwide propagation of its revolutionary ideas of 1789. As I have shown before, the "Rights of Man and of the Citizen" proclaimed by the French revolution cannot be derived from a "natural right". But this fact should not prevent people from proclaiming them as moral and juridical norms. That is what France did.

From it beginnings, the universal character of the *Déclaration des*

---

[44] W. Lippmann, "National Purpose", in *The National Purpose* (New York, 1960), p. 127.

Droits de l'Homme et du Citoyen was obvious. The French revolution of 1789 could have proclaimed the "rights of the French citizen". It proclaimed, however, "the rights of man and the citizen" without qualification, and, thus, France brought about the first supra-national revolution in history. *"Le peuple français vote la liberté du monde,"* said Saint-Just — the French are voting for the freedom of the world. Thus, the blood shed on the barricades of Paris was shed for mankind. That is what many foreigners coming to Paris feel. Contemplating the historical sites where the great events of the French revolution took place, many a foreigner says to himself: *De te fabula narratur* — your story is being told. One remembers the sublime verses in *Hermann und Dorothea*, where Goethe says that, thanks to the Declaration of the Rights of Man and the Citizen, Paris deserved more than ever the "magnificent name of the world's capital"[45]

To be sure, America's *Declaration of Independence*, likewise, contains some universal principles of great nobility. Nevertheless, as its name and its contents show, it was of a more particular character; for it basically proclaimed that the "United Colonies are . . . Absolved from all Allegiance to the British Crown". The American Declaration of Independence was a manifesto in which a new nation tried to justify its acts toward another nation with which it had been previously linked. On the contrary, the *Déclaration des Droits de l'Homme et du Citoyen* was a message from a nation to mankind. It still is.

For more than a century and a half, France has been the main ambassadress of this message. Even during the epochs of restoration, the French nation never totally denied the equalitarian message of its revolution. It was always alive in the people's heart. Speaking of the wars of Napoleon I, Chateaubriand said: *". . . nous allions l'épée dans une main, les Droits de l'Homme dans l'autre"*[46] — we marched with the sword in one hand, the Declaration of Human Rights in the other.

Of the three words which form the motto of the French revolution, *Liberté, Égalité, Fraternité,* the second probably expresses its most original creation. The story of Louis-Philippe-Joseph, Duke of Orléans, is well known. A revolutionary of royal blood, he had renounced all his privileges and sat in the Convention on the extreme left. Having asked for and received a new family name from the City of Paris, he was called Philippe Égalité. The word *égalité* (equality) expressed the

---

[45] Goethe, "Hermann und Dorothea", *Klio, Das Zeitalter, Sämtliche Werke* (Stuttgart, 1857), 5. Band, p. 39.
[46] *Napoléon raconté par Chateaubriand* (Paris), p. 32.

characteristic of the French revolution much better than the word liberty. Indeed, liberty was at home in England a long time before it could manifest itself in France. It conquered America some years before triumphing in France. However, equality is a conquest of the French revolution. Professor Brogan says that "England ... is a country in which *in*equality is cherished".[47] To what extent this is still true could be seen during Queen Elizabeth's II coronation. On this occasion, even the public rest-rooms of London reflected the social hierarchy of the United Kingdom, bearing the inscriptions "Peers", "Gentlemen", "Men", and "Peeresses", "Ladies", "Women". Professor Brogan, who himself is British, feels that in the United States there is much more equality than in England — except in the economic field, where the *Social Register* replaces the German *Gotha* almanac.

I shall not go so far as to affirm that France has achieved the ideal of total equality, but it seems that, in the hierarchy of the French code of values, equality occupies a place beyond comparison. France made her entrance into modern history with the ideas of her Encyclopedists and with the realization of these ideas in the French revolution. The great majority of the French identified themselves with the revolutionary project of bringing about the triumph of these ideas. This project became a real collective project, and it greatly contributed to the molding of the modern Frenchman's national character. Since the idea of equality is one of the most important normative postulates of the French collective project, it is understandable that it had a decisive influence on the formation of the French code of values. Therefore, Daninos may be right when he says that the French pedestrian who sees a millionaire passing by in his Cadillac dreams of the day when he will be able to force him out of his car, so that he will have to walk like everybody else. If the policy of France is often criticized by her friends, it is, also, because they always expect France to live up to the equalitarian principles which she symbolizes for the world.

France has, also, other collective projects; for example, that of being the world's teacher in all questions of good taste and refinement. She tries to teach what Pascal called *l'esprit géométrique* and *l'esprit de finesse*, the latter being that kind of intuition which makes the French masters of the art of writing psychological novels and plays. French civilization tries to create a balance, an Aristotelian μεσότης between the *vita contemplativa* and the *vita activa* — an equilibrium so necessary in our modern world with its frantic activity. All these

[47] D. W. Brogan, *The English People* (New York, 1943), p. 111.

projects have been crystallized in the code of values of the modern Frenchman.

Our analyses of some nations' codes of values and of the ways in which these codes depend on the nations' collective projects seem to justify our doctrine, according to which a nation is a community of values and ideals to the extent to which it is or was united by a collective project and its postulates. We wish only to add one example of recent history which shows how a group's code of values changes as soon as it adopts a new project with which it identifies itself. For centuries, the Jews lived in dispersion without any collective project. They had only a mediocre appreciation of manual work, farming and military virtues. But the realization of the collective project which the new State of Israel represents — that of reviving Jewish national life on its historical ground — requires manual work, tillage of the land and needs military virtues. Representing indispensable means for promoting the nation's collective project, manual work, tillage and military virtues suddenly became first-rate instrumental and radiated values. Today, they occupy the highest levels in the hierarchy of values of the young Israeli nation.

However, the nation is not the only community of values and ideals, since history knows also supra-national collective projects. They existed in the Middle Ages, and we see them now in modern times. At the beginning of the eighteenth century, the French ethnologist, Father Lafiteau, wrote: *"La religion influoit autrefois tout ce que faisoient les hommes"*[48] — in bygone times, religion influenced everything men did. This held not only for primitive man but, also, for the Middle Ages. At that time, the Europeans were engaged in a common project of other-worldly orientation: the project of striving for man's eternal salvation. As soon as this eternal salvation was postulated as an intrinsic normative value and accepted as such by the great majority of Europeans, everything which, according to the ideas of that epoch, could promote its realization became a positive instrumental value. Considered as the appropriate means for furthering the project of eternal salvation, charity, confession, religious painting, poetry and music became instrumental religious values and were accepted as such by the Europeans. Soon these instrumental values became radiated values reflecting the intrinsic value of the supreme religious project. Only later, when the secularization of values took place, did charity become a moral value independent of the religious project with which it had

[48] Lafiteau, *Moeurs des sauvages américains comparées aux moeurs des premiers temps* (Paris, 1724), p. 453.

been bound up. And painting, music and poetry became purely aesthetic values, free from any instrumental, religious character. Only at that time, did these values begin to shine with their own light instead of reflecting the light of a supreme religious value.

The search for eternal salvation was a project common to the Europeans, but it was not a collective project, which always consists of a joint effort. Only in the crusades did the common project of the Occidental Christian nations become a collective project. This supra-national collective project created a code of supra-national values which transformed the Christian nations of the Occident into a community of values and ideals. The ideal of medieval knighthood with its moral and artistic values, permeated with religious spirit, with its *troubadours* and *trouvères*, its *minstrels* and *Minnesänger*, its *chansons de geste* and its Arthurian sagas is to be found in France, England, and Germany. It crystallized there as a result of the collective project of the crusades which united these nations axiologically and politically.

A supra-national community of competing values and ideals had constituted itself in the opposite camp among the Moslem nations. They, too, were engaged in a common collective project with other-worldly aims: that of spreading Mohammed's message by fire and the sword. Later on, in the Thirty Years' War, we see the Protestant nations united by a collective project which likewise created a supra-national community of values and ideals with its specific code.

The hierarchy of values of the medieval Christians was guaranteed by divine authority, exemplified by Christ and interpreted by the Church. Since the religious values formed the summit of the medieval axiological hierarchy, they totally governed the lives of people. Deriving from a supreme other-worldly project, the execution of which was required, the medieval values involved rites and other human acts. Thus, they created a specific way of life. Therefore, in the Middle Ages and at the beginning of modern times after the Reformation, a symbiosis of people with different religions in the same family and even in the same town or country was practically impossible, because the different value systems, bound up with different religions, brought about different ways of life. The principle, *cuius regio, eius religio* — whose realm you live in, his religion you have to profess — sanctioned the ghettos, the autos-da-fe, the expulsions of the Jews, of the Moors and, finally, of the Protestants.

Since the seventeenth and, especially, the eighteenth century, a progressive secularization of values has taken place. A pluralism of value systems has replaced the medieval monistic value pyramid with its summit of religious values. Now, each domain of values develops a hierarchy of its own and is no longer subject to the domain of religious values. The collective project uniting the Occidental nations is no longer religious; it no longer implies religious acts and no longer imposes a religious style of life. Therefore, in our day, the way of life of a Catholic is no longer basically different from that of a Protestant, of a Jew or of an atheist. With this evolution, the coexistence of different religions in the same country and mixed marriages have become possible in the Western world.

For certain Eastern civilizations, the situation is different. There, the value systems which govern man's everyday life are still basically religious, and their secularization advances only slowly. Rhadakrishnan's antithesis of "Eastern religion-Western thought"[49] can also be interpreted in the sense that while the Western way of life is, today, governed by secularized value systems based on rational thought, the Eastern way of life is still governed by religious evaluations. While rational thought is common to all modern men, religions are different, owing to their different historical heritages. Where religious values govern man's life, peoples professing different religions have difficulty in living together.

The difference between the secularized Western value systems and the religious Eastern value systems may explain the fact that, in the West, religion has ceased to be a factor tracing frontiers between nations, while, in the East, religion still can fulfil this function. The recent separation between India and Pakistan again demonstrated this.

In modern times, the Western world has been engaged in another supra-national collective project. This time, it is no longer an other-worldly but a worldly project: the realization of scientific and technological civilization on a world-wide scale. In this collective project, the positive value of rational and empirical methods is postulated as a norm and confers a positive instrumental value upon all means able to promote the realization of this project and a negative value on everything hindering or delaying its execution. Also, the degrees of these instrumental values are determined by the extent to which they further the realization of the project of a universal scientific technological civilization.

Many instrumental values of this civilization have changed into radiated values reflecting the intrinsic value of the collective project. Thus, the intrinsic value affirmed in the collective project of establishing

[49] Sir S. Radhakrishnan, *Eastern Religions and Western Thought* (Oxford, 1939).

a world-wide scientific and technological civilization brought about the crystallization of a new code of values, common to the nations of Western civilization. While these nations are separated by their national codes of values, they are united by the supra-national code of the civilization to which they belong, owing to their contributions to the common collective project.

But, besides this supra-national collective project of realizing our scientific technological civilization on a world-wide scale, there are other supra-national collective projects. While the project we have just analyzed tends to unify the value codes of different nations, the other collective projects we refer to rather tend to multiply these codes. We mean the collective projects based on classes. These historical projects are also supra-national. When Marx launched his appeal "Proletarians of all countries, unite!" the classes were exclusively groups within nations. In our day, we may also say that the nations are groups within classes, for, now, the Capitalist nations are face to face with the Communist nations.

What distinguishes these two groups of nations from each other are, obviously, their collective projects and the codes of values ensuing from them. The collective project of the Communist nations consists in the world-wide realization of a social order based on the collective ownership of the means of production. On the contrary, the collective project of the Capitalist nations consists in the conservation of a social order based on individual ownership of the means of production.

As soon as the collective project of Communism and its normative postulates are adopted, its whole code of instrumental and radiated values follows automatically. The main postulate of the Communist project is that the welfare of the working class is the highest moral and social value and that the welfare of the whole society depends on it. According to Communism, this welfare can only be guaranteed by the collectivization of the means of production and by the establishment of a planned economy. Since, in this system, class struggles and revolutions are considered the only means able to bring about the collecivization of the means of production and to assure the welfare of the working class, class struggles and revolutions become high-ranking instrumental values. They also change into high radiated values, giving whoever has adopted the collective project of Communism, the moral satisfaction of serving the cause in which he believes.

Something similar happens with the collective project of Capitalism which, likewise, rests on certain postulates adopted as norms and entails, therefore, a specific code of instrumental and radiated values. The main postulate of the Capitalist project is that the welfare of society is solely assured by private ownership of the means of production which, in its turn, requires the free play of individual forces, the economic *laissez-faire*. In this system, the free play of individual forces is considered the highest instrumental value capable of assuring the conservation of private ownership of the means of production. At the same time, this free play of individual forces acquires a positive radiated value, giving the man engaged in free enterprise a feeling of sovereignty.

Within each of these two systems, every value belonging to it can be derived from the postulates adopted as standards, and its validity can be tested against the latter. But how can one prove the inferiority or superiority of the one or the other of the two groups of normative values adopted as standards in the two antagonistic projects? At first, such a demonstration appears to be theoretically impossible, for only the postulates adopted as norms and standards in each of the two projects can confer validity on the values ensuing from them. In order to be able to determine the superior or inferior value of the basic postulates adopted in the projects of Capitalism and Communism, it would be necessary to have a third standard against which the normative values of these two projects could be tested. But where is such a *common* standard?

One of the highest normative values postulated in the Capitalist project is freedom — not only economic but also moral and intellectual freedom — the right to individual creation. On the other hand, one of the highest normative values postulated in the Communist project is security — not only economic but also moral and intellectual security — the asurance against doubt. How is it possible to prove that freedom is a higher value than security, when the feelings of millions of persons place security above freedom? On the other hand, it seems impossible to prove that security is a higher value than freedom as long as millions of persons feel that freedom — especially intellectual freedom — is the highest of all values. Each of these two values is intrinsic, each is a value of the first degree against which those of the second degree can be tested. But against which common standard can they be tested? They seem to be irreducible; they cannot be proved but only felt. *"Wenn ihr's nich fühlt, ihr werdet's nich erjagen,"*[50] says Goethe — if you do not feel it, you will not catch it.

Man has the tendency to postulate as norms the intrinsic values he feels as such. Of the collective projects offered to him at a given histor-

[50] *Goethes Faust*, I, p. 28.

ical epoch, he will choose those which embody the intrinsic values in which he believes. In the case of the collective projects called Capitalism and Communism, there is still another factor which may influence the choice: the class situation of the one who chooses, and the class interest bound up with it. This factor is, however, not always decisive. Friedrich Engels, son of a capitalist and owner of factories in Germany and England, wrote, with Marx, the *Manifesto of the Communist Party* and thus inaugurated the movement supposed to destroy the class to which he belonged. It is true that often our value feelings are only the reflections of our interests, but sometimes they are the contrary of them. However this may be, at this moment in history the world is divided between the two great supra-national collective projects called Capitalism and Communism; and, as in an electrolysis, the human ions are attracted to the one or the other project either by their interests or by their value feelings.

Let us, however, not forget that we have found two collective projects which are more general than those of Capitalism and Communism and which also have their specific codes of values. The one was the collective project of establishing scientific technological civilization on a worldwide scale. This project is more general than Capitalism and Communism, since it embraces both of them. For both Capitalism and Communism tend to expand the scientific technological civilization all over the world, although they try to do this by different methods.

Being more general than these two collective projects, the project of establishing our scientific technological civilization on a world-wide basis could serve as a standard against which the values achieved by Capitalism and Communism could be tested. From this point of view, the one of the two antagonistic projects which contributes more to the universalization of our scientific technological civilization would appear to be the higher value. In choosing this standard of values, we must, however, not forget that the project of universalizing our scientific technological civilization is historically conditioned and could not, therefore, serve as a suprahistorical standard. Besides, this project only involves intellectual and pragmatic values but does not include moral and social values. For, as Aldous Huxley and other fiction writers have shown, a scientific technological civilization may also be abused for the purpose of degrading man into a robot.

Besides the project of a world-wide scientific technological civilization, we have, however, met a more fundamental project, the most universal which exists: that of living. It is more fundamental than all other projects for, unlike them, the human project of living does not depend upon history but solely on the human condition, which is transhistorical. The project of living, which is the condition of all history, is, of course, also more general than that of Capitalism, of Communism and of the universal scientific and technological civilization, for it is common to the adherents of these and all other projects.

As we showed earlier, the code of values derived from the universal human project of living constitutes *basic human or existential ethics.* Since the human project of living is suprahistorical, the code of values derived from it is, likewise, of suprahistorical validity. Therefore, it can be used as a suprahistorical standard against which such historical collective projects as Capitalism and Communism can be tested. Since the welfare of mankind is postulated as a normative value by both Capitalism and Communism, the question is, which of these two antagonistic collective projects gives better guarantees for human welfare and for the preservation of the basic existential values, human life and health? Finally, which of these projects offers more possibilities for the development of human potentialities? In the long run, only history will be able to answer these questions.

Max Weber compared the world's competing values to an "eternal struggle of the gods" without any possibility for men to decide which of these gods one should follow. Let each man choose in his own way his god or his devil! But, since all choices are historically conditioned and philosophically arbitrary, man has no reason for preferring one choice to another.[51] This scepticism of Weber entails a kind of equivalence of all values and is, thus, tantamount to nihilism.

If, however, we recognize that the human project of living is the *a priori* condition of all other projects — of individual as well as of collective historical projects — and that it is, itself, transhistorical — then we avoid Historicist nihilism; for, then, the values implied in all historical projects can be tested against the suprahistorical standards of the values bound up with the transhistorical human project of living. Since these existential values reflect the objective conditions necessary for the conservation of human life in nature, society and history, they have precedence over all other values — individual and collective. The hierarchy of values emerging in the course of history, from the realization of the diverse collective projects, will then be determined by the degree of their compatibility with the values of our transhistorical basic human ethics. Hence, the different historical and other projects are no

---

[51] M. Weber, "Wissenschaft als Beruf", *Gesammelte Aufsätze zur Wissenschaftslehre* (Tübingen, 1922), pp. 550-551.

longer equivalent, and a person has good reasons for choosing Albert Schweitzer's project rather than Adolf Hitler's.

All these analyses lead us to a final definition of history as a sequence of attempts to carry out collective projects and to realize the values bound up with them. For the achievement of these projects, work is needed, and, therefore, Professor Paul Schrecker is right in calling work "the elemental historical process".[52]

The historical experience of all epochs shows us that collective projects cannot succeed, unless they take into account the social, economic, technological and cultural forces of their epochs. Historical projects are likewise doomed to failure if they do not correspond to the needs of the groups which adopted them and unless they are compatible with the vital interests of competing groups. If these groups consider their interests to be threatened by foreign collective projects, they will resist them. The result will be conflicts. Thus, history manifests itself as a sequence of clashes between collective projects and between the codes of values bound up with them.

If one looks for a *meaning* in this sequence of attempts to carry out collective projects which constitute history, one may find it in the fact that every realization of a collective project results in the crystallization of new values. Thus, history would be *justified*, in as much as it enriches the patrimony of mankind's values.

---

[52] P. Schrecker, *Work And History* (Princeton, N.J., 1948), p. 12.

INDEX OF NAMES

Alembert, J. d', 144.
Alexander the Great, 32, 76, 115.
Altenstein, K. von, 20.
Amenhotep III, 162.
Ampère, A. M., 115.
Apollinaire, G., 218.
Archimedes, 187.
Aristotle, 42, 49, 74, 100, 103, 105, 106, 139, 163, 199, 236.
Arndt, E. M., 116.
Aron, Raymond, 17, 25, 29, 65, 75, 77, 114, 127, 135, 184.
Ayer, A. J., 105.

Babeuf, F. N., 155.
Bacon, Sir F., 32, 71, 90, 105.
Ballvé, F., 17.
Balzac, H. de, 11, 30.
Bancroft, G., 98.
Battaglia, F., 48, 159, 160.
Beard, Ch. A., 78, 98, 128.
Beaulavon, G., 19.
Beauvoir, S. de, 179.
Becker, C. L., 19, 22, 125, 130.
Bell, Gr., 115.
Bergson, H., 11, 21, 29, 47, 48, 106, 129.
Berkeley, G., 85.
Bernard, C., 97, 106, 107.
Berthelot, M., 109.
Bismarck, O. von, 222.
Blakeslee, A. L., 233.
Bloch, M., 82, 84.
Bloch, P., 78/79.
Böckh, A., 147.
Boltzmann, L., 45.
Bonaparte, Napoleon, 10, 11, 31, 32, 40, 41, 73, 90, 115, 120, 145, 164, 217, 235.
Bopp, F., 147.
Bossuet, J. B., 9, 10, 11, 53, 55, 56, 59, 98.
Bowers, C. 129, 130.
Boyle, R., 115.

Brogan, D. W., 236.
Brunschvicg, L., 19, 20, 22.
Buckle, H. Th., 61.
Buddha, 115.
Bunge, M., 110.
Burckhardt, J., 65, 119, 120, 126, 127.
Burke, E., 132, 133.
Byron, Lord G. G. N., 218.

Caesar, J., 20, 32, 59, 72, 80, 83, 115, 234.
Calvin, J., 115.
Camus, A., 32, 33, 34, 35, 36, 79, 162.
Carlyle, Th., 49, 119, 123, 125, 126.
Carnot, N. L. S., 44.
Cassirer, E., 61, 123, 161.
Castro, A., 225.
Cervantes, M. de, 223.
Chamberlain, H. St., 218.
Chateaubriand, F. R. de, 235.
Cheyney, E. P., 113, 114.
Chrysippos, 140.
Churchill, Sir W., 20, 26, 83.
Cicero, M. T., 24, 140.
Claparède, E., 89.
Clausius, R. E., 44.
Cleanthes, 140.
Clemenceau, G., 20.
Clovis, 179.
Collingwood, R. G., 17, 81, 82, 106, 107, 128.
Commager, H. St., 230, 231, 232.
Comte, A., 55, 57, 60, 61, 65, 92, 112, 195, 197.
Condorcet, M. J. A., 16, 60, 92, 193, 197.
Coolidge, C., 233.
Copernicus, N., 187, 188.
Corts-Grau, J., 149.
Cournot, A., 49, 105.
Croce, B., 10, 18, 19, 22, 25, 26, 43, 47, 49, 113, 122, 123, 129, 159, 160, 184.
Curie, P. and M., 115.

Curie-Sklodowska, M., 218.
Curtius, E. R., 33.

Daninos, P., 228, 229, 230, 236.
Darwin, Sir Ch. G., 115.
Darwin, Ch. R., 11, 108.
Davis, J., 113.
Descartes, R., 14, 26, 28, 57, 58, 72, 76.
Destutt de Tracy, A. L. C. de, 90.
Dewey, J., 103, 204.
Diderot, D., 143, 144, 155.
Dilthey, W., 49, 67, 68, 70, 72, 105, 121.
Dostoevski, F. M., 11, 116, 122.
Dray, W., 110.
DuBridge, L.A., 94, 95.
Dühring, E., 167, 168.
Duhem, P., 45, 191.
Durkheim, E., 26, 28, 31, 80, 92, 133, 134.

Edwards, E., 89.
Einstein, A., 22, 44, 76, 115, 116, 162, 172, 187, 192.
Eisenhower, D., 20, 26, 83.
El Greco, 218, 226.
Elisabeth II, Queen, 236.
Engel-Janosi, F., 165, 169.
Engels, F., 15, 37, 78-79, 90, 91, 126, 164, 165, 166, 167, 168, 171, 172, 198, 242.
Euclid, 187.
Eusebius, 53.

Feuerbach, L., 164, 166, 170.
Fichte, J. G., 29, 67, 126, 145, 154.
Filmer, Sir R., 154, 155.
Foch, F., 20, 83.
France, A., 88, 89.
Frank, T., 77.
Franklin, B., 29.
Frazer, Sir J., 63.
Frederick William IV, 130, 131.
Freeman, 28.
Fresnel, A., 171, 172.
Freud, S., 27, 102.
Frondizi, R., 187, 205, 218.
Fulton, R., 115.

Galbraith, V. H., 18.
Galileï, G., 115, 163, 176, 187.
Galle, J. G., 114.
Gardiner, P. L., 110.
Gaulle, Ch. de, 26.
George III, 133.
Gervinus, G. G., 116.
Gibbon, E., 49, 61, 62, 76, 77, 98, 109.
Gilson, E., 20.
Gödel, K., 44.

Goethe, J. W. von, 14, 28, 33, 40, 60, 62, 63, 125, 184, 194, 221, 235, 241.
Gregory VII, 80.
Grimm, J., 147.
Grotius, H., 144, 152, 153, 154.
Grünbaum, A., 44.

Halbwachs, M., 83.
Hannibal, 73.
Hartmann, N., 126, 183, 214, 218.
Haydn, J., 30.
Hayek, F. A., 197.
Hayes, C., 129, 130.
Hegel, G. W. F., 10, 12, 13, 14, 18, 19, 20, 21, 23, 24, 25, 28, 30, 31, 32, 40, 41, 43, 50, 53, 57, 61, 62, 67, 70, 80, 81, 89, 112, 113, 126, 147, 157, 158, 159, 160, 161, 167, 174, 176, 183, 188, 189, 214, 224.
Heidegger, M., 11, 23, 25, 36, 80, 98, 172, 173, 174.
Heiden, K., 81.
Heine, H., 116.
Hempel, K., 110.
Heraclitus, 42, 43, 66, 147, 162, 175.
Herbart, J. F., 159.
Herder, J. G., 29, 57, 80, 145, 146, 159.
Herodotus, 49, 50, 51.
Heyde, J. E., 205.
Hieronymus, 53.
Hippolytus, 42.
Hitler, A., 12, 32, 41, 116, 118, 121, 186, 213, 244.
Hobbes, Th., 152, 153, 154.
Hook, S., 61.
Huizinga, J., 17, 126.
Humboldt, W. von, 126.
Hume, D., 60, 61, 147.
Huntington, E., 77.
Husserl, E., 41, 69, 70, 86.
Huxley, A., 242.
Huygens, Chr., 22, 172.

Isabel, the Catholic, Queen, 223.

James, W., 170.
Jaspers, K., 18, 24, 25, 53.
Jefferson, Th., 28, 90, 115.
Jellinek, A., 146.
Jenkins, I., 204.
Jerusalem, W., 92.
Jolivet, R., 23.
Jung, C. G., 27, 94.

Kant, I., 25, 26, 27, 53, 57, 65, 66, 67, 71, 74, 79, 81, 84, 85, 87, 118, 125, 145, 153, 154, 162, 163, 172, 193, 209, 210, 212.

Kaphahn, F., 77.
Kautsky, K., 124.
Kelsen, H., 150, 151, 152, 153, 154, 155.
Kepler, J., 192.
Korn, A., 49, 73.
Kraft, V., 105, 205.

Lafiteau, J. F., 147, 237.
Lalande, A., 17, 139, 152, 198.
Lapshin, J., 196.
Laube, H., 30.
Lavelle, L., 191.
Lavoisier, A. L., 115.
Le Bon, G., 80, 84.
Leibniz, G. W. von, 86, 87.
Lenin, 115, 126, 168, 169.
Lerner, M., 232.
Lessing, G. E., 96.
Lessing, Th., 72, 99.
Leverrier, U. J. J., 114.
Lévy-Bruhl, L., 34, 92, 94, 148, 149.
Liebig, H., 77.
Lifshitz, M., 169.
Linné, C., 76.
Lippmann, W., 233, 234.
Locke, J., 152, 154.
Lossky, N. O., 196.
Louis XIV, 58, 59, 185.
Ludwig, E., 12.
Lukács, Georg, 11, 166, 170.
Luther, M., 115.

Mach, E., 191, 192.
Machiavelli, N., 9, 10, 11, 40, 90.
Maistre, J. de, 124.
Malraux, A., 176, 199.
Malthus, Th. R., 115.
Mandelbaum, M., 77, 78, 124.
Mannheim, K., 27, 91, 92, 93, 94, 95, 98, 133, 139.
Marconi, G., 115.
Marcus Aurelius, 140.
Maritain, J., 196.
Marrou, H.-I., 17, 20, 24, 65, 77, 78, 98, 127.
Martin du Gard, R., 190.
Marx, K., 28, 36, 37, 43, 53, 80, 90, 91, 92, 113, 115, 126, 145, 164, 166, 167, 168, 169, 170, 171, 198, 214, 240, 242.
Masson-Oursel, P., 27.
Maurois, A., 228.
Meinecke, F., 55, 60, 146.
Meyer, Ed., 130.
Meyerson, E., 198.
Michelet, J., 55, 57, 124.

Miller, F. T., 81.
Mirabeau, H. G. de, 80.
Mises, R. von, 108, 139.
Mohamet, 115.
Molière, J. B. P., 73, 120.
Mommsen, Th., 76, 98.
Montesquieu, Ch. de S., 30, 142, 146.
Moses, 115.
Mozart, W. A., 30, 205.
Musonius Rufus, 140.
Mussolini, B., 32.

Naville, P., 37, 38.
Nero, 76.
Newton, Sir I., 22, 28, 76, 115, 162, 172, 187.
Niebuhr, B. G., 147.
Niebuhr, R., 129.
Nietzsche, F., 10, 13, 14, 23, 34, 35, 48, 50, 68, 69, 152, 160, 161, 162, 174, 222, 227.

Odoaker, 224.
Offenbach, J., 218.
Oppenheimer, J. R., 199.
Ortega y Gasset, J., 11, 19, 68, 80, 87, 99, 148, 172, 174, 175, 176, 179, 215, 216, 217, 218, 225.
Ostwald, W., 46.
Ovid, P. N., 45.

Paoli, P., 217.
Pareto, V., 92.
Parmenides, 42.
Pascal, B., 205, 236.
Pasteur, L., 115.
Peirce, Ch. S., 170.
Pericles, 59.
Philip of Macedonia, 76.
Philip II of Spain, 99.
Philippe Egalité, 235.
Pico della Mirandola, G., 193.
Piganiol, A., 77.
Planck, M., 93.
Plato, 42, 45, 48, 49, 54, 59, 73, 100, 101, 103, 139.
Pleyel, I., 30.
Plutarch, 76.
Poincaré, H., 151, 191, 192.
Polybius, 9.
Popper, K. R., 65, 96, 97, 117, 138.
Proudhon, P. J., 165.
Proust, M., 33.
Ptolemaeus, C., 188, 189.
Pufendorf, S., 152, 153.
Pythagoras, 187.

Radhakrishnan, Sir S., 239.
Raleigh, Sir W., 88, 89.
Ranke, L. von, 49, 71, 126, 147.
Reichenbach, H., 54.
Remarque, E. M., 12.
Renan, E., 49, 51, 80, 109, 160, 215, 216, 217, 218.
Renouvin, P., 126.
Rickert, H., 44, 67, 72, 73, 81, 109, 118, 119, 120, 121, 122, 123, 124, 130, 131, 133, 134, 135, 136, 186, 190.
Ricoeur, P., 69.
Rolland, R., 161.
Rosenberg, A., 222.
Rostovtzeff, M. I., 77.
Rothenstreich, N., 163, 164.
Rousseau, J.-J., 2, 30, 31, 80, 152, 154, 162, 164, 227.
Royce, J., 31, 80.
Russell, Lord B., 49, 109.

Saint Augustine, 28, 39, 40, 44, 48, 51, 52, 53, 54, 55, 56, 64, 65, 141.
Saint Isidore, 141.
Saint Paul, 141.
Saint Thomas Aquinas, 141, 142, 143, 144.
Saint-Just, A. de, 235.
Saint-Simon, C. H. de, 84, 92, 197.
Salieri, A., 30.
Sand, George, 30.
Santayana, G., 53, 54.
Sartre, J.-P., 11, 14, 21, 30, 80, 129, 172, 173, 174, 176, 177, 178, 179, 180, 199, 211, 216.
Savigny, F. C. von, 13, 147, 148, 149, 150.
Scheler, M., 23, 53, 91, 92, 97, 98, 218.
Schiller, J. C. F., 16, 57.
Schmidt, W., 112.
Schmitt, C., 222.
Schneider, H. W., 156.
Schopenhauer, A., 57, 85, 206.
Schrecker, P., 244.
Schweitzer, A., 244.
Scipio, P. C. S., m., 140.
Seeck, O., 77.
Seneca, L. A., 8, 44, 140, 186, 213.
Simmel, G., 23, 49, 72, 73, 75, 78, 79, 80, 81, 89, 118.
Socrates, 139, 214.
Solon, 42.
Sombart, W., 91.
Sommerville, J., 169, 170.
Sorokin, P. A., 92, 195, 196, 197, 198.
Spaak, P. H., 85.
Spencer, H., 198.

Spengler, O., 28, 41, 43, 47, 59, 62, 65, 109, 110, 111, 126, 170, 187, 188, 189, 190, 201.
Spinoza, B. de, 104, 123, 219.
Stalin, J., 15, 32, 116, 213.
Standen, A., 197.
Stephenson, G., 115.
Sterling, J. E. W., 28.
Stern, A., 31, 41, 100, 116, 145, 172, 212, 218.
Stern, W., 22, 89, 135, 220.
Stobaeus, 140.
Strauss, L., 156, 157, 182, 186.
Sue, E., 30.

Taine, H., 61, 119.
Thales, 187.
Thiers, L.-A., 30.
Tolstoy, L., 62.
Toynbee, A. J., 28, 41, 43, 49, 51, 59, 61, 62, 63, 64, 65, 77, 111, 112, 126, 188, 196.
Treitschke, H. von, 124.
Troeltsch, E., 22, 53, 55, 91, 98, 129, 135, 137, 160, 183, 184.
Turgot, A. R., 60, 193, 197.

Unamuno, M. de, 224, 225.

Vaihinger, H., 78.
Valéry, P., 77, 106.
Varro, M. T., 51.
Vassiliev, A. T., 77.
Vercingetorix, 234.
Vico, G., 28, 29, 43, 51, 53, 56, 57, 66, 71, 125, 147, 197.
Vigny, A. de, 43, 106.
Virgil, P. M., 59.
Volta, A., 115.
Voltaire, 15, 16, 18, 30, 39, 55, 57, 58, 59, 60, 62, 73, 93, 120, 126, 185, 188.
Vorländer, K., 145.

Wagner, C., 218.
Wagner, R., 69.
Weber, A., 112.
Weber, M., 72, 74, 75, 77, 91, 122, 127, 128, 156, 157, 243.
Werkmeister, W. H., 204.
Whyte, W. H., 232.
Windelband, W., 49, 72, 105, 106, 107, 108, 118, 119, 120.
Winstanley, W., 89.
Wundt, W., 121.

Zoroaster, 54.